Mary (Beaumont) Welch

Mrs. Welch's Cook Book

Mary (Beaumont) Welch

Mrs. Welch's Cook Book

ISBN/EAN: 9783744786515

Printed in Europe, USA, Canada, Australia, Japan

Cover: Foto ©Andreas Hilbeck / pixelio.de

More available books at **www.hansebooks.com**

PREFACE.

In this volume are included, besides many others, the receipts used in the Department of Domestic Economy of the Iowa State College of Agriculture and Mechanic Arts.

These, and all others, have been gathered with great care from many sources. Having had exceptional advantages for the study of cookery, and access to the most complete library on food and kindred subjects in the west, I feel sure, in presenting this book to the public, I am offering a work of practical value. Like all similar books, it is, in great measure, a compilation. I do not claim to be original, I have simply gleaned the best from the highest authorities.

Each receipt has been either personally tested, or is vouched for by competent housewives among my friends. Wherever possible I have given credit for such receipts as I have copied. Many, however, have been gathered from papers, or sent to me by friends through a term of years, and their origin is lost. While studying in Germany and England, I collected much that was valuable, all of which I have proved by actual trial to be good. I am under obligations also, to that excellent English paper "The Queen," for a number of capital receipts. Many of these I have altered to suit our markets and taste, making the original instructions simply a basis for final results.

I desire to call especial attention to the chapters that close this book by Prof. Macomber, Prof. Pope, and Dr. Fairchild. These are all valuable and come from gentlemen, each of whom is recognized author ity on the topic of which he treats.

MARY B. WELCH.

Ames, Iowa.

CONTENTS.

5

CHAPTER X.

CHAPTER XI.

CHAPTER XII.

CHAPTER XIII.

CHAPTER XIV.

CHAPTER XV.

CHAPTER XVI.

CHAPTER XVII.

CHAPTER XVIII.

CHAPTER XIX.

CHAPTER XX.

CHAPTER XXI.

CHAPTER XXII.

CHAPTER XXIII.

CHAPTER XXIV.

CHAPTER XXV.

CHAPTER I

THE COMING COOK.

GENUINE civilization and good cooking are more closely related than is usually appreciated. Savages live on food either wholly or partially raw and have not the faintest conception of the routine of meals, variety of diet, and combination of flavors that are to us absolute necessities. They gorge themselves when food is plentiful, and starve when it is scarce. They eat the coarsest and grossest substances without subjecting them to the refining effects of fire, or the transforming influence of condiments, herbs, or extracts. They know nothing of the subtle combinations by which the palate may be tickled and the digestive powers stimulated to easy and effective work.

To their habits of eating may be ascribed, in great measure, their imperfect physical development, their mental dullness, and their moral obtuseness. Improve their diet and you have taken the first step towards a better life. Philanthropists and missionaries of all kinds are beginning to understand that no appeal can be effectually made to the higher nature until the stomach has first been revived, and that all reforms in the individual must proceed from this center to the head and heart.

Coarse food, even though perfectly digested, produces coarse natures. Indigestible food is even worse in its effect, for it results in actual disease, and disease of such a character as to influence in marked degree the whole mental outlook. A sour stomach is apt to produce a sour temper. Melancholy, suspicion, envy, false and distorted views of men and things, follow dyspepsia as the shadow follows substance.

The effect of diet in stimulating evil passions is well known. Its effect also in disease is acknowledged and respected. The

9

wise physician supplements his medicines by carefully selected and skillfully prepared food. More than this, he is often able to cure without the medicine by judicious advice to his patient as to the kind, quality, and amount of nourishment he shall take. The success of many sanitariums, where attention to diet is a special feature in the treatment of disease, proves this beyond dispute. No one will deny the further proposition that the sensualist, the drunkard, the debauchee in general, is the victim of over-indulgence in eating and drinking, and that his vice cannot be cured and self-control re-established without a minute and persistent attention to the needs of the stomach. The man or woman whose vile business it is to pander to the animal passions and to corrupt our youth, seem to appreciate the mental and moral effect of eating and drinking, much better, alas! than the cook, the mother, or the minister. Many a boy or girl has been ruined for life *after* the preliminary work had been accomplished by a feast, set out with the express design on the part of the provider to inflame the passions, dull the finer sensibilities, and fire the blood.

The influence of what we eat and drink on the growth and development of the body is so patent that little need be said about it. I have dwelt particularly on its mental and moral effect, since these are less visible to the careless observer. Comparative values are not sufficiently considered, even by those who urge most strenuously the advancement of the human race. Those who decry the claims of the body, and at the same time attempt to exalt the power of mental and spiritual growth, forget that the body is the medium through which mind acts, and that one cannot be abused or depressed without very sensibly affecting the other. The only possible way to have a "sound mind" is first to secure a "sound body."

The cook exercises, then, a most important function. Her duties may well command the respect of her employers. Her wages should be in some just proportion to the value of her work, and her social position should be graded according to her fitness for her heavy responsibilities. The teacher looks down with something akin to contempt upon the cook, who should rather be regarded as her natural ally. The child, who goes daily to school with a stomach full of badly selected and worse cooked food tugging at every vital force, is ill prepared for the reception of mental aliment, and the teacher suffering from the same cause is absolutely unfit to administer it acceptably. Both are at the mercy of the one whose power they least suspect. If the cook but knew what influence she might exert, and if the world valued her services properly, what a revolution would be wrought in human affairs.

When the tired man can say to his cook: "I am weary—refresh me with that which will be easy to digest, which will stimulate and energize without reaction," and forthwith the cook does as she is bid; when the poet or the philosopher, the artist or the artisan, the teacher or the taught, each can ask and receive confidently the exact food needed, then will human effort reach its highest achievement. Then, too, will cookery take its proper rank, and the cook receive her just reward.

In order to prepare the cook for such service, what are some of the things she must know? Unless the whole routine of her work be hap-hazard and unreliable she should have intelligent and well defined opinions concerning the relation of food to physical growth, so that she can prepare that which is best adapted to the needs of the entire household, fit to build up symmetrical and healthy bodies for the children, as well as to furnish to the mature workers in the family the necessary nutriment to keep good the balance between supply and demand. And not only should these bodies be robust and sound, but fit temples also for the indwelling of a pure spirit, a calm and courageous temper, and a keen, searching intellect.

All this implies a practical application of the principles taught in physiology and chemistry, as well as a knowledge of the kind and quality of nutriment stored in plants, flesh, fish, and fowl. Earth, air, and sea, furnish her with the materials which she must understand how to prepare, so they can be easily transformed into bone, blood, and muscle, in such proportions that each shall have its normal growth. She must be both too wise and too humane to concoct any dish or brew any drink that will induce dyspepsia, headache, or dullness.

The kitchen will be a laboratory wherein zeal and knowledge join hands in the experiments continually being made. It will also be a school in which enthusiastic pupils are willing to work hard as a previous condition to future skill. Fertility of resource, a quick and ingenious wit, knowledge of details, a complete understanding of the materials the whole world furnishes for culinary manipulation, these are but a few of the qualifications that must fit a man or woman to be the coming cook.

CHAPTER II.

BREAKFAST, DINNER, TEA.

HESE may be called our National rotation of meals. Though in the larger cities the routine becomes, breakfast, luncheon, dinner, still by far the greater proportion of housekeepers in the United States adhere to the first programme. In country towns and villages, in farm house, and rural hamlet, on prairie and hillside, in the sunny South and fair Northwest, farmer, merchant, lawyer, mechanic, or minister, gathers his family about him three times a day, at breakfast, dinner, and tea. Some general directions as to the manner in which these may be best served should, therefore, precede the receipts which will form the bulk of this book. While it is impossible to give advice which can be accurately followed under all circumstances, it is never waste of time to urge system and order in the setting out and dishing up of any meal. No matter how plain the repast, nor how humble the home, a certain order in these can be profitably observed.

The table should be set according to a fixed method and the dishes follow each other in regular succession. While, in the parlor, a certain elegant and apparently careless arrangement is allowable, on the dining table straight lines, right angles, and a strict attention to geometric figures should be the rule. We must trust to a pleasing variety in the forms of dishes, to sparkling glass, highly polished silver, spotless linen, and the charming effect produced by contrasting yet harmonious colors, for attractive and artistic effect. Breakfast and tea are comparatively simple meals, and sometimes housekeepers who pride themselves on elegant and stately dinners are careless and indifferent regarding them. There are many theories afloat as to the proper kind and amount of food for breakfast. One insists that a cup of

13

coffee and a roll are all that any man needs to fit him for the work of the day, and substantiates his position by citing the Germans who, he says, are a long-lived, wise, and happy people, and require nothing more for their first meal. He forgets to state, however, that a heartier breakfast follows a little later in the morning, and that any German would think himself greatly abused if obliged to do a full morning's work on the energy supplied by a cup of coffee and a roll. Another urges that oatmeal should form the basis of every breakfast, and quotes the robust and canny Scot as a striking example of the ability of this grain to supply working power. The third pleads that our climate is stimulating, our people filled with a feverish unrest that impels to an abnormal and exhausting activity, and that we need, therefore, a great variety of hearty and stimulating food, to fit us for the hurry and worry of the morning's scramble.

I suspect there is a grain of wisdom in each of these statements. The German does thrive on his "early morsel," followed soon by a heartier supply, and either by reason of, or in spite of, his six meals a day has reached a high position among nations mentally and physically. The Scot does relish his oatmeal, and adding to this the needed amount of stronger aliment, has become a shining example of sturdy independence in both mind and body. And we do differ from either, both in climatic conditions, nervous susceptibility, and eager energy, and our bill of fare must not, therefore, be too closely modeled after theirs. We have three meals a day to the German's six and the Scotchman's four. We breakfast, as a rule, earlier than either, and work more hours before the next meal is served. We must, therefore, have a larger amount and greater variety to keep the stomach (paradoxically speaking) in good heart until the noon meal.

Then again no meal should be prepared with reference simply to one or two members of the family circle. The young, the middle-aged, the very old, each should be considered and a sufficient variety presented to meet the necessities of all. It is too much the custom to offer at the table food fit only for active and robust men, and neglect altogether to provide that suited to the digestive capacity of young children and delicate women, or the feeble, assimilative powers of the aged. This thoughtlessness may be remedied without great trouble and with the most beneficial results. There can be oatmeal or similar food, with an abundance of good milk and cream, as well as brown bread and white, for both young and old. Juicy, tender beefsteak, a nourishing stew, or delicate, well cooked chops are easily digested and yield much nourishment, while eggs are, as a rule, fitted to satisfy and benefit alike the child, the father, and the father's father. Fresh ripe fruit is, in general, a healthful food for breakfast, and may be partaken of by all with advantage, unless some peculiar condition or special disease make it literally "forbidden." One need not despair, therefore, at being told to suit her meals to the dietetic wants of the whole family. While thus urging a suitable variety, I by no means advocate a heavy or elaborate breakfast. It is true that the average American who goes forth to his daily work at half past seven o'clock or earlier, and cannot expect his next meal before twelve or one, must have something substantial and nourishing, but this does not imply four or five courses, or a succession of meats followed by hot cakes or doughnuts.

A breakfast may be plain, wholesome, and nutritious, and at the same time offer a sufficient number of viands to tempt the appetite and warm the blood of all who partake of it. Variety may be farther secured by taking pains that no breakfast shall, in the same week at least, repeat itself. Zest for food, which is renewed by novelty and dulled by sameness, is an important factor in digestion. Hence, I imagine, the long lists of different methods of preparing the same food, as well as the illimitable variety of materials offered us by our bountiful friend, generous Dame Nature. The American breakfast on many a farm, the year round, is fat pork, fried potatoes, and, perhaps, pancakes occasionally, as an extra relish, and in many a town and village, fried beef—emphatically not beefsteak—fried potatoes, and as before hot cakes and molasses, when great luxury is desired. I have personal knowledge of a family, a rich and generous family, too, whose morning meal in winter invariably consists of sausage and buckwheat cakes. There is no excuse for such willful and reckless neglect of every law of digestion. We live in a land of plenty, and if we suffer from any such intolerable sameness in diet, it is because we are too lazy, too indifferent, or too ignorant to secure anything better. If we can get no meat but beef, there are many ways of preparing it so as to secure variety. Codfish, mackerel, white fish, and herrings can usually be had at the smallest grocery. Oatmeal, cracked wheat, graham flour, Indian meal, and eggs are almost always cheap and abundant. She who wills may, by the exercise of a little thought and ingenuity, secure almost anywhere in this country an appetizing variety for every meal.

And after the bill of fare for the breakfast has been decided on, some attention must be given to the manner of presenting it to the family. How shall the table be set and in what order shall the dishes be served? For this and for every other meal, the first thing to be considered is the table linen. One of the great luxuries within the reach of wealth is the possibility of unlimited clean tablecloths and napkins. No array of delicate food can be either pleasing to the eye or tempting to the palate, when placed against a background of dingy and rumpled linen. Ordinary housekeepers, with ordinary incomes, must exercise care and ingenuity in order to secure, without increasing the weekly washing to a burdensome degree, tablecloths and napkins for every meal that are not unpleasant to refined eyes. There are several expedients that will help at least to this much to be wished for result. To begin with, great care must be taken in clearing the table. Oftentimes table linen is more soiled by the carelessness of servants in this operation than by actual use during the meal. Glasses of water and cups of coffee are needlessly spilled, gravy and morsels of food are dripped from plate to plate, or dirty knives and forks are laid full length on the table cloth, leaving their grimy impress to offend the taste of the family at the next meal. Then, after the table is cleared, the cloth should never be shaken, but neatly brushed, then .folded in the exact lines the iron left when it came fresh from the laundry, and carefully laid away, under a weight if possible, until needed again. Wrinkles and the general mussy appearance of a cloth shaken first and then carelessly folded, are thus avoided. A heavy felt or Canton flannel cover under the linen much improves its appearance, and at the same time, lessens in a marked degree the noise of the clatter of dishes as they are moved about, which is always an unpleasant accompaniment to a meal. It saves also the surface of the dining-room table from spot or blemish, and the texture of the outer cover likewise from hard wear. It is altogether a great improvement, and any housewife who tries it once will never again be satisfied to set her table the old way. Heavy, doublefaced white Canton flannel, wide enough for the purpose, can be bought for from seventy-five cents to a dollar a yard. If ordinary caution is exercised not to soil the outer cloth unnecessarily, such an inner covering does not need frequent washing. A coarse white blanket will serve this purpose also, if one cannot conveniently buy the other.

Great pains must be taken to lay the cloth perfectly straight and exactly in the middle of the table. It is exceedingly unpleasant to see it awry in any way, lopped down this side or that, or the center fold straggling uncertainly at any sort of a diagonal across the table. The coffee or tea service should stand before the "mistress of the manse," the cups and saucers be ranged symmetrically about her plate—and cold bread, butter, salt, cream, etc., should be in their respective places. If there be oatmeal or any similar dish for breakfast, that should be served first, and while it is being disposed of, the beefsteak or omelette, the smoking coffee, and all the other hot dishes, except cakes, fried mush, or anything of that sort to be eaten with sweets, can be brought in from the kitchen. The oatmeal is then removed and the substantial dishes placed before the head of the house to be dished out by him on well warmed plates and handed by the waiter to each person at the table. The coffee is served by "my lady" and the butter, bread, etc., offered on a small tray carried by the waiter for this purpose. The attendant should watch the progress of the meal, and if cakes are to follow, as soon as a part of the family are ready she should notify the cook that she may commence to bake them, quietly remove the plates, substitute clean ones, also warmed, and bring the cakes from the kitchen. It is not necessary to wait for every one to finish the first course before beginning to offer the second. If many servants are kept, of course there can be no difficulty in serving every meal in the most approved style. Even with two, the above will be found the easiest, simplest, and pleasantest way of managing breakfast. If fruit, oatmeal, meat, potatoes, and hot cakes are all put on the table at the same time, the effect is confused and the very abundance palls the appetite. No one can partake of all simul-

2

taneously, and the beefsteak and coffee are cold by the time the oatmeal is eaten, and the cakes have long ceased to be hot before it is possible to serve them. On the contrary, by following the first plan, the cook has a few moments for the finishing touches needed by the hot dishes, can make an omelette so it can be served steaming from the pan, and after these have gone in, can have time to get everything ready to bake her cakes.

Where a single servant is maid of all work it is somewhat more difficult, but a little ingenuity will still compass it. She can put the oatmeal on the table and summon the family to breakfast. While they are eating this first course, she can dish up the remainder of the breakfast and bring it in, then quietly remove the first plates and return to the kitchen to see to her cakes. The butter, bread, etc., must be passed in this case by different members of the family, and if each one knows what is expected and the table is arranged with reference to this, it can be done quickly, without noise and without confusion. Where no help is kept, the younger members of the family should, as soon as possible, be trained to wait, each in turn, on the table. Of course, the whole method of living must, under these circumstances, be simplified and made to conform to the strength of the inmates and the character of the surroundings of the home. But in the plainest farm house, or the poorest mechanic's dwelling, system, a well settled routine of work, and a definite notion of the fitness of things, are necessary factors in good housekeeping. Table manners and habits of eating, as well as the quality of the food and its proper preparation, exercise great influence on both character and physique, and every mother should realize the fact, that a well ordered meal, served as perfectly as her circumstances will allow, makes a part of that subtle influence which is silently and powerfully evolving the future man or woman from the crude boy or girl under her care.

The inequality of incomes and the wide diversity of circumstances surrounding different housekeepers, make it absolutely impossible to lay down fixed and invariable rules for all. I am anxious to be useful to the largest possible number, and shall therefore remember in all my suggestions and all my receipts, that the greater proportion of the housewives this book will probably reach are not likely to be the wives of millionares, nor

the mistresses of homes in which expense is of no account. She
who can live elegantly on a small income, whose refined taste,
cultivated intellect, and hearty interest in home duties, take the
place in great measure of the extra dollars of her rich neighbor,
achieves a triumph well worth time and thought. During the
season of flowers there is no housekeeper so busy that she cannot,
if she will, have her table beautified by their presence. Not a
month from April to November on our western prairies that
does not spontaneously furnish some bloom and fragrance for
household adornment. From the hepatica in early spring to the
golden rod and aster in the fall there is a constant, ever varying
succession of leaf and blossom. Through all gradations of coloring from tender blues and faintest pinks to flaming scarlets,
rich purples, and glowing yellows, Nature tempts every taste,
and yields without money and without price bounteous largesse
to all her friends. Can we not learn of her to make the common
things of our every day life and work attractive by uniting with
them some form of beauty.

Dinner is the important meal of the day. If it come at noon
it should be well studied, as we depend on the warmth, nutrition,
and stimulus it furnishes to repair the waste caused by the
morning's work, to fortify the system to withstand the fatigue
of the remainder of the day, and to furnish sufficient strength to
carry us through, with the aid of a light tea, to the next morning. If it come in the after part of the day still more does it
need careful thought. The stomach is likely to be weakened
from long fasting, and the whole physical tone depressed. One
is not fit to digest hearty food at once, yet he is so hungry he
will be tempted to eat hastily and ravenously whatever is set before him. All these things should be considered by the intelligent housewife.

The best stomachic to prepare for the easy digestion of a hearty
dinner is soup, not a rich, heavy, and greasy liquid, but one of
the light, clear soups, which are simply strong extracts of meat,
entirely free from grease, clear and sparkling, and almost as
stimulating as wine. The sense of warmth and comfort produced
by a few tablespoonfuls of such a broth, testifies to its efficacy
as a preparatory dish. It dulls the first keen edge of appetite,
without in the least degree producing a feeling of satiety. It

gives tone to the stomach, and is, moreover, almost at once assimilated, refreshing the whole inner man. He can then proceed deliberately to discuss the remainder of his dinner, and eating slowly, will not only enjoy it but digest it without trouble in due time. Liebig says: "The extractive substances of flesh, when added to food do duty as true nutritive materials," and Dr. Letheby adds: "As they are at once absorbed into the circulation requiring no effort of digestion, *they not only create force, but they also economize it.* They are, therefore, among the most valuable constituents of food." The hostess who offers her guests at a German a cup of strong broth early in the evening, may do it in blind obedience to what she regards as an arbitrary fashion, but the custom had its origin in a genuine dietetic philosophy. Great physical exertions are expected of her guests, and the cup of meat extract "not only creates force but also enconomizes it."

There are many ways of serving dinner. No doubt the style of setting the dinner table with the dessert alone, and adorning it with a profusion of flowers, makes it a thing of beauty. No doubt also it relieves the host and hostess of all care, to have the substantial part of the dinner presented by servants entirely from the sideboard, course after course, coming regularly, quietly, and systematically as if by magic; but no doubt again, this requires trained servants and plenty of them, and is practically impossible to the ordinary housekeeper. A compromise can be effected however if you have a quick, bright maid who can be trained to her work.

The table may be set partly after the old style and partly after the more modern or so called Russian way. Some low ornamental dish may occupy the center, and on either side, arranged with due regard to harmony of color and general effect, may be placed fruit, flowers, and any light, sweet dishes intended for dessert, such as custards, creams, or blanc manges, nuts, raisins, etc., etc. These should extend in a straight line through the middle of the table and compose its main ornamentation. Button hole bouquets, napkins handsomely marked with colored monograms, etched figures or flowers, or suggestive mottos, each enfolding a thick slice of bread, low glass forms for flowers here and there, goblets or tumblers of thin glass, some one, or a variety of the numberless fanciful devices for supplying salt to each plate, these break up any tendency to too great formality in the general arrangement. The large, clumsy, and conspicuous caster is now banished from the dinner table. All condiments, except salt, are served from the sideboard as they are required. It is also the present custom, and saves time and confusion, to have as many knives, forks, and spoons by the sides of each plate as will be needed in the course of the meal.

When dinner is first announced, the soup and soup-plates are found before the hostess, and the former is dished out by her, a small ladleful in each soup-plate, and carried by a waiter on a tray and handed over the left shoulder to each person at the table. No one is expected to ask for soup a second time, and the turreen is now quietly removed. As soon as anyone has evidently got through with his soup-plate, it is at once replaced by a fresh plate without waiting for all to finish. If fish is to come after the soup, that is then placed before the host to be carved by him, or being previously cut in suitable portions is handed to each person so he may select his own morsel. Plain Irish potatoes are often passed with the fish. The waiter removes these plates as before, and then the joint is placed before the host who carves it and sends to each his favorite slice. The vegetables, side dishes, etc., are then offered by the waiter, each person helping himself as he desires. The last course before dessert is frequently a salad with thin slices of bread and butter. The clearing of the table is a very simple matter if this method is followed. There are only the plates and the roast, or the fowls, birds, etc. that may have followed the roast, to be removed, then the table is brushed, or the crumbs removed with a silver scraper. The hostess serves the dessert, and lastly small cups of *café noir* or coffee without cream, and sometimes bits of bread and butter and cheese, conclude the meal. I shall say nothing about wines in this connection, since I never offer them at my own table and have not made a study of them for my friends.

Or the good, hospitable, old fashioned, usual custom may be followed, and indeed, must be in many homes where but one servant is kept, of having first the soup and then the heavy course all placed at once on the table to be served by the heads of the family, and last the dessert. Even then a regular routine should be established and followed every day. There will still be room for flowers to brighten the table, and the girl can be trained to remove each course, to brush the table, and bring in the dessert in an orderly and quiet manner. She should also be taught to make herself tidy by the addition of a white apron to her usual dress, and any other device that will not take too much time. The younger members of a family can soon learn to be of great assistance in the progress of any meal, if some specific thing is regularly trusted to their care, and they will early come to enjoy and be proud of the want of friction, and the perfect smoothness characteristic of all the routine of a well ordered table.

And now comes tea, the pleasant evening meal, around which, the day's work being done, the family gather to relate the day's experience, forget its worries, and plan the evening's pleasure. To me it is the most attractive meal of the three. The unrest and hurry of the day are over. The children are home from school, the father free from care, and the dear mother ready at last for rest and comfort. It is a light repast, and yet the fragrant and steaming tea-pot is even more indicative of good cheer than all the formal array of smoking viands at the midday meal.

The tea table should by its brightness and beauty prepare all who approach it for cheerfulness and good fellowship. The silver and glass should reflect serene faces, the bread or biscuit be as light as the heart that beats in each bosom, and the fruit and cake fit companions for these. Then will quick and perfect digestion prepare for "balmy sleep," and balmy sleep ensure an awakening like that of the happy, healthy child, who springs from his bed, bright as a sunbeam, with eyes clear as a dew-drop, eager for the day's fun, refreshed in every member.

CHAPTER III.

TERMS USED IN COOKING.

BAKING.

HIS is the process by which we as a people cook our so called roasts. It is simply cooking by confined hot air. Baked meat is inferior to roasted because the ventilation of the oven can never be so perfect as that of the spit, and the dry heat evaporates juices so rapidly as to make the joint comparatively hard and tasteless. Any meat baked should therefore be frequently basted.

Every dripping pan should be furnished with a rack so that the meat need not come directly in contact with the bottom of the pan, and also that the heated air may be able to surround the meat on all sides.

BOILING.

The manner of this culinary process depends on the effect to be produced. If it is desired to prepare a stew, combining the good features of both soup and meat, then cold water is used at first as the medium for cooking. Salt meats, like ham and corn-beef, must also be put on the fire in cold water. A " pot roast " on the contrary is partly covered at once with boiling water, turned often, and boiled rapidly for the first few moments, the temperature then reduced and the boiling continued more moderately. When fish are boiled they must first be carefully tied in cloth so they will not break. Boiling pieces of meat, birds, etc., should also be securely tied in shape before boiling.

If puddings are to be boiled in a bag, it must first be wrung out of hot water and then thickly floured; if in a mold, it should be well buttered. Never fill the bag or mold full but leave room for the contents to swell. The water must be kept boiling con-

23

stantly the required time or the pudding will surely be ruined. As the water evaporates, the kettle must be replenished with boiling water which should be kept ready for this purpose.

STEAMING is a modification of boiling whereby the article cooked is boiled in the heated vapor of water. Puddings, dumplings, and many vegetables are better cooked in this way than boiled, if care be taken to keep the water under the steamer boiling all the time. It takes longer to cook by this method than by boiling.

STEWING is another modification of boiling. Here, too, time is a matter of great importance. The fire should be even and regular, and the thing to be stewed put into cold water and kept carefully skimmed. When the water has once boiled up, the kettle should be moved to the back of the stove, and the broth allowed just to bubble slowly and evenly around the edges of the pot. After the liquor has been skimmed until it is clear, cover closely, and do not remove the cover except when absolutely necessary.

From "Wholesome Fare" a standard English book on cookery, I extract the following: "Stewing, another modification of boiling, is especially open to the observation "the more haste, the worse speed." It is an eminently economical branch of cooking. By it, coarse joints, old poultry, hard portions of animals, feet, gizzards, tendons, and even bones, are made to supply savory and wholesome nutriment. Time and slow cooking are the secret of success; if a thing cannot be stewed tender in one doing, it must be done in two or three, supplying as required, from time to time, the moisture absorbed and evaporated." And Dr. Letheby, an eminent authority on food, says: "Stewing is a delicate and safe process when the object is to retain the nutriment of meat, and to render it succulent and tender. All kinds of tough and strong-flavored meat may therefore be cooked with great advantage in this manner." And Dr. Smith, whose valuable work on foods is so well known, adds: "A slow fire, or water at a temperature of 160 degrees, will suffice to expand the fibres, and in some degree to rupture them, whilst it separates these and other structures and renders the whole mass more fitted for mastication and digestion."

BONING.

With a sharp knife, patience, and plenty of time, this is not so difficult an operation as is often thought. In boning a fowl the first thing to do is to lay open the back by one straight cut its entire length. Now cut towards the wings and disjoint them at the body. Then cut the flesh from the carcass to the thigh bones and disjoint these also at the body. Then cut the flesh entirely from the remainder of the skeleton, taking great pains not to cut through the skin where it joins the ridge of the breast bone. If the shape of the bird is to be preserved it is best not to remove the wing and leg bones, though this may be done if preferred. It is more common now, however, not to undertake to preserve the shape, and the flesh of the wings and legs is cut away to the last joint, which is severed by the cleaver. The wings and legs are then turned in, the fowl laid skin down on the table, stuffed and rolled in compact form, sewed or tied tightly in a stout cloth bandage and then boiled.

The bones from a shoulder of lamb, or the ribs from a rib roast can likewise easily be removed with a little practice.

BOUQUET-GARNI.

A *bouquet-garni* or more commonly a bouquet of herbs, is a bunch of herbs, tied together and used to flavor soups, stews, sauces, etc. It is usually composed of a few sprigs of thyme, parsley and a bay leaf. A little celery, sweet marjoram, or indeed any of the sweet herbs may be added according to the effect desired. I append a few extracts in regard to herbs from Miss Corson's "Cooking-School Text Book." "A *bouquet* of herbs is made by tying together a few sprigs of parsley, thyme, and two bay-leaves. The bay-leaves, which have the flavor of laurel, can be bought at any German grocery or drug store, enough to last for a long time, for five cents. The best herbs are sage, thyme, sweet marjoram, tarragon, mint, sweet basil, parsley, bay-leaves, celery seed and onions. If the seed of any of the seven first mentioned is planted in little boxes on the window sill, or in a sunny spot in the yard, enough can be raised for general use. Gather and dry them as follows: parsley and tarragon should be dried in June and July, just before flowering; mint in June and

July; thyme, marjoram, and savory in July and August; basil and sage in August and September; all herbs should be gathered in the sunshine, and dried by artificial heat; their flavor is best preserved by keeping them in air-tight cans, or in tightly corked glass bottles."

"DRIED CELERY AND PARSLEY.—In using celery, wash the leaves, stalks, roots and trimmings, and put them in a cool oven to dry thoroughly; then grate the root, and rub the leaves and stalks through a seive, and put all into a tightly corked bottle, or tin can with close cover; this makes a most delicious seasoning for soups, stews, and stuffing. In using parsley, save every bit of leaf, stalk, or root, and treat them in the same way as the celery. Remember, in using parsley, that the root has even a stronger flavor than the leaves, and do not waste a bit."

"TARRAGON VINEGAR.—Use a bunch of fresh tarragon in summer, or the dried herb in winter; put it in an earthen bowl, and pour on it one pint of scalding hot vinegar; cover it and let it stand until the next day; then strain it and put it into a bottle tightly corked. Either put more hot vinegar on the tarragon, or dry it, and save it until wanted to make more; a gallon or more can be made from one bunch; only every time it is used it must stand a day longer."

"CELERY SALT.—Mix celery root, which has been dried and grated as above, with one-fourth of its quantity of salt; it makes a nice seasoning, and keeps a long time."

"SPICE SALT.—This can be made nicely by drying, powdering, and mixing by repeated siftings, the following ingredients: one-quarter of an ounce each of powdered thyme, bay-leaf and pepper; one-eighth of an ounce each of marjoram and cayenne pepper; one-half of an ounce each of powdered clove and nutmeg; to every four ounces of this powder add one ounce of salt, and keep the mixture in an air-tight vessel. One ounce of it added to three pounds of stuffing, or force meat of any kind, makes a delicious seasoning."

BRAIZING.

Braizing is a method of cooking by the application of heat both above and below the thing to be cooked. It is accomplished by means of a kettle having a deep lid which can be filled with lighted charcoal, or live embers or coals of any sort. The cover must fit perfectly tight, and the kettle be just large enough to contain the joint, bird, or other meat to be cooked. This must be partially surrounded with stock for basting, and the herbs, spices, or vegetables intended for seasoning. Braizing is an operation requiring great care, as the heat should be evenly applied, the pot kept as much as possible closely covered, and the basting very frequent. If the heat below is too strong, a plate is sometimes put in the bottom of the pot, and the meat placed on that. An oiled paper, cut just to fit, is placed between the meat and the lid, if that becomes too hot. This, of course must be lifted every time any basting is done.

BRAIZING KETTLE.

BROILING.

This method of cooking is, as a rule, applied only to small things, such as steaks, chops, birds, pan fish, etc. It is a delicate operation and needs constant care. The stew-kettle, the dripping-pan, and the stock-pot may, at times, be left to take care of themselves, but the cook must stand over her gridiron until the process is complete. It needs a clear, hot fire, the best for the purpose being

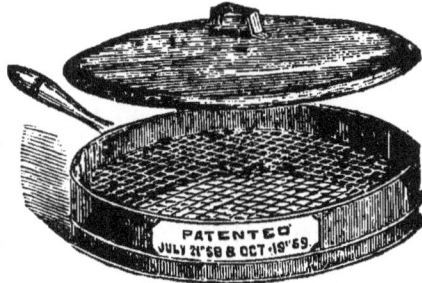

AMERICAN BROILER.

thoroughly ignited charcoal. The gridiron should be hot, and the bars greased before the steak or chop is placed on it. There have been great improvements made of late in the manufacture of gridirons. Instead of the plain iron bars formerly in use we may purchase now broilers of almost any shape to suit our convenience. The circular gridiron made to fit any range and tightly covered like the American, illustrated above, is exceedingly convenient, especially over wood coals. The Henis is also a superior gridiron, the best indeed I have ever tried. There is less smoke, and less dripping, and, being light, it is easily turned.

I can heartily recommend it. The broiler should be turned frequently, so as to cook the steak evenly, and to prevent also tho

THE HENIS BROILER.

escape of the juices. If obliged to turn the meat, instead of the gridiron, care must be exercised not to stick the fork in the muscle, as in that case a hole is made for the escape of the juices. It must be turned either with tongs which come for the purpose, or the fork may be inserted in the fat, or put under the steak and used as a lever to turn it over. Fish or birds that are split, should be broiled inside first. The best gridiron for fish is the

wire broiler. They can be purchased of almost any size and it is convenient to have a set of them. Thin cuts of meat will bear a much hotter fire than thick ones. In the latter case sear the STEAK

outside quickly and then remove to a TONGS. greater distance from the coals, or moderate the fire, to give time for slower cooking, being sure to turn frequently in either case. If

WIRE BROILER.

the fire flames up too much, or is too hot, sprinkle salt over it.

FRYING.

This is simply boiling in hot fat. Nothing is fried in the proper meaning of that word unless immersed in the hot oil. We have no English word that accurately expresses the idea conveyed to the majority of minds by the monosyllable " fry." The French word *sauté* is used by all cooks for this purpose. This process will be fully described a little later.

The causes of failure in frying are thus described in "Wholesome Fare ":

"1. An insufficient quantity of fat in the pan.
"2. Putting in things to fry before the fat is hot enough.
"3. Too much moisture adhering to the surface of things to be fried."

Many things that would be ruined by boiling in water can be quickly and delicately cooked in hot fat. If there be plenty of fat in the pan, if this be of the right temperature, and if the article to be cooked be not wet so the hot liquid can take immediate hold of it, it need never be greasy or fat-soaked. On the contrary, the surface will be seared over or hardened as soon as it comes in contact with the hot fat and thus become impervious. Boiling water penetrates and finally dissolves most substances long exposed to its influence. Hot fat hardens and finally reduces that which is immersed in it to a cinder. If properly managed the frying-pan is one of the most useful and indispensable utensils. Here is an instance in which there's a great deal in a name. By applying the term "fry" to altogether the wrong operation it has come into great disrepute.

For frying small things, a wire basket, similar to the cut below, is used as a help in handling them. Croquettes, Saratoga potatoes, etc., are first put in the basket, and then the whole lowered into the hot fat. The basket should never quite reach the bottom of the fry-kettle. The temperature of the fat can be tested by dropping a bit of bread in it. If it brown in five or six seconds, the heat is right. When a light, hardly perceptible smoke begins to curl up from the kettle the fat is also generally of the right temperature.

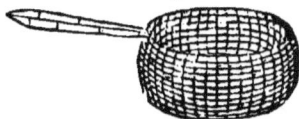

The fats used for frying are olive oil, butter, lard, or any sweet, clear, dripping. Any one of these may be used again and again if it is properly cared for. It should be kept clear of both dregs and scum, and carefully strained into earthen vessels containing a little water, so that any sediment may fall to the bottom each time after using. Fat used for frying fish should be kept separate from that used for meats, and that in which sweets, such as doughnuts, are fried, should be kept separate from either. The fry-kettle must be scrupulously clean. Too much pains cannot be taken in regard to this. Croquettes, oysters, small fish, etc., should be laid for a moment on blotting-paper, near the fire, when taken from the fat. This will entirely absorb any superficial grease, and render them dry and crisp. The fry-kettle should be at least six inches deep.

Brillat-Savarin, in his most entertaining book on "Gastronomy as a Fine Art," makes a learned professor discourse as follows on "The Theory of Frying," to a delinquent cook who had spoiled a fine fish in the operation.

"The liquids which you expose to the action of fire become charged with different amounts of heat, in virtue of some property impressed upon them by Nature, the secret of which is yet reserved from us. Thus, you might with impunity dip your finger in spirits of wine when boiling, but you would draw it out quick enough from brandy, and quicker still if it were water, while even a hasty immersion in boiling oil would hurt you cruelly—the capacity of oil for heat being at least three times that of water.

"Hence it is that an alimentary substance in boiling water softens, becomes dissolved, and forms a soup; and in oil, it contracts, assumes a darker color, and at last has its surface carbonized. In the former case, the water dissolves and draws out the juices contained by the sapid substance; in the latter, the juices are preserved, because the oil cannot dissolve them. It is to the second process, boiling in oil or fat, that the term 'to fry' is properly applied.

"The beauty of a good fry is carbonizing or browning the surface by sudden immersion—the process known as the 'surprise.' It forms a sort of vault to enclose all that is valuable, prevents the fat from reaching it, and concentrates the juices, so as best to develop the alimentary qualities."

LARDING.

This is one method of garnishing and at the same time seasoning meats naturally dry and deficient in fat, such as fillet of beef, the breast of fowls, liver, etc. It is done by running strips of pork, called lardoons into the surface of the article to be larded. A larding needle [see cut] greatly facilitates the work. These

lardoons should be cut from the firmest dry salted pork or bacon and must be even in size and of equal length, these being determined by the proportions of that for which they are intended to be used.

The process is as follows: A puncture is made with the sharp point of the larding needle on the surface of the article operated on, the needle is pushed partly through and one end of a lardoon is then inserted in the split extremity or eye of the needle, which closes tightly on it as it is drawn to the opposite side. The lardoons are placed at regular intervals and arranged according to any fanciful design that may please the cook. Their projecting ends should be of equal length.

The following illustration shows a fillet of beef partly larded and will explain the whole operation better than words can:

LEMON ZEST.

This is obtained by rubbing loaf sugar over the yellow surface of a lemon, thus extracting the oil which gives this portion of the rind its peculiar pungency. This sugar is then used to sweeten and flavor custards, creams, puddings, etc. It is also pounded fine and sifted into meringues when it is desired to impart to them a taste of lemon. It is simply a more delicate and safer way of obtaining the flavor than by grating the rind, since this is contained only in its yellow surface. The white part is bitter and indigestible. This fact should be remembered when a receipt directs that the grated rind of a lemon should be used.

ROASTING.

This is almost a lost art to American cooks. It can only take place before an open fire and is utterly impracticable in connection with a modern cook stove or range. Mrs. Beeton says: " Of the various methods of preparing meat, roasting is that which most effectually preserves its nutritive qualities. Meat is roasted by being exposed to the direct influence of the fire. This is done by placing the meat before an open grate, and keeping it in motion to prevent the scorching of any part. When meat is properly roasted, the outer layer of its albumen is coagulated, and thus presents a barrier to the exit of the juice. In roasting meat the heat must be strongest at first, and it should then be much reduced. To have a good juicy roast, therefore, the fire must be red and vigorous at the very commencement of the operation. In the most careful roasting some of the juice is squeezed out of the meat; this evaporates on the surface of the meat, and gives it a dark brown color, a rich lustre, and a strong aromatic taste. Besides these effects on the albumen and the expelled juice, roasting converts the cellular tissue of the meat into gelatine, and melts the fat out of the fat-cells."

ROUX.

This is butter and flour melted together and cooked, and it is the foundation of many savory sauces. The common method of making gravies and sauces is to add an uncooked flour paste to the stock or liquor of which these are to be made and thus thicken it. A much better flavored and smoother sauce is obtained, however, by cooking the flour and butter and adding the stock very slowly to it. Roux is of two kinds, brown and white. The former is used as a foundation for dark sauces; the latter for drawn butter, Bechamel and light sauces. The difference in the color of the roux depends upon the length of time the mixture is cooked. If the ingredients are simply melted together and simmered a moment or two, the roux will be white; if exposed to the effect of heat until the flour is browned, it will be dark.

SAUTÉING.

Frying, as I have already explained, is cooking by immersion in hot fat. Sautéing is a modification of this process by which a small quantity only of fat is used, and the thing cooking must be constantly turned or tossed about, if the operation is to be successful. Hence, the word, from the French *sauter*, to jump or *faire sauter*, to make jump, to toss. In this method, as in frying, the fat should be hot at the beginning of the process. It is a favorite method of cooking potatoes, cutlets, chops, small birds, etc. Doughnuts, croquettes, and small fish are fried. Pancakes, omelettes, cutlets, are sauté. In all cases it requires careful attention to sauté well, and the cook cannot leave her work with impunity until it is entirely finished. This is a cut of the most approved style of sauté pan.

SAUTÉ PAN.

GLOSSARY OF TERMS USED IN MODERN COOKING.

(COMPILED FROM THE BEST AUTHORITIES.)

Angelica.—A plant, the tender, tubular branches of which, after being preserved in syrup, are used to decorate puddings, jellies, etc.

Assiette (plate).—*Assiettes* are the small *entreés* and *hors d'oeuvres*, the quantity of which does not exceed what a plate will hold. At dessert, fruits, cheese, etc., if served upon a plate, are termed *assiettes*.

Assiette volante.—A dish which the servant hands round to the guests, but is not placed upon the table.

Aspic.—A savory jelly, used as an exterior molding for boned chicken, tongue, cold game, etc. This being of a transparent nature, allows that which it covers to be seen through it. It may also be used in other ways for decorating and garnishing.

Au bleu.—Fish dressed in such a manner as to have a bluish appearance.

Bain-marie.—An open saucepan or kettle of nearly boiling water, in which a smaller vessel or vessels can be set for cooking and warming.

Bechamel.—French white sauce.

Bisque.—Soup made generally with shell fish.

Blanch.—To whiten nuts, vegetables, fruits, poultry, etc., by plunging them into boiling water for a short time, and afterwards plunging them into cold water, there to remain until they are cold.

Blanquette.—A sort of fricassee.

Bouilli.—Beef or other meat boiled; generally speaking, boiled beef is understood by the term.

Bouillie.—A French dish resembling hasty pudding.

Bouillon.—A rich beef broth.

3

Braize.—To cook meat in a kettle having a lid so arranged as to hold coals, and thus apply direct heat above and below.

Braisiére.—A saucepan or kettle having a lid with ledges, to put fire on the top.

Brider.—To truss poultry, game, etc., to keep them in shape.

Bouquet-garni.—A bunch of soup herbs tied together.

Caramel.—Burnt sugar dissolved in boiling water, used to color soups, gravies, etc.

Casserole.—A crust.of rice which, after having been molded into form, is baked, and then filled with a fricassee of white meat, or fried chicken.

Compote.—A stew, as of fruit or pigeons.

Consommeé.—Rich, clear stock or soup.

Croquettes.—Rolls or balls of minced meat, rice, potatoes, etc., fried.

Croutons.—Dice, or sippets of bread, fried brown, and used in soups. These words both signify something crisp.

Daubiére.—An oval stewpan in which *daubes* are cooked; *daubes* being meat or fowl stewed in sauce.

Désosser.—To bone.

Entrées.—Small side or corner dishes, served with the first course.

Entremets.—Small side or corner dishes, served with the second course.

Escalopes.—Collops; small pieces of tender meat, or fish, chopped and served on toast.

Espagnole and veloute.—The two main sauces from which all others are made; the first is brown and the other white.

Farce.—Is a coarse kind of force meat used for pies.

Feuilletage.—Puff-paste.

Flamber.—To singe fowl, or game, after they have been picked.

Foncer.—To put in the bottom of a saucepan slices of ham, veal, or thin, broad slices of bacon.

Galette.—A broad, thin cake.

Gateau.—A cake, correctly speaking; but used sometimes to denote a pudding, and a kind of tart.

Glacer.—To glaze, or spread upon hot meats, or larded fowl, a thick and rich sauce or gravy, called *glaze.* This is laid on with a feather or brush. In confectionery the term means to ice fruits and pastry with sugar, which glistens on hardening.

Hors doeuvres.—Small dishes, or *assiettes volantes* of sardines, anchovies, and other relishes of this kind, served to the guests during the first course.

Jardiniere.—A mixed preparation of vegetables, stewed down in their own sauce.

Lit.—A bed or layer; articles in thin slices are placed in layers, other articles, or seasoning, being laid between them.

Macedoine.—The same as a *jardiniere*, when of vegetables; when of fruits, a kind of jelly.

Maigre.—Broth, soup, or gravy, made without meat.

Matelote.—A rich fish stew, made with wine.

Mayonnaise.—Cold sauce, or salad dressing made with the yolk of egg and olive oil.

Menu.—The bill of fare.

Meringue.—A kind of icing, made of whites of eggs and sugar well beaten, and used to spread over the top of a pudding or pie, and then slightly browned in the oven.

Miroton.—Slices of meat.

Mouiller.—To add water, broth, or other liquid, during the cooking.

Nougat.—A mixture of almonds and sugar.

Nouilles.—A kind of vermicelli.

Paner.—To cover with very fine crumbs of bread.

Piquer.—To lard with strips of fat pork or bacon.

Poelée.—Stock used instead of water for boiling turkeys, sweet breads, fowls, and vegetables, to render them more highly flavored.

Purée.—Vegetables or meat reduced to a very smooth pulp, which is afterwards mixed with enough liquid to make it of the consistency of very thick soup.

Quenelle.—A delicate sort of force meat.

Ragout.—Stew or hash.

Remoulade.—Salad dressing.

Rissoles.—Pastry, made of light puff-paste, and cut into various forms and fried. They may be filled with fish, meat, or sweets.

Roux.—French thickening; brown, and white.

Salmi.—Ragout of game previously roasted.

Sauce piquante.—A sharp sauce, in which an acid flavor predominates.

Sauter.—To cook in a saucepan with hot lard or butter, repeatedly stirring or moving it about.

Soufflés.—The word *soufflé* means strictly something puffed up, and is generally applied to a very light and delicate kind of pudding.

Tamis.—Tammy, a sort of open cloth or sieve, through which to strain broth or sauces.

Tourte.—Tart; fruit-pie.

Trousser.—To truss a bird.

Vol-au-vent.—A rich crust of very fine puff paste, which may be filled with various delicate preparations of fish, flesh fowl, or fruit.

CHAPTER IV.

UTENSILS.

HE utensils for woman's use in domestic matters are quite as important in their relation to results, as the apparatus in the laboratory, or the tools in the work-shop. Under inspection, most kitchens could offer only an array of ill-selected, worse cared for implements, few in number, worn and battered, and entirely inadequate to the needs of the cook if she be expected to do good work. The wonder is that the results of her labor are even as satisfactory as they are. A cook can no more produce dainty food with means unsuited to that end, than an artisan can do good work without fit tools. The carelessness of housekeepers in providing proper conveniences for kitchen use is due in great measure to their ignorance rather than their penuriousness. I have been astonished at the curiosity and interest excited in my classes by my array of working tools, and the eagerness with which lists of modern utensils have been copied and forwarded to dealers under my directions. "We did not know there were such things to be had" has been the almost universal exclamation. Especially is this true in the country, where, no call being made for better things, the shelves of hardware merchants repeat forever the same display of iron pot and tin pan our grandmothers used in Revolutionary times, or before. Woman is naturally conservative, and unless her attention is called to improved ways and means, will travel indefinitely the well beaten but difficult path worn into ruts by the weary feet of those who have preceded her. But she is quick also to see and imitate, and if once guided into easier ways will follow them eagerly.

I shall endeavor in this chapter to illustrate and explain some of the newer and more valuable devices for making the culinary art easier to practice and surer in its results. Should a few think me somewhat too minute, I am sure the many will find no fault with the full and specific directions here set forth in regard to improved utensils. I have not confined myself strictly to cooking conveniences, but in a very few instances have mentioned tools I have found exceptionally useful in other departments of housework.

APPLE CORER.—This simple contrivance explains itself. This form is preferable to any other I have tried. If the tube is not sharpened as at *a* it is almost impossible to avoid splitting the apple.

a

THE BAIN MARIE is a heavy pan of sufficient size to hold several sauce-pans. It is partly filled with hot water and kept on the back of the range.

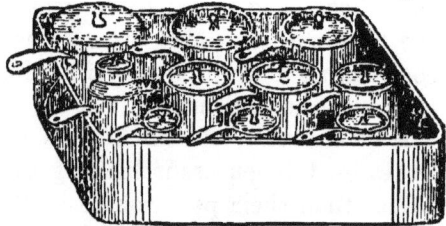

BAIN MARIE SAUCE-PAN.—The small sauce-pans containing gravies, sauces, etc., being immersed in the hot water, are kept at the proper temperature until needed. The *bain marie* is kept on the back part of the range where the water will keep hot, yet not actually boil. Food kept warm in this way does not deteriorate in quality nor dry up like that kept on the top of the range or in the oven. The *bain marie* is almost indispensable in the preparation of a dinner of many courses. It is well nigh impossible in any ordinary kitchen, or with the usual number of servants, to prepare all the different garnishes and sauces at the last moment. Nor is it necessary if only they can be kept hot and fresh as in the *bain marie*.

BROWN BREAD PAN.—This is the most convenient shape for a pan in which brown bread is to be steamed. The cover fits closely and laps over far enough to ensure against the possibility of coming off accidentally, or of permitting the steam or water to enter the pan.

CAKE BOX.—The upright cake box with shelves for different varieties of cake, is much more convenient than the old fashioned box with trays, each of which had to be successively lifted out to get at the contents below. It has this advantage, too, that the amount and kind of cake on hand can be determined at a glance. It is easy to keep clean and convenient in every way. It may be obtained in several sizes, either with or without lock and key, and answers as well for bread as for cake.

CASSEROLE.—This is simply a rice border in which may be served a stew of meat, *sautéd* chicken, vegetables, or something sweet, as preserved fruit. The rice, boiled soft and mashed with a wooden spoon until perfectly smooth, is either pressed in a mold and then after it has cooled and hardened, the mold is unclasped and carefully removed, leaving the rice form, the center of which is scooped out and the *casserole* filled and placed in a very hot oven for a few moments before serving, or the *casserole* may be moulded into shape by hand, then baked, the center removed, etc. This latter is a delicate and difficult operation and is seldom attempted except by professional cooks. Francatelli greatly prides himself on the deftness and artistic skill with which he can shape and decorate a *casserole*. He says: "A *casserole* of rice is justly considered one of the most elegant *entrées;* it requires great care throughout its preparation, especially in the treatment of the rice, that being its basis, and upon the success of this much of the beauty of the *casserole* depends. If the rice be not sufficiently boiled, and effectually worked into a smooth paste, it becomes a difficult matter to mold it, and any apparent roughness would spoil the looks of the *casserole*."

CASSEROLE MOLD.

CHARLOTTE RUSSE CUP AND MOLD.—These are lined with sponge cake and filled with a preparation of whipped cream, a cup for each person, or the mold for the

whole number. After the cream has remained long enough in the cake, the molds being surrounded by ice, or standing in a very cold place, to become firm, the whole will slip out, retaining the form of the mold.

CIRCULAR MOLD.—A is a circular, open tin mold to be filled with wine jelly, corn starch, *blanc mange,* Bavarian cream, rice, or anything of the sort which can be molded. After the circle of jelly or *blanc mange* is removed from the mold, the center can be filled with whipped cream, fruit, jelly, chocolate, etc. The filling may vary indefinitely according to the taste of the cook. If the border is rice, fried chicken, green peas, or something of that kind may compose the filling. Figure *a* represents a circle of wine jelly filled with whipped cream, *b* a more ornamental border of *blanc mange* filled partly with berries and the center heaped with whipped cream; *c* is the same mold empty.

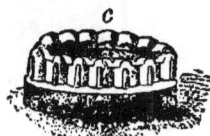

A small sized CLEAVER similar to the illustration is a most convenient utensil. To be sure a hatchet will do, provided a sharp one is kept for the sole purpose of disjointing fowls, breaking the bones of steaks, etc., to make he carving easier, or for the many similar purposes for which it may be needed. A good cleaver, however, costs little more than a hatchet, and being heavier in the blade, shorter handled and a better shape, is much to be preferred.

CLOTHES SPRINKLER.—Any housewife who has ever used this, costing as it does but a few cents, will never again waste time and water sprinkling clothes the old way.

COPPER STEW-PAN.—Copper cooking utensils have many things

to recommend them. They are very durable, retain the heat a long time, are flat-bottomed, and show every particle of dirt, so that at a glance it is easy to tell whether they are properly cared for or not. Both stew pan and cover are coated with tin on their inner surface, so that any danger of poisonous compounds caused by the action on the copper of acids, oils, or salt, is completely avoided. If this lining wears off they can easily be retinned, and the first expense in purchasing them, which is comparatively heavy, is more than compensated for by their great durability. Since copper is a good conductor of heat, less fuel is required for cooking in a copper stew pan than in one of iron or tin. Food should never be allowed to stand in any copper cooking utensil to cool. The stew pans should be kept scrupulously clean. A good preparation for cleaning them is a mixture of turpentine and fine brick-dust rubbed on with flannel. After being cleaned with this they should be wiped with a dry, soft cloth and finally polished with a dry chamois skin and powdered whiting. Miss Corson says in her "Cooking School Text Book": "One of the best *chefs* belonging to the New York Cooking School always had the coppers cleaned with the following mixture, rubbed on with the hand, and then washed off with clean, cold water, and always employed a soft towel to dry them thoroughly; the mixture consisted of equal parts of salt, fine sand, and flour, made into a thick paste with milk or buttermilk." At the South Kensington National Training School of Cookery, fine sand, soap and lemon juice are the polishing materials used in cleaning the coppers. This is rubbed on with the palm of the hand, and the coppers, when spotlessly bright within and without. are washed and dried.

CONFECTIONER'S TUBE.—This is used for decorating the icing on cakes, the *méringues* on pies and puddings. The tubes come having the opening at the small end cut in various ornamental shapes.

BAG FOR USING WITH TUBE.—The bag is made of some closely woven, strong material through which the *méringue* will not leak. The tube A is put in the bag B, the bag is then filled with icing, and this can be squeezed at will in any desirable form through the ornamental opening at the bottom of the tube by compressing the bag. Mottoes are thus formed, monograms, flowers, or borders, as the fancy may dictate. Any tinner can make the tube, and any housewife the bag. In deft hands they will be found capable of producing an infinite variety of pleasing effects.

CORN CAKE PANS.—Here are shown two styles, joined together as in A, or single as in B. They are deeper than the ordinary gem pan. They can be bought in agate or tinware and are comparatively inexpensive. Corn muffins or cakes served in this shape are much nicer than in loaves, and, cooked in small quantities as in these cups, are more certain to be light, tender, and above all, evenly and thoroughly cooked than when baked in loaves.

CRULLER AND POTATO FRYER.—This ingenious utensil combines the advantages of a wire basket and fry-kettle. The perforated kettle hangs on the hook while the lard below is heating. When that is at the proper temperature the crullers, or potatoes, or doughnuts are placed in this vessel and the whole lowered into the hot fat. As soon as they are cooked the pan is again suspended from the hook until its contents are thoroughly drained, they are then removed, a fresh supply takes their place, and the process is repeated.

CUSTARD KETTLE.—This double kettle is a great boon to the housewife. The lower compartment *a* is partly filled with boiling water, the upper one *b* with milk for custards, tapioca-cream, or any like preparation. This can then be left to heat without constant anxiety lest it may

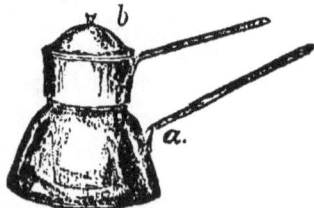

burn. Who cannot remember agonizing over a stew-pan of milk, with a dozen other things requiring immediate attention, and being tormented by the painful certainty that if the milk be left for a single moment it will surely scorch, though it can be watched and waited for half an hour without getting appreciably hotter. Or if the milk be put in a pail, and this placed in a kettle of hot water, either the pail obstinately refuses to stand upright, or the water boils up into the milk. I shall not soon forget the comfortable sense of satisfaction I experienced when I first tried this double kettle. What had before been a serious and harassing business became easy and comfortable, and the making of a smooth, velvety custard ceased from that moment to be drudgery.

DIGESTER.—This is a kind of iron stock-pot, the lid of which fits in a groove, thus effectually preventing the escape of the steam. A self-regulating valve at the top permits the outgo of superfluous steam. This is a valuable utensil, as by its use more nutriment can be obtained to the pound of meat and bone than in any other way. They can be procured in all sizes, and the smaller ones are very useful in making sauces, gravies, etc. They should always be placed over a very slow fire and plenty of time be given for the extraction of all the juices from the meat.

DOUGHNUT CUTTER.—This illustration explains itself and will suggest a means of relief to those who have been accustomed to cutting doughnuts first with a biscuit cutter, and then removing the center with the top of the pepper-box. This cutter is a good substitute also for a jumble-mold.

EGG BOILER. To those who are exceedingly particular as to the exact second their eggs must be boiled, this copper egg boiler will offer a great luxury. It can be used at the breakfast table and the water can be kept boiling, if desired, by a spirit lamp underneath.

Egg Fryers.—Egg fryers are iron spiders, molded after the manner of the illustrations, which are filled with hot lard or drippings, and the eggs are dropped separately in each form. They can be turned if desired, and when sufficiently cooked are slipped out, retaining the imprint of the mold, on thin slices of broiled ham.

Egg Poacher.—This illustration presents one form of the egg poacher. They are offered in many patterns and with sauce-pans to correspond. They are immersed in boiling water, the eggs dropped in, and when these are cooked the poacher is lifted out of the sauce-pan. Each little perforated cup is movable and can be removed from the stand and the egg carefully emptied out on a slice of toast.

Egg Whisk.—For beating a large number of eggs, from eight or ten to a dozen or more, this is preferable to any egg beater. It is also convenient to whip cream. Cream can be beaten to a stiff foam with a good egg whisk in half the time it would take to do it with a "Whipped Cream Churn."

Drip-pan Grate or Trivet.—No dripping-pan or meat roaster should be used for baking meats without having adjusted to it such a grate, to lift the meat from direct contact with the bottom of the pan.

The Fish Kettle is almost indispensable for boiling a fish of any size. Each kettle is fitted with a flat strainer, having a handle to lift it by. The fish is placed on the strainer and lowered into the boiling water. When done, the strainer is carefully lifted out and the fish gently slipped off.

In this way the danger of breaking it in dishing up is almost wholly avoided.

FELT JELLY BAG.—These can be purchased in all sizes and are used in connection with the jelly strainer illustrated a little farther on. They are stronger, strain more perfectly, and are much more durable than any home-made bag.

THE FLOUR DREDGE is used to sprinkle flour over fish, meats, and all things that need it. A similar box is also employed to dredge cookies, buns, etc., with sugar. It is convenient also for flouring the pastry board.

FLUTED KNIFE.—Vegetables for garnishing, such as potatoes, carrots, and turnips, can be cut into a variety of pleasing shapes with this knife. Below are found a few illustrations of the easier forms. With a little ingenuity many fanciful effects can be produced.

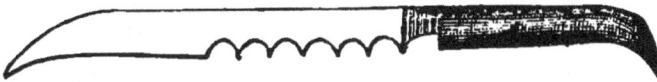

SABATIERE'S, AND FRENCH COOKS' KNIVES.—When these have once been tried, they seem absolutely indispensable to the cook. The smallest size is also called a *boning knife*. The second size is the style and shape of *Sabatiere's carving knife* which I can also cordially recommend. These knives are strong, of excellent material, easily kept sharp, and of the right shape.

GRAVY STRAINER.—If gravy and sauces, very unsightly from lumps, were not so common, I should not think it necessary to illustrate so simple a utensil. The above is an excellent style, as it can be held over a small gravy, or sauce boat, and at the same time it is large enough to hold a reasonable quantity. A wooden handle is to be preferred to a tin one as it does not heat through so quickly, and is also pleasant to hold.

INDIVIDUAL ICE CREAM MOLDS.—These are made of lead lined with porcelain, and come in a great variety of shapes. The cream is partly frozen, then the molds are filled, closed and packed in ice. When they are to be removed they are immersed *for a second* in hot water. They then turn out easily, and furnish a much more ornamental way of serving ice cream than the ordinary method of dishing it out by the spoonful. In a city one can order such things from the confectioner, but there is no reason why any good housewife in a small town or on a farm, who has milk and cream in abundance should not have ice cream as often as she desires it. Ice is coming to be considered a necessity, and the wife of a well-to-do and thrifty farmer can almost always command it. With proper utensils she may rival her city friends in the elegance of her entertainments.

JELLY OR SOUP STRAINER.—Something of this sort is almost indispensable in a house where jellies and soups are often made. The felt jelly bag described on page 45, is drawn securely over the frame *a* which fits exactly the top of the stand. This frame is then adjusted to the stand, and the hot liquid poured in without fear of spilling or leaking. A soup stand should, of course, be larger than the jelly stand, and the bag should be made of strong factory, or crash.

LADY-FINGER CAKE PANS.—Of course if one lives in or near a town of any size, where the baker will furnish "lady-fingers" whenever they are needed for Charlotte Russe, cabinet puddings, or dainties of that sort, one need not stop to manufac-

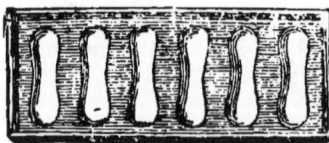

ture them herself. But in many villages, and on many farms it is impossible to get them at any price, unless they are manufactured at home. Sponge cake is easily made, and when eggs are cheap and abundant, is as inexpensive as it is delicious. With the pans illustrated above, lady-fingers are not so much trouble to make as ordinary cookies.

LEMON SQUEEZER.—The porcelain lined lemon squeezer, as here shown, is the best style for use, as the acid corrodes a metal one, and is apt to receive an unpleasant flavor from one made wholly of wood.

MEAT PIE MOLD.—This cut represents the mold closed and ready for use. It is first well buttered, the paste then pressed into it, then filled, the cover put on and ornamented, and then baked. When taken from the oven, the wire pin A is drawn out, and the mold opens and is taken away from the pie, instead of the pie being lifted from it. There is therefore no danger of breaking or disfiguring the crust. Empty cases, to be filled with meat, game, or anything of the sort, are often made in these molds. The paste must necessarily be stiff and rather tough to take and retain the imprint. It is often not intended to be eaten at all, but simply to serve as an ornamental dish, the contents of which can be served as from any other receptacle.

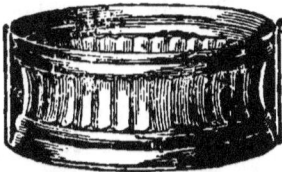

MEAT SQUEEZER.—This is used to press the juice from rare cooked beef. An excellent food for invalids or those convalescing from wasting disease, is made by toasting delicately a piece of bread, and then squeezing over it the juice of beef, and adding enough salt to make it palatable. If strong beef extract is needed quickly in an emergency it can be obtained in this way.

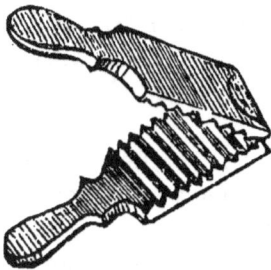

MORTAR AND PESTLE.—This old-fashioned convenience is so useful it ought never to be omitted from a housekeeper's list. The accompanying cut shows one made of wedgewood, which is much to be preferred to iron.

MUFFIN CUPS AND RINGS.—The cut A represents the plain deep muffin cup, B a more ornamental shape, and C the old style rings. The first is the most convenient form, as both the other designs require a dripping pan to hold them. The rings are placed in a pan, then filled and baked.

PASTRY BRUSH.—Such a brush is used to varnish over pastry, buns, tea-cakes, etc., with the white or yolk of egg. It also serves to apply glaze to meat.

PASTE JAGGER.—The wheel A is used for cutting pastry for the borders of pies, strips to criss-cross on cranberry, or other open tarts, and the ornamental figure B is imprinted on the outer edge of the pie.

POTATO CUTTERS.—By means of these cutters uniform and shapely pieces can be cut from potatoes or other vegetables. These, if of potatoes, are first parboiled in salted water, and then fried a delicate brown in hot fat and used, in general, to garnish meat dishes, such as boiled beef, beef á-la-mode, etc.

POTATO MASHER.—This style is much to be preferred to the solid wooden masher. When this is used the potato can be thoroughly mashed, and at the same time made light and creamy.

POTATO QUIRLERS.—With these, carrots, turnips, or potatoes may be cut into the forms illustrated. The quirls of carrot are boiled in salted water until tender, the potatoes usually fried in hot lard like Saratoga potatoes. They make a handsome garnish, or they may be served by themselves. The quirler is forced into the vegetable as far as A. The handle, as is shown, is separate from the quirlers, fitting them all, and must be taken off each time in order to remove the quirl, the vegetable having first been cut through to meet the steel.

SIEVE FOR PURÉES.—Anyone who has tried to rub pea, or bean, or any vegetable purée, through an ordinary sieve with a spoon will welcome this as a valuable addition to their kitchen tools. The handle A is attached to a wooden masher which fits the sieve loosely enough to admit of being moved about sufficiently to press the contents through. The sieve itself is very strong and will admit of the necessary strain.

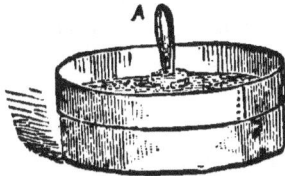

SQUASH STRAINER.—This is a strong, well made strainer somewhat coarser than an ordinary flour sieve, and much stronger. The purée sieve will do nicely for squash also.

TAPER STRAINER.—A most excellent form for straining sauces, custards, etc. It holds a convenient quantity, and offers a large surface for the liquid to pass through, and thus enables the work to be done quickly.

TEA-KETTLE STEAMER.—This steamer fits the opening in the top of a tea-kettle, and is so made as to hold almost as much as the common steamer. If the stove is crowded it saves the need of an extra kettle of water and thus economizes space.

4

TRUSSING NEEDLE.—A needle of this sort should be long enough to reach entirely through a turkey, or better still, one should have several needles graduated in size. A fowl *cannot* be properly trussed unless the cord which holds it in shape is first passed through the body at the second joint, and again at the wings.

VEGETABLE BASKET.—A wire basket of this sort is used to hold eggs, potatoes, etc., which are to be boiled. By placing these in the basket before plunging them into the boiling water, they can all, when done, be lifted out of the water at once. Salads can be washed and left to drain in such a basket, and thus frequent handling, so detrimental to their crisp freshness, can be avoided.

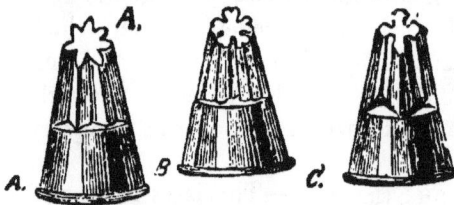

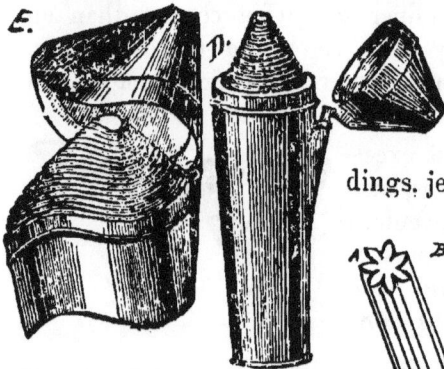

VEGETABLE CUTTERS.— Here are represented a few of the shapes of these pretty tin cutters. They are useful not only in cutting vegetables for soups or for garnishing, but they may be employed in many other ways. They furnish tasteful forms for *croutons* or sippets of bread; and puddings, jellies, and cakes can be beautifully ornamented by their aid. The illustration shows the shapes of the cut pieces also.

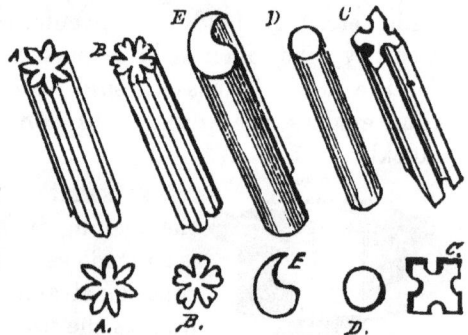

CHAPTER V.

MARKETING.

VERY sensible housekeeper should know enough about marketing to select her supplies wisely and intelligently. Economy begins here. Tradesmen soon discover who may be imposed on safely. The fine cuts of meat, the freshest eggs, the crispest salads, the soundest vegetables go to the house whose mistress has posted herself on all these matters and cannot therefore be deceived, while she who does not know a porter-house steak from a round, nor a young and tender fowl from the "oldest inhabitant" of the barn-yard, will continually be disappointed because her meat is tough and tasteless, and her supplies in general poor in quality. A little attention will soon compass the more important items of information, and the time employed in learning how to market to the best advantage is certainly well spent.

BEEF.

This is the most important animal food. How essential, then, that it should be selected with care and that infinite pains should be taken to distinguish healthy sound beef from that which is diseased, or in any way unfit for use. Fortunately the characteristics of good beef are so marked that they can be easily distinguished, and a little experience will enable one to tell with tolerable accuracy its condition in regard to health and tenderness. The necessity for care in securing meat free from disease is so vital that every one should know precisely the marks by which to be guided in its selection. I therefore append Dr. Letheby's instructions in regard to the character of sound meat. Dr. Letheby had charge of the London markets for some years, and paid special attention to the quality and condition of the meat supply. I give this extract, consequently, with perfect

51

confidence in the facts it presents. He says: "Good meat has the following characters:—

"1st. It is neither of a pale pink color nor of a deep purple tint, for the former is a sign of disease, and the latter indicates that the animal has not been slaughtered but has died with the blood in it, or has suffered from acute fever.

"2d. It has a marbled appearance from the ramification of little veins of fat among the muscles.

"3d. It should be firm and elastic to the touch, and should scarcely moisten the fingers—bad meat being wet, and sodden, and flabby, with the fat looking like jelly or wet parchment.

"4th. It should have little or no odor, and the odor should not be disagreeable, for diseased meat has a sickly, cadaverous smell, and sometimes a smell of physic. This is very discoverable when the meat is chopped up and drenched with warm water.

"5th. It should not run to water or become very wet on standing for a day or so, but should, on the contrary, dry upon the surface.

"6th. When dried at a temperature of 212 degrees or thereabout, it should not lose more than from 70 to 74 per cent of its weight, whereas bad meat will often lose as much as 80 per cent.

"7th. It should not shrink or waste much in cooking."

The color of the best beef is a deep bright red, and the suet a light cream color. In tender beef the fat is interspersed through the muscle giving it what is called a marbled appearance. The suet of tender beef is dry and firm, will crumble easily, and contains but little fibre. When the suet is oily, or full of stringy fibre, and is small in quantity, it may be regarded as certain proof that the beef is tough, dry, and tasteless. Tough beef will also have an open and coarse grain as well as tough cartilages, sinews, ligaments, and muscle. The best beef animals carry a large amount of flesh in proportion to the size of the bones. If the animal has been killed immediately after too hard driving, or when overheated from any cause, the flesh will spoil quickly, and both flesh and fat will have a dark look, caused from excess of blood. Such beef is, of course, to be avoided.

The ox when slaughtered is cut into sides, the division line being the back-bone. These sides are again subdivided into quarters. The choice roasting pieces, and most delicate steaks are cut from the hind quarter. The sirloin extends along the back-bone from the hip to the ribs, that nearest the rump being called the thick-end sirloin, and that next the ribs, thin-end sirloin or porter-house. The sirloin makes good steaks or prime roasting pieces.

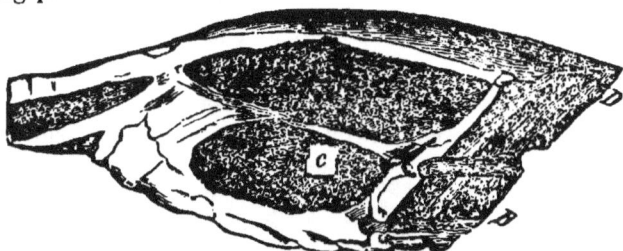

SIRLOIN ROAST.

This represents, what is sometimes called the middle-cut sirloin. That is, it is taken from between the thick or hip-sirloin and the thin-end or porter-house. *B B* are the ridge of the back-bone—*d* that portion of the back-bone that helps to form the arch of the back, *c* the tenderloin steak, lying under the bone on the kidney side.

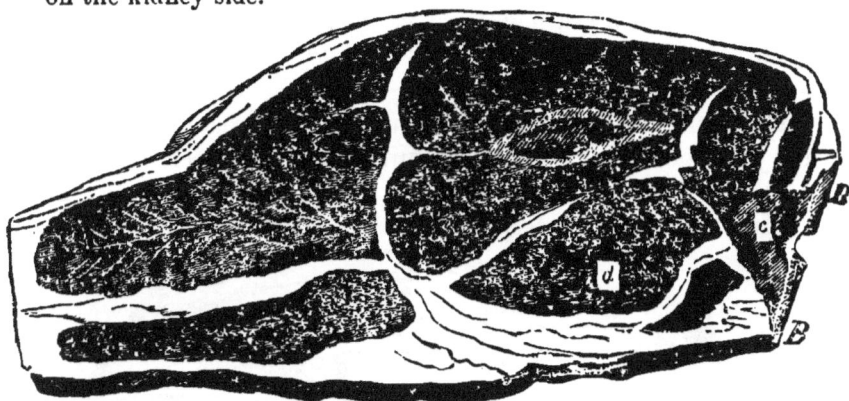

SIRLOIN STEAK.

This 'fine steak comes from the thick or hip end of the sirloin and contains the most tenderloin of any of the sirloin steaks. *BB* is the back-bone, *c* the flange of the back-bone and *d* the tenderloin. The thick end is much more profitable for steak for family use than the porter-house or thin end.

Excellent steaks are also cut from the rump, these being the

favorite steaks in England.   Steak, to be tender, should be cut
across the grain.

The small or thin end sirloin is cut either into steaks, called
porter-house, or into small roasts.

PORTER-HOUSE STEAK.

B B the back-bone, *c* the continuation of this bone, *d*, the
tenderloin.

This is a delicious morsel, but more wasteful than any other
steak, as all the thin part beyond *c* is practically of little account.

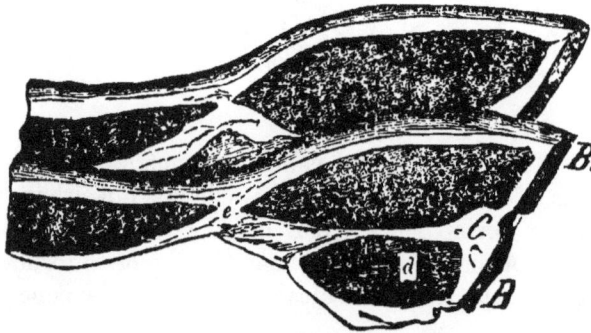

It is, of course,
weighed before
it is trimmed,
and considera-
ble of this is
cut away be-
fore it is sent
to the house.
Many butch-
ers, indeed,
trim off the

PORTER HOUSE STEAK.

whole of the thin end and only send to their customers the
portion between *c* and B B.

The round lies below the rump, and from it are obtained excellent cuts for boiling, stewing, corning, a-la-mode beef, etc.

The leg furnishes soup-bones and meat.   The first seven ribs,
cut from the fore-quarter, are called " prime ribs " and make ex-

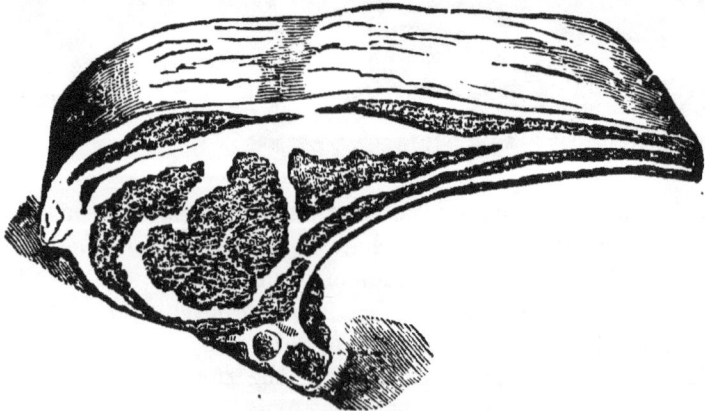

MIDDLE-CUT RIBS.

cellent roasts. Indeed, they are considered by many as richer in flavor than the sirloin. The first two, joining the thin-end sirloin are most suitable for small families. The third and fourth are known as the middle-cut ribs and are highly prized.

The remaining six ribs are likewise used for roasts, though they do not furnish such delicious eating as the prime ribs. From the four ribs next the neck the chuck steaks are cut, and in a first-class animal these are by no means to be despised. The shin-bone makes good soup, and excellent pieces for boiling, corning, and stewing are obtained from the remainder of the fore-quarter.

FILLET OF BEEF, OR TENDERLOIN.

This choice morsel extends the whole length of the sirloin, and lies on the under or kidney side of the back-bone. Its tenderness is due to the fact that the muscles composing it are little used during the lifetime of the animal, as it is so situated as to be protected on the under side by the suet or kidney fat, and on the upper side by the back-bone. Although so tender it is by no means the best flavored or most nutritious portion of the animal. The very want of exercise referred to above, renders it less juicy and rich than those parts to which a constant flow of blood is attracted by regular exertion. It is an expensive roast, costing often a dollar a pound. It is so dry and deficient in fat that it must be larded and highly seasoned to render it agreeable. It rarely weighs more than eight or ten pounds, and more frequently less. It is sometimes cut in small pieces, larded and broiled and served on toast, as a course at breakfast or luncheon.

THE LIVER, THE HEART, THE TONGUE, THE KIDNEYS, AND TRIPE

or a portion of the stomach, all are eaten with relish by many people. The heart, the liver, and the kidneys are not very easily digested, but they are extremely nutritious, and since they are among the cheapest parts of the ox, are valuable food for those who can eat them. Tripe is both digestible and nutritious.

VEAL.

Veal should not be killed younger than from six to eight weeks old. In France and Germany they are required to be ten months old before they can be butchered. The flesh should be a clear, bright red, the grain fine and close, the fat white and firm. Veal is the leanest of all meats and cannot be considered either very nutritious or very digestible. It is, indeed, as difficult to digest as pork, requiring from four to five hours. It is a luxury to be indulged in sparingly, as a means rather of securing that variety essential to zest for food, than as a necessity which will furnish warmth, strength, and energy.

Veal is divided like beef into fore and hind quarters. These terms apply also to mutton and pork. The hind-quarter furnishes the loin which may be roasted whole or divided into two parts, each making a roasting piece, or may be cut into fine veal chops, and the leg, which likewise may or may not be divided. The loin is the choicest roasting piece, though the leg is not much inferior. From the leg veal cutlets are taken. The knuckle or lower part of the leg is used for soup or stew.

From the fore-quarter come the shoulder, neck, and breast. The shoulder is frequently boned, stuffed, and roasted, and cooked in this way makes an excellent dinner. The breast is usually made into pot-pie, stew or similar dish, though it can be roasted if preferred.

There is scarcely any part of the calf which is not considered edible. The *head*, after being well scalded and shaven, is boiled and served whole, or made into a soup or stew. The *tongue* is either cooked with it or removed and eaten separately. *Calves' feet* make excellent jelly; the *kidneys* are considered a toothsome dainty, and the *sweet bread* and *liver* are justly regarded as great delicacies. The liver of no other animal can compare with that of the calf. Sweet-breads are, in cities, where the demand for them is usually great, so expensive that they may be regarded as among the most extravagant of luxuries. They are said to be "the most delicate in flavor of any meat with which we are acquainted." Even the *eyes* and the *brains* are considered good eating by epicures, though the sauce in which they are served must, I fancy, be depended on to give them relish.

MUTTON.

The lean of mutton should be a deep red color, its texture firm, the fat white, clean, and hard. In poor or diseased mutton the fat will be yellowish and the flesh flabby. To be prime the animal should be from three to five years old when slaughtered. The leg furnishes the choicest roasting or boiling piece as it contains the least fat and is more solid, juicier, and more nourishing than any other joint.

HIND QUARTER OF MUTTON.—From the hind quarter are cut

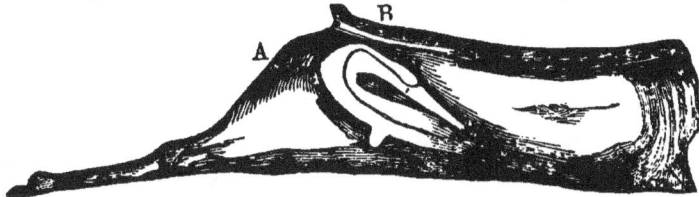

the leg A and the loin B. The loin is either roasted whole or cut into chops.

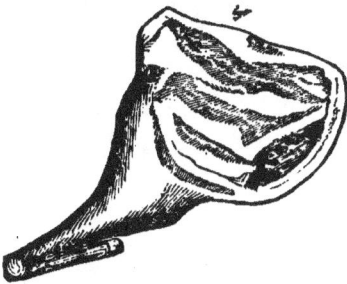

SHOULDER OF MUTTON.—From the fore-quarter we get the shoulder of mutton, which also makes an excellent roasting piece. It is a little lower in price than the leg, but if the shoulder-blade is removed and the opening filled with a savory stuffing it is little, if any, inferior to it.

MUTTON CHOPS.—These are cut from the breast, each chop containing one rib. They are somewhat smaller than those cut from the loin. The loin chops are sometimes called "English Chops." The breast is the lowest priced cut in the whole carcass, though not the most economical to purchase after all, since the proportion of fat is very large and the shrinkage great in cooking. The lean, too, is stringy and deficient in flavor.

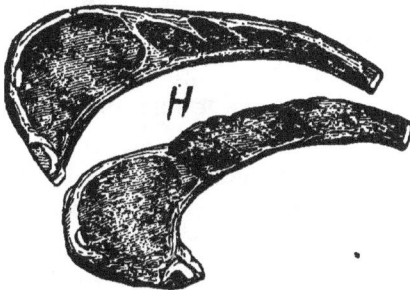

LAMB.

Before the age of twelve months the joints are known as *lamb* instead of *mutton*. They correspond exactly with the cuts just described, being called "lamb chops," "shoulder of lamb," etc. As in beef and veal, almost every part of the sheep is eatable. The head, the tongue, the brains, the liver, the heart, the stomach, the sweet-bread, the kidneys, and even the eyes are considered edible.

PORK.

The importance of great care in selecting pork is so extreme that I quote from the best authority (De Voe) the following minute directions: "The skin should present a semi-transparent appearance, approaching white in color; the fat on the back should not be less than half an inch thick, white and firm, and the lean of a pale reddish color, and sappy. The skin of the older animals, or bacon hogs, is thicker and coarser, while the lean is of a darker color but equally sweet, juicy, and tender.

Measly Pork.—The flesh of the hog with this disease, when slaughtered, is exceedingly unwholesome, and is not fit to be used for any purpose. It may be known by the many yellowish lumps or kernels seen through the fat and lean, as well as the flesh having a heavy, dull appearance."

POULTRY.

Under this general term are included all domesticated fowls. When fresh, the eyes are full and bright, the feet and legs moist, soft, and limber. If they have been kept long after killing and have become stale, the eyes are shrunken, and the legs and feet are stiff and dry, and when beginning actually to spoil, the body will begin to change color and oftentimes present a spotted and greenish appearance.

A young chicken or turkey will have the tip of the breast-bone pliable and limber, so that it can be bent easily by the fingers. In the young fowl this is hardly more than cartilage but it hardens into bone as the bird matures. If the flesh on the breast yields readily to the pressure of the thumb or finger it is an evidence of tenderness. The spurs of a young cock are soft, loose, and short. When old, the comb and legs are rough, and the spurs become hard. When the legs of a turkey-cock are rough, the spur long and firm, the breast-bone hard, and the skin covering it hard and fat, you may be sure the bird under inspection has reached years of discretion, and will need long and careful cooking to make him palatable.

A full grown and mature turkey, is, however, preferred for boiling and boning, since the skin is elastic and sufficiently strong to bear the dressing and sewing without tearing.

YOUNG DUCKS AND GEESE have also a soft tip to the breast-bone, the skin is very tender and easily torn, and the legs and wind-pipe are brittle and it requires little effort to break them.

PIGEONS when full grown are rather dry and tasteless eating, but their young, called "*squabs*" are tender and delicate. The signs of age are long, thin legs, and very dark colored flesh. *Giblets* usually consist of the heart, liver, and gizzard. These are often chopped and added to the sauce or gravy served with roasted fowl, or are made into soup, the neck, wings and feet being added. In city markets, these parts come also under the term "giblets."

GAME BIRDS as a rule are heavier in proportion to their size, than barn-yard fowls. The meat is darker and stronger, having generally a fine rich flavor, known as a "gamey taste." Both the wild turkey and wild goose, when young and in good condi-tion, are considered choicer eating them the tame ones.

VEGETABLES AND FRUITS.

These should be selected with reference to their perfect sound-ness and full maturity. No food supply is more important in its relation to health and vigor. The acids and various salts they furnish help materially to keep us in good condition. In summer, when they chiefly abound, they are both cooling and stimulating in just the right degree. Their actual value is hardly appreciated until, being deprived of them, as on long sea voy-ages, in miner's camps, or on the frontier, health fails, skin dis-eases of various kinds make their appearance, and the whole system suffers.

At the same time probably more illness, especially in hot weather, is due to eating unripe or partly decayed fruit and veg-etables, than from any other source. If chosen with care and judgment, if sound, ripe, and fresh, they are invaluable. If bought at random, unripe, tough, decaying, and wilted, they are absolutely dangerous.

CHAPTER VI.

BREAD AND BREAKFAST CAKES.

READ is one of the most important of foods. Its common use proves its value, and teaches us how necessary it is that it should be well made, and consequently sweet and nutritious. The waste in badly baked, sour, and indigestible bread is enormous. She is a true philanthropist who helps to reduce it in any appreciable quantity. The waste of raw material in this direction is but a fragment of the general loss. The actual diminution in working power in those who consume bad food is the important element to be considered. This can scarcely be computed. Indigestion affects mind as well as body. It undermines both intellectual force and physical vigor, and, as upon the combination' of these two depends the advancement of the world in any direction, religious, social, political, or commercial, some notion can be gained as to the responsibility of those who prepare food. Not until the relations of food to progress are clearly understood and recognized, can the importance of good cooking be fully appreciated. To be well fed in the best sense of the word, means to be thoroughly equipped for the day's work, to be nourished in every part of the body, to be built up, strengthened, invigorated, cheered, stimulated, energized, ready for every task. With a stomach full of indigestible and unfit food, urging every physical force to help in disposing of it, no man can do his best, and the world is a loser by just so much as he falls short of this. Every time, therefore, that you make bad bread you defraud yourself and your family of a certain amount of actual force. Be too conscientious and too honest to join those who through ignorance or carelessness are daily hindering instead of helping humanity on.

Bread can only be made from flour having gluten in such proportion and of such quality as to make it capable of complete vesciculation. The flour from wheat meets these requirements better than any other grain. The quality of the gluten contained in Indian meal, for instance, is not suitable to such vesciculation. This is the case, indeed, with almost every variety of flour except wheat and rye. By vesiculation is meant the diffusion of small bubbles of carbonic acid gas or air throughout the dough. These bubbles are retained by the toughness and elasticity of the gluten, which forms little sacks or vescicles from which they cannot readily escape. When the dough is sufficiently swollen or distended, it is baked and the cells fixed by heat, and the result is our light bread.

How shall we raise or vesiculate our bread with the least waste? There are three methods. In one the carbonic acid is generated chemically within the sponge. In the second it is introduced from without physically.

In the first, as a result of the chemical action of the yeast plant, whereby it appropriates the starch of the flour and sets free carbonic acid, we have left a small amount of broken down and partly decayed material which, of course, is not wholesome food. The amount is so small, when the vesiculation is carried just to the proper point, as to be generally considered harmless, but if it goes too far the bread becomes sour, and the longer it continues after this the greater the amount of putrified material consumed when such bread is eaten. The immense importance of arresting the vesiculation at the right time may be seen from this.

When by the second process, the gas is introduced into the dough by physical means solely, being prepared outside of the sponge, and forced into it under great pressure, no such waste is possible, and the so-called aerated bread is therefore freest from impurities and the most wholesome. This method of raising bread is, however, impracticable for the housekeeper, since the machinery needed is both too complicated and too expensive for ordinary use.

Air may, however, be introduced into dough and then expanded by heat, as in the pulled or beaten bread of the Maryland housewife. Dough, mixed with very cold water, and pulled, and stretched and beaten in a cold place, becomes filled with bubbles of air which are retained by the gluten. Such dough put into a heated oven will swell and rise by the expansion of the confined air from the action of the heat, and will when baked make sweet and wholesome bread. This method is expensive too, of time and muscle, but has been practiced largely in the south, where help was cheap and abundant. A valuable hint can be gained from it however, and I look confidently forward to the time when some shrewd Yankee will act upon it, and invent a simple and economic machine for pulling the dough, thus bringing this sort of bread within the reach of the busiest woman.

The action of baking powders, soda, etc., all bring about the same result, the introduction of gas into dough, whereby it is vesciculated and made ready to bake, and all are injurious if not judiciously used.

To insure good bread the following things must be carefully attended to:

The flour must be made from good grain, must not be musty, must contain the proper proportion and the right kind of gluten. Dr. Kedzie, of the Michigan Agricultural College, has invented a simple and inexpensive method for determining the quantity of the gluten in flour, which I hope he will soon give to the world in such shape as to be available in every home.

The yeast should be sweet and active.

The dough should be thoroughly kneaded so as to distribute the yeast evenly throughout the mass and to make the gluten firmer and tougher.

Enough salt should be added to the sponge to make the bread palatable, to toughen the gluten and whiten the loaf.

It should be baked in separate loaves so that the heat will reach the center of the loaf in all directions equally, and the temperature of the oven should be so regulated that the crust will be light colored and tender. To effect this the loaves should be small, weighing, when baked, not more than one or one and one-half pounds.

The ideal proportions for bread, when all the conditions are perfect are: One quart of flour, one-fourth of a quart of water, one-fourth of a cup of yeast, one-fourth of a tablespoonful of sugar, and one-fourth of a tablespoonful of salt.

Alum is added to flour to strengthen the gluten and thereby make it capable of retaining a great deal of water, the baker making so much clear profit when he can sell water at the price of bread. The reasons why bread will retain so much water are thus given by Prof. Johnston in his "Chemistry of Common Life:" "During the baking a portion of the starch is converted into a kind of gum called dextrine, which is known to hold water stronger than the starch does; the gluten of the flour, if it once becomes thoroughly wet, is very difficult to dry again, and it forms a tenacious coat round every little hollow cell in the bread, which coating does not readily allow the gas contained in the cell to escape, or the water to dry up and pass off in vapor. The dry crust which forms round the bread in baking is nearly impervious to water, and like the skin of a potato which we bake in the oven or in the hot cinders, prevents the moisture from escaping." Alum will also toughen the gluten of poor flour so as to make it better capable of vesciculation, and by preventing the discoloration of such gluten by heat make the loaf whiter.

Sulphate of copper has a similar effect and is much more injurious to the consumer than alum.

The addition of a small quantity of potato can scarcely be called an adulteration. The starch of the potato is eagerly appropriated by the yeast plant and the sponge is rendered more active and lively when it is present. It does become an adulteration, however, when added in such quantity as to make the potato in an appreciable manner a substitute for the flour.

Rice flour is often added to make the bread white and fine grained, and though not actually injurious as alum and copper are, makes the bread less nutritious by increasing the proportion of starch to gluten and the other nitrogenous elements of the flour.

Shall we eat brown bread, or bread made from flour containing the bran or outside coverings of the grain, or white bread made from flour containing largely the kernels of the grain? There are several sides to this question as to every other. While the bran contains much that is nutritious, its outside covering is largely composed of silica and is almost, if not entirely indigestible. If not separated from the inner coatings, which contain certain valuable nutritive material, such as gluten and cerealine, it acts as an irritant, hurrying the food along the alimentary canal, and does not, therefore, allow sufficient time for the absorption of such nutritive material. It consequently causes waste, and while it may supply the place of medicine to such as need a laxative, it cannot be called an economical food for those who engage in active work. Physical exercise will, in most cases, act as a sufficiently strong stimulant to digestion, and the laboring man or woman needs condensed, not laxative food.

Brown bread, made from whole meal, is therefore a luxury, to be indulged in by the rich, and is too wasteful a food for the poor.

YEAST.

English recipe, in which the food is prepared for the yeast plant, and time allowed for it to germinate and increase, no plant being introduced to hasten the operation. If the directions are carefully followed, sweet, strong yeast will be obtained. The conditions being right, success is certain.

Ingredients.—Two ounces of hops; four quarts of water; one pound of flour; three pounds of potatoes; two table-spoonfuls of salt; one-half pound brown sugar.

Time to boil, half an hour; to make, four days.

First day—Boil two ounces of hops in four quarts of water for half an hour; strain it, and allow to stand until lukewarm, then add the salt and sugar; add this gradually to the pound of flour making a smooth batter.

Third day—Boil and mash the potatoes, and add to the mixture.

Fourth day—Strain and bottle for use.

It must be stirred frequently while it is making, and kept near the fire. It should be mixed and left to ferment in an earthen jar. Keep in a cool, dry place. The bottles must be kept tightly corked.

POTATO YEAST.

Ingredients.—Four potatoes, one quart of boiling water, one tea-spoonful of salt, one-half cupful of brown sugar, one-half cupful of good yeast.

Pare the potatoes and boil till tender; press them through a colander with one quart of boiling water; add the salt and sugar, and when lukewarm, stir in the yeast. It will rise in five or six hours if set in a warm place.

5

HOP YEAST.

(From the Appledore Cook Book.)

"Pare and boil one dozen mealy potatoes; as soon as you put
the potatoes on to boil, put a handful of hops into another kettle containing three quarts of cold water; cover and boil. When
the potatoes are boiled, drain and mash fine; then strain the hops
through a fine sieve on the potatoes, and be sure the hops are
boiling; stir well. Then add one-half a cup of sugar, one-fourth
of salt, and one pint of flour; mix this well and strain through a
colander; let it stand until it is milk-warm and then stir in one
cup of good yeast; set it to rise where it will be warm. It will
rise in about five hours if the yeast is good. You can tell when
it is risen by the white foam which will rise to the top. When
risen pour in a stone jug, cork tightly, and keep in a cool place."

Both these receipts are "never-failing" if directions are carefully followed and the ingredients are good. In summer it is,
perhaps, easier to use the *potato yeast*, making it fresh every
week.

YEAST BREAD.

To be set in the morning and baked early in the afternoon.
An excellent receipt for summer.

Ingredients.—Four good-sized potatoes, one quart of boiling
water, one cup of yeast, one table-spoonful of sugar, one table-
spoonful of salt, one table-spoonful of lard, about four quarts of
flour.

Take four good sized potatoes, pare, boil and mash and pour
over them one quart of *actually boiling water;* strain the whole
through a colander. Let this get lukewarm and then stir in one
cup of yeast, one table-spoonful of sugar, one table-spoonful of
salt, and enough flour to make as stiff a dough as you can
beat thoroughly with a wooden spoon. Now beat vigorously
until sure that the yeast is evenly distributed throughout
the entire mixture, and set in a warm place to rise. If the
yeast is good it will rise in from four to five hours. When
well risen, add enough flour so that it can be kneaded without sticking. Turn out on a kneading board and rub in one
table-spoonful of lard; knead for at least twenty minutes. Let
all the movements be light and quick. It requires skill rather

than muscle. Add as little flour as possible while kneading.
Now put the dough into the pan again and let it rise one hour,
and then form into loaves. This quantity will make eight small,
brick-shaped loaves. Let the loaves rise until light, about three-
quarters of an hour, and bake three-quarters of an hour.

YEAST BREAD.

To be set at night and baked in the morning.

Ingredients.—Four quarts of flour, one quart luke warm water,
one cup of yeast, one table-spoonful of salt.

Put the flour in a bread pan, make a well in the center, into
which pour the yeast; mix in gradually and thoroughly the quart
of warm water, stirring down the flour from the sides of the
pan, but using only enough to make a moderately thick batter;
beat this well, sprinkle flour over the top, cover and put in a
warm place to rise. In the morning it should be very light and
foamy. Add the salt and stir in the remainder of the flour. It
may be necessary to add a little more flour to prevent the bread
from sticking, but if the flour is first class four quarts will be
quite enough. Knead for half an hour and leave to rise. When
light mould into loaves and bake. This will also make eight
loaves and they will bake in three-quarters of an hour.

BREAKFAST ROLLS.

(National Training School of Cookery, South Kensington, London.)

Ingredients.—One pound of flour, one-half ounce of German
yeast, or one large table-spoonful of home-made yeast, one ounce
of butter, one-half tea-spoonful of salt, one-half tea-spoonful of
sugar, one egg, one-half pint of lukewarm milk.

Mix the above ingredients thoroughly together and set in a
warm place to rise. When light knead down and set to rise
again. Form into rolls and leave until light. Bake half an
hour. As soon as they come from the oven glaze with a little
warm milk in which a small quantity of butter has been melted.

Whenever the German compressed yeast is used it should be
worked into a smooth cream with a small quantity, say a tea-
spoonful to an ounce, of white sugar, before it is mixed with the
other ingredients.

GALETTES.

(National Training School of Cookery.)

Ingredients.—One pound of flour, one-half ounce German compressed yeast, or one generous table-spoonful of home-made yeast, one tea-spoonful of sugar, one-third of a tea-spoonful of salt; one and one-half gills of sweet milk mixed with the yeast, four ounces of butter, three eggs.

Mix one-half pound of the flour with the yeast, milk, sugar, and salt; beat thoroughly and set in a warm place to rise. When light add the remaining half pound of flour, the butter and the eggs. Beat well and set to rise again. When light form into round cakes, handling the dough as lightly as possible. Set to rise again, and then bake fifteen minutes in a hot oven. Beat a dessert spoonful of sugar with one egg. When the galettes are baked and while still very hot, brush them over with this mixture.

These are the most delicate and delicious tea cakes imaginable. They are to be eaten hot, or they are allowed to cool and are then split open and toasted on the inside.

ENGLISH BUNS.

Ingredients.—One and three-fourths pounds of flour, one ounce of German compressed yeast, one pint of milk, one-fourth of a pound of butter, two eggs, one-fourth of a pound of sugar, one-fourth of a pound of sultanas, two ounces candied peel (orange, lemon, and citron).

Mix together one-half pound of the flour, the ounce of yeast and the pint of milk; beat well and set to rise. When light mix in the remainder of the flour and the other ingredients and set to rise again. When sufficiently risen the second time form into buns, or round biscuits, and when these are light bake fifteen or twenty minutes in a moderately hot oven. Glaze while hot with a mixture made by heating one dessert spoonful of sugar with one egg.

BROWN BREAD.

Ingredients.—One quart of sweet milk, two quarts of Indian meal, one pint of Graham flour, one tea-spoonful of saleratus, three-fourths of a cupful of molasses.

Mix together the Indian meal, Graham flour, milk, and molasses; dissolve the saleratus perfectly in one-fourth of a cupful of boiling water; beat thoroughly into the mixture, pour into brown bread tins and steam two and one-half hours, and then bake one-half hour.

BROWN BREAD.

Ingredients.—Three pints of sour milk, one cupful of molasses, one table-spoonful of salt, one table-spoonful of soda, five cupfuls of wheat or rye flour, five cupfuls of Indian meal.

Dissolve the soda in the sour milk and mix with the other ingredients. Bake three hours in a moderate oven.

BROWN BREAD.

Ingredients.—Two cups of flour, three cups of corn meal, one cup of molasses, one table-spoonful of salt, one table-spoonful of soda.

Mix the soda and molasses thoroughly together; add the other ingredients and make into a stiff batter with cold water. Steam three hours, and bake one-half hour.

GRAHAM BREAD.

(*Miss Parloa.*)

Ingredients.—One pint of water or milk, one pint of flour, one large pint of Graham, half a cup of sugar, half a cup of yeast, one tea-spoonful of salt.

Have the milk or water blood-warm; add the yeast to it. Have the flour sifted in a deep dish; add yeast and milk gradually to the flour, beating until perfectly smooth; set in a rather cool place to rise over night. In the morning add the salt, sugar, and then the Graham, a little at a time, beating vigorously all the while. When thoroughly beaten, turn into two bread pans, and let it rise one hour. Bake one hour.

Muffins.—Graham muffins are made the same as the bread. Fill tin muffin cups two-thirds full and let the mixture rise to the top of the cups; then bake in a rather quick oven twenty minutes.

CORN BREAD OR JOHNNY CAKE.

Ingredients.—One pint of sweet milk, one pint of Indian meal, one pint of flour, two eggs, one-half cup of sugar, one table-spoonful of melted butter, two table-spoonfuls of baking powder.

Sift the Indian meal, flour and baking powder together; add the sugar, melted butter and eggs, and mix with the milk. Bake either in loaves, in gem-irons, or in muffin rings.

CORN MEAL BREAD.

Ingredients.—One pint of corn meal, one table-spoonful of butter, one table-spoonful of yeast, two eggs, sweet milk to make · a batter.

Rub the butter into the corn meal; add the two eggs and make into a batter with sweet milk; add the yeast and set by the fire one hour to rise. Bake in gem-irons.

LIGHT BISCUIT.

Ingredients.—One quart of sweet milk, one-half cup of good hop yeast, two-thirds of a cup of shortening (nice, sweet drippings, butter, or half butter and half lard), two table-spoonfuls of sugar, one tea-spoonful of salt, flour.

Boil the milk; when lukewarm mix with flour to form a thick sponge, add the yeast, and beat twenty minutes. Let it rise four or five hours; then add the shortening, sugar, and salt, stirring in flour with a wooden spoon, until the dough cleaves from the spoon. Roll out to an inch or a little less in thickness; mold into biscuit, and let them stand in a warm place till thoroughly light. Bake in a quick oven.

PARKER HOUSE ROLLS.

Scald a generous pint of milk; let it stand till lukewarm; take two quarts of flour and rub into it a table-spoonful of lard or butter, make a hole in the center and add one-half tea-cupful of yeast, a tea-spoonful of sugar, one of salt, and the milk, and cover with the flour. Do not beat much. Let it stand until morning, or if mixed in the morning, until afternoon, then work smooth about fifteen minutes. When light roll out and cut with a large biscuit cutter; rub over the tops with a little melted butter, and lap over like a turnover. Then let them rise, and when light bake in a rather quick oven twenty minutes.

SODA AND CREAM TARTAR BISCUITS.

Ingredients.—One quart of flour, one heaping table-spoonful of butter or lard, one salt-spoonful of salt, one tea-spoonful of soda, two tea-spoonfuls of cream tartar, sweet milk or cold water nearly two cups.

Let all the ingredients be as cold as possible. Sift soda and cream tartar with the flour several times, so the soda and cream tartar will be evenly and thoroughly distributed. Rub in the shortening as expeditiously as possible and then quickly add the milk or water. These, and all biscuits raised with baking powder, should be mixed just as soft as it is possible to handle them. Roll from half to three-quarters of an inch thick and bake at once in a quick oven. Success depends in great measure on quickness.

BAKING POWDER BISCUITS.

These are made exactly like the soda and cream tartar biscuits, substituting three tea-spoonfuls of baking powder for the soda and cream tartar.

RAISED MUFFINS.

Ingredients.—One quart of flour, one pint of milk, one-half cup of yeast, two eggs, one tea-spoonful of salt, two table-spoonfuls of butter.

Mix the flour, milk, yeast, and salt together over night. Let stand until morning to rise; add the eggs and the butter and bake in muffin rings.

BAKING POWDER MUFFINS.

(Mrs. Henderson.)

Ingredients.—Two eggs, one pint of flour, one tea-cupful of milk or cream, butter half the size of an egg, a little salt, and one tea-spoonful of baking powder.

Mix the baking powder and salt in the flour. Beat the eggs; add to the yolks, first, milk, then butter (melted), then flour, then whites. Beat well after it is all mixed, and bake them immediately in a hot oven, in gem pans or muffin rings. Take them out of the pans or rings the moment they are done and send to the table.

SALLY LUNN.

Ingredients.—One cup of butter, two table-spoonsful of sugar, two eggs, one pint of sweet milk, one tea-spoonful of soda, two tea-spoonfuls of cream tartar, one quart of flour, and a salt-spoonful of salt.

Sift the flour, cream tartar, soda, and salt together. Blend the butter and sugar, add the eggs, then the flour and milk alternately until all of both is used. Bake in a rather quick oven.

BREAKFAST CAKES.

Ingredients.—One quart of flour, one table-spoonful of baking powder rubbed in the flour, two eggs, one table-spoonful of butter, one table-spoonful of sugar, flour to make a thin batter. Bake in gem irons well heated.

POP OVERS.

Ingredients.—Four eggs, four cups of flour, two cups of milk, butter the size of an egg. Bake in patty pans in a hot oven.

SCONES.
English Recipe.

Ingredients.—One pound of flour, one-half pint of milk, three ounces of butter, one-half ounce of cream tartar, one-fourth of an ounce of soda, one ounce of sugar. A few raisins, split and seeded, or a few sultanas.

Sift the cream tartar, soda, and sugar with the flour; rub in the butter; add the raisins, and then blend the whole together with the milk. Form the dough into triangular pieces about an inch thick. Bake in a quick oven. They can be eaten warm, or allowed to cool and then be split open and toasted.

WAFFLES.

Ingredients.—Two eggs, one pint of flour, one and one-fourth cupfuls of milk, one tea-spoonful of baking powder, one dessert-spoonful of butter, one salt-spoonful of salt.

Sift the baking powder, salt and flour together; blend these with the milk, then add the beaten yolks of the eggs, and the butter melted; lastly, mix lightly in the well beaten whites. They should be baked immediately after the whites are added.

RICE WAFFLES.

Ingredients.—One cup of boiled rice, one pint of milk, two eggs, one tea-spoonful of salt, one tea-spoonful of lard or butter, one-half tea-spoonful of soda, one tea-spoonful of cream tartar, flour to make a thin batter.

RICE WAFFLES.

(Mrs. Henderson.)

Ingredients.—One and one-half pints of boiled rice, one and one-half pints of flour, half a tea-cupful of sour milk, half a tea-cupful of sweet milk, one tea-spoonful of soda, three eggs, and butter the size of a walnut.

RICE PANCAKES.

are made as in the last receipt, by adding an extra half cupful of milk.

FLOUR GRIDDLE CAKES.

To every pint of sour milk allow one tea-spoonful of soda, two eggs, yolks and whites beaten separately, and flour enough to make a thin batter.

BUCKWHEAT CAKES.

Three Receipts from The Home Messenger Receipt Book.

No. 1. One pint of buckwheat, half pint of sifted corn meal, two level tea-spoonfuls of salt, four table-spoonfuls of yeast, one and a half pints of lukewarm water, or one pint of water and one cup of milk. Beat well and set to rise over night.

No. 2. One pint cup of very fine oatmeal, set to soak in the morning with one quart of water, into which two table-spoonfuls of yeast have been stirred. At night add one quart of buckwheat flour, and one quart of water, and three tea-spoonfuls of salt; beat well and let rise until morning.

No. 3. One pint of buckwheat flour, three table-spoonfuls of yeast. One quart of lukewarm water. Stir well and let rise till morning.

If your cakes sour, add just before baking a half tea-spoonful of soda dissolved in a quarter of a tea-cupful of boiling water.

BREAD CRUMB CAKES.

Soak the bread crumbs in sweet milk over night. In the morning press them through the colander. To two tea-cupfuls of bread crumbs add two eggs, one cupful of flour or corn meal, and sour milk enough to make a thin batter. Dissolve half a tea-spoonful of soda in the sour milk before mixing.

CHAPTER VII.

CAKE.

HE subjoined directions for mixing cake must be carefully followed when the receipts in this chapter are used, except when specific instructions as to methods are appended to particular receipts. The ingredients composing the different cakes will be given, and then it will be taken for granted that they will be compounded according to instructions.

The first step to be taken in preparing to bake is to get everything that will be needed ready before the mixing begins. The pans should be lined with paper and greased, bowls, spoons, eggbeater, sifted flour, weighed or measured, ready for use; milk, eggs, etc., should be right at hand. The oven, too, should be at the proper temperature and all things so arranged, that when once the eggs are broken and the mixing has actually begun, nothing need interrupt or delay proceedings until the process is complete and the cake in the oven. Flour should be sifted *before* it is measured unless the contrary is expressly advised; if baking powder is to be used that should be sifted with the flour; soda and cream tartar should *both* be added dry to the flour and perfectly distributed through it by several siftings; cups or measures should not be heaped. When all things are ready the order of mixing is, in general, as follows:

1. Cream the butter.

2. Mix gradually with it the sugar and blend both together until they make a smooth, light paste.

3. The beaten yolks of the eggs are next added.

4. Stir in a little flour, then a part of the milk, then flour, then milk, until all the milk has been added. This process should use at least half the flour.

75

5. The flavoring extract, if any is used, should go in next.

6. Sift in gradually a part of the remaining flour, add the whites of the eggs, well beaten, and at the same time the remainder of the flour.

7. All cake should be put at first into a moderate oven so it may have a chance to rise before the crust begins to form. Otherwise the batter will burst through and make an ill-shaped loaf. It cannot be so light and tender if part of it bakes before it is wholly risen, and part of it bakes after it has risen.

MEASURES.

The ordinary stone china tea-cup is used for measuring unless coffee-cup is mentioned. I append here the three tables of weights and measures most used in household affairs, for easy reference.

AVOIRDUPOIS WEIGHT.

27 $\frac{11}{32}$	Grains	=1 Dram (dr.)
16	Drams	=1 Ounce (oz.)
16	Ounces	=1 Pound (lb.)
25	Pounds	=1 Quarter (qr.)
4	Quarters	=1 Hundred weight (cwt.)
20	Hundred weight	=1 Ton.

LIQUID MEASURE.

4	Gills	=1 Pint (pt.)
2	Pints	=1 Quart (qt.)
4	Quarts	=1 Gallon (gal.)

DRY MEASURE.

8	Quarts	=1 Peck (pk.)
4	Pecks	=1 Bushel (bu.)
8	Bushels	=1 Quarter (qr.)

The following are approximate substitutions of measures for weights. They are correct enough for all ordinary purposes. They are compiled from various sources.

Ten eggs are equal to one pound.

One quart of sifted flour equals one pound.

Two cups of butter packed are one pound.

One pint of granulated sugar is one pound.

Sixteen table-spoonfuls are half a pint.

Eight table-spoonfuls are one gill.

A common sized tumbler holds half a pint.

Four tea-cupfuls of liquid equal one quart.

In the following receipts for cake it will be noticed that soda and cream tartar are largely used in place of baking powder. Baking powder can, however, always be substituted, using one table-spoonful of baking powder for one tea-spoonful of soda and two of cream tartar.

Many of the old-fashioned but excellent receipts for cake contain wine or brandy. I have given them as they have been handed down to me, and can vouch for their quality. The amount of liquor used is so small as to give no decided flavor. Indeed its presence would never be suspected. In a rich cake it acts as a preservative, and it also makes the cake less indigestible. If any one has scruples as to its use in these small quantities, cold water or milk can be substituted.

WEDDING CAKE.

Ingredients.—Three pounds of butter, three and one-half pounds of sugar, three pounds of flour, one pound of citron, thirty-six eggs, nine pounds of currants, six pounds of raisins, one ounce of cloves, one ounce of cinnamon, one ounce of nutmegs, one gill of brandy, one gill of wine.

FRUIT CAKE.

Ingredients.—Two pounds of flour, two pounds of sugar, two pounds of butter, six pounds of stoned raisins, three pounds of currants, one pound of citron, fifteen eggs, four nutmegs, one wine-glass of brandy, a variety of spices if liked; a slow oven.

FRUIT CAKE.

Ingredients.—One pound of flour, one pound of sugar, three-fourths of a pound of butter, two pounds of seedless raisins, two pounds of currants, one pound of citron, one-fourth of a pound of almonds, one-half an ounce of mace, one tea-spoonful of rose water, one wine-glass of brandy or wine, ten eggs.

FRUIT CAKE.

Ingredients.—Fifteen eggs, one and one-half pounds of butter, one and one-half pounds of sugar, one and one-half pounds of flour, two pounds of seeded raisins, two pounds of currants, one and one-half pounds candied peel (citron, lemon, orange), one pound of sliced figs, one pound of blanched almonds sliced, a half pint of molasses, one ounce of ground mace, and one ounce of cinnamon.

This is my favorite fruit cake and it always gives satisfaction. It keeps well, looks well, and tastes good.

BLACK CAKE.

Ingredients.—One pound of flour, one pound of sugar, three-fourths of a pound of butter, five eggs, one gill of cream, one tea-spoonful of soda, one gill of wine, two pounds of fruit, one ounce of cloves, one ounce of cinnamon.

REPUBLICAN CAKE.

Ingredients.—One pound of sugar, one-half pound of butter, one pound of flour, four eggs beaten separately, one cup of sweet milk, table-spoonful of baking powder, raisins, wine-glass of wine or brandy, one nutmeg.

COMPOSITION CAKE.

Ingredients.—Six eggs, beaten separately, three cups of sugar, two cups of butter, one pound of fruit, six cups of flour, one cup of sweet milk, one nutmeg, one glass of brandy or wine, one tea-spoonful of soda, two tea-spoonfuls of cream tartar or one table-spoonful of baking powder.

DARIOLES A LA DUCHESSE.
(French Receipt.)

Thoroughly mix four ounces of flour with the yolk and white of one egg; add the yolks only of three eggs besides; one ounce of powdered sugar, four macaroons thoroughly crushed, and another whole egg. These ingredients should be added to each other singly, and when thoroughly mixed stir in a tea-cupful of cream, a half tea-spoonful of vanilla essence, a pinch of angelica, minced very fine, and a little mixed preserved fruit. Pour this mixture into buttered moulds and bake in a quick oven.

Citron can be used in place of angelica if that is difficult to procure.

FANCY NUT CAKES.

Ingredients.—Two-thirds of a cup of butter, two cups of sugar, one cup of milk, three eggs, three cups of flour, three tea-spoonfuls of baking powder, one cup of nuts.

Bake in shallow tins about two inches thick, cut in squares, frost and put walnut meat on each piece.

DOUGH CAKE.

Ingredients.—Two cups of bread dough, one heaping cup of sugar, one-half cup of butter, one cup of raisins, one-half of a nutmeg.

BREAD CAKE.

Ingredients.—Four cups of light bread dough, two cups of sugar, one cup of butter, one cup of cream, four eggs, one glass of brandy, a handful of flour, or sufficient flour to make a rather stiff dough.

POUND CAKE.

Ingredients.—One pound of butter, one pound of sugar, one pound of flour, ten eggs, beaten well, grated rind of one lemon, one glass of wine.

SOUTHERN POUND CAKE.

Ingredients.—One pound of flour, one pound of eggs, one pound of sugar, three-fourths of a pound of butter, one glass of brandy, one nutmeg, one tea-spoonful of mace.

Cream half the flour with the butter, and add the brandy and spice. Beat the yolks until very light, add the sugar, then the beaten whites and the rest of the flour alternately. Put all together and beat steadily half an hour. This is a splendid cake.

POUND CAKE.

From "76."

Ingredients.—One pound of butter, one pound of flour, nine eggs leaving out two yolks, grated peel of one lemon.

Beat the whites to a stiff froth and the butter to a cream; add the sugar and the yolks, and beat till very light; then the flour and whites of eggs alternately. Bake in a moderate oven.

FIG CAKE.

Ingredients.—One cup of sugar, three-fourths of a cup of butter, one-half cup of sweet milk, yolks of seven eggs and one whole egg beaten together, one and three-fourths cups of flour, one and one-half tea-spoonfuls of baking powder, one pound of figs.

Pour half of the batter into the tin and lay on one pound of halved figs; sift lightly with flour; pour on the rest of the batter and bake in a moderate oven.

FIG CAKE.

Ingredients.—One cup of butter, one cup of brown sugar, one pint of molasses, one and one-half cups of sour milk, one small table-spoonful of soda, three eggs, one wine-glass of brandy or whiskey, one cup of chopped raisins, a little citron, spices of all kinds, one pound of figs.

Stir it about as stiff with flour as for a pound cake. Fill the layer cake tins, and have the figs cut in thin slices and strew them through the cake. Alternate a layer of this dark mixture with a layer of any white or silver cake, after it is baked, and put them together with a little icing, so that they will not separate.

A GOOD WHITE CAKE, FOR THE FIG CAKE.

Ingredients.—The whites of four eggs, two cups of sugar, one cup of sweet milk, four cups of flour, two tea-spoonfuls of baking powder mixed with the flour.

CHOCOLATE CAKE.

Ingredients.—Two and one-half cups of sugar, one cup of butter, one cup of milk, six eggs (save out the whites of two), four cups of flour, four tea-spoonfuls of baking powder.

Icing.—One-third of a cake of chocolate set to melt on the back part of the stove, whites of four eggs, sugar enough to make a stiff icing. Flavor with vanilla. Bake in a baking sheet about one inch thick, put the icing on as thickly as possible and cut it in squares.

CHOCOLATE CAKE.

Ingredients—White part.—Two cups of sugar, two-thirds of a cup of butter, one cup of sweet milk, three cups of flour, two tea-spoonfuls of baking powder, whites of seven eggs.

Dark part.—The same as the white, with seven yolks and one cup of grated chocolate.

Bake in layers and put together with the white of eggs, alternating a white layer with a dark one. Frost with chocolate icing.

COCOANUT CAKE.

Ingredients.—Two cups of sugar, one cup of butter, four eggs, one cup of milk, one tea-spoonful of soda, two tea-spoonfuls of cream tartar, four cups of flour.

Bake in layers, then take the whites of three eggs and make icing as for icing cake;. grate into it as much cocoanut as it will take and spread between the layers of cake. Ice on the top and grate on as much cocoanut as will lie smoothly. This receipt makes one large cake.

COCOANUT CAKE.

Ingredients.—Whites of six eggs, one and one-half cups of sugar, one-half cup of butter, one-half cup of water, one and one-half cups of flour, one-half cup of corn-starch, one-half tea-spoonful of soda, one tea-spoonful of cream tartar.

Bake in three round tins; then take the whites of three eggs, beat to a froth, six table-spoonfuls of sugar, one cup of grated cocoanut; mix together and frost.

CORN STARCH CAKE.

Ingredients.—Whites of eight eggs, two cups of sugar, one cup of butter, one-half cup of milk, one tea-spoonful of cream tartar, one-half tea-spoonful of soda, one and one-half cups of corn starch, one and one-half cups of flour.

CORN STARCH CAKE.

Ingredients.—One cup of butter, two cups of sugar, two cups of flour, one cup of corn starch, one cup of sweet milk, two tea-spoonfuls of cream tartar, one tea-spoonful of soda, whites of seven eggs.

CORN STARCH CAKE.

Ingredients.—One cup of sugar, one cup of flour, one-half cup of butter, one-half cup of corn starch dissolved in one-half cup of sweet milk, whites of four eggs, one-half tea-spoonful of soda, one tea-spoonful of cream tartar, one tea-spoonful of lemon juice.

LEMON CAKE.

Ingredients.—Three cups of white sugar, one cup of butter, one cup of sweet milk, four cups of flour, five eggs, full tea-spoonful of baking powder, juice and grated peel of one lemon.

LEMON CAKE.

Ingredients.—Three teacups of sugar, one cup of butter, one cup of milk, five cups of sifted flour, five eggs, one tea-spoonful of soda, one tea-spoonful of cream tartar, grated peel of two lemons and the juice of one and one-half.

SILVER CAKE.

Ingredients.—One pound of sugar, three-fourths of a pound of sifted flour, six ounces of butter, the whites of fourteen eggs, mace, and citron, if you like.

WHITE CAKE.

Ingredients.—One and one-half cups of sugar, two-thirds of a cup of butter, two-thirds of a cup of sweet milk, one tea-spoonful of cream tartar, one-half tea-spoonful of soda, whites of four eggs, two cups of flour.

DELICATE CAKE.

Ingredients.—Whites of ten eggs, three cups of sugar, four cups of flour, one cup of butter, one cup of sweet milk, one tea-spoonful cream tartar, one-half tea-spoonful of soda.

DELICATE CAKE.

Ingredients.—Whites of seven eggs, two cups of sugar, one cup of butter, one cup of sweet milk, three and one-half even cups of flour, two tea-spoonfuls of baking powder.

DELICATE CAKE.

Ingredients.—One pound of sugar, one-half pound of butter, one pound of flour, the whites of sixteen eggs well beaten.

DELICATE CAKE.

(Mrs. Henderson.)

I copy this cake exactly—I have tried it many times and always with success. Mrs. Henderson says:

"I venture to say there is not to be found a better receipt for white cake than the following. The cake is mixed contrary to the usual rules for making cake, but it is the best mode for making it fine-grained and delicate.

Ingredients.—Whites of six eggs, scant three-quarters of a cupful of butter, one and one-quarter cupfuls of pulverized sugar, two cupfuls of flour, juice of half a lemon, one-quarter of a tea-spoonful of soda.

If soda is used mix it well with the flour, and pass it through the sieve several times to distribute it equally. Beat the butter to a light cream, and add the flour to it, stirring it in gradually with the ends of the fingers until it is a smooth paste. Beat the whites of the six eggs to a stiff froth, and mix in them the pulverized sugar; now stir the egg and sugar gradually into the flour and butter, adding also the lemon juice, and mix it smoothly together with the egg-whisk. As soon as it is perfectly smooth put it into the oven, the heat of which should be rather moderate at first. When done and still hot, spread over it a frosting made in the following manner:

Use a heaping tea-cupful of fine pulverized sugar to the white of each egg, or, say, a pound of sugar to the whites of three eggs. Beat the whites until they are slightly *foaming* only; do not beat them to a froth. The sugar may all be poured on the egg at once, or if considered easier to mix, it may be gradually added. Either way, as soon as the sugar and eggs are thoroughly stirred together, and flavored with a little vanilla or lemon, the icing is ready to spread over the cake. The icing made with the white of one egg is quite sufficient to frost an ordinary sized cake.

This cake may be made with one tea-spoonful of baking powder, or with prepared flour, or with one-quarter tea-spoonful of soda, and one-half tea-spoonful cream tartar, when the essence of lemon should be used instead of the lemon juice."

WHITE SPONGE CAKE.

Ingredients.—One tumbler of sugar, one tumbler of flour, whites of six eggs, tea-spoonful of baking powder.

SPONGE CAKE.

Ingredients.—One cup of sugar, one cup of flour, four eggs, two table-spoonfuls of water, one tea-spoonful of baking powder.

Mix the yolks of the eggs and sugar, then add the water, then the whites beaten to a stiff froth. The flour and baking powder the last thing.

SPONGE CAKE.

Ingredients..—Twelve eggs, one pound of sugar, one-half pound of flour, the rind and juice of two lemons.

Beat the eggs separately, beat the sugar into the yolks gradually and then add the rind of the lemons; next add the whites, well beaten, then stir in the flour. Do not beat at all after stirring in the flour.

SPONGE CAKE.

This is the best of the sponge cake receipts. A little more knack is required in mixing than in those which contain baking powder, but it is altogether superior to them.

Ingredients.—One pound of pulverized sugar, one-half pound of sifted flour, ten eggs, the grated rind and juice of one lemon, a salt-spoonful of salt.

Beat both yolks and whites *very thoroughly;* blend them lightly and quickly together; add the sugar gradually, then the lemon juice and rind and salt, and lastly the flour. Do not beat it after the flour is added. Bake in a moderate oven.

FLORENTINE CAKE.

Bake sponge cake after the preceding receipt in two layers, about an inch thick. Spread between them a custard made as follows:

Boil one quart of fresh milk; beat the yolks of four eggs with four table-spoonfuls of sugar; when the milk has boiled up once, pour it boiling on the beaten eggs, stirring rapidly all the time; when well mixed return to the fire. Of three light table-spoonfuls of corn starch make a paste with a little cold milk, which stir immediately into the custard on the fire. Let it cook until well thickened, stirring all the while. Take off the fire and flavor while hot with one tea-spoonful of vanilla.

After the cakes are put together with the custard between, ice with the following chocolate icing.

CHOCOLATE ICING.

Three table-spoonfuls of chocolate, six table-spoonfuls of white sugar, two table-spoonfuls of sweet cream, and a very small piece of butter, say half an ounce. Let this icing simmer over the fire for a few moments, when it can be immediately applied to the cake. Sprinkle granulated sugar over the top while hot.

This is a delicious chocolate icing for any chocolate cake. The amount of custard will do for three cakes—the icing for two.

IMPERIAL CAKE.

This is a superb cake and will keep as long as fruit cake.

Ingredients.—One pound of sugar, one pound of butter, ten eggs, grated rind and juice of one lemon, one pound of flour, one pound of almonds blanched and split, one-half pound of raisins stoned and halved, one-half pound of citron cut in thin slips, two table-spoonfuls extra flour for dredging the fruit, one tea-spoonful of extract of nectarine in one tea-spoonful of water, and one table-spoonful of rose water in one table-spoonful of water.

QUEEN CAKE.

Ingredients.—One large cup of butter, three cups of sugar, four cups of flour, one cup of sweet cream, two tea-spoonfuls of baking powder, the yolks of seven eggs and the whites of four, one tea-spoonful of vanilla.

GOLD AND SILVER CAKE.
(Home Messenger Cook Book.)

A simple but good receipt, making one loaf of each.

Ingredients.—One-half cup of butter, one cup of sugar, one and one-half cups of sifted flour, one-half cup of sweet milk, one and one-half tea-spoonfuls of baking powder, whites of four eggs, one-half tea-spoonful of vanilla.

Make the gold cake the same, only substitute the yolks for the whites, and lemon for vanilla.

ANGELS' FOOD.

Success is certain if the following receipt is carefully followed.

Ingredients.—Whites of eleven eggs, one and one-half tumblers of granulated sugar, one tumbler of sifted flour, one tea-spoonful of extract of vanilla, one tea-spoonful of cream tartar.

Sift the flour four times, then add cream tartar and sift again, but have only one tumbler after sifting. Sift the sugar and measure; beat the eggs to a stiff froth, add the sugar lightly, then the flour very gently, then vanilla. Do not stop beating till ready to put the mixture in the pan. Beat the eggs on a large platter, and mix the batter on the same platter. Use a pan that has never been greased. A brick-shaped pan made with short feet so as to raise it a quarter of an inch or so from the bottom of the oven should be kept especially for this cake. Bake forty minutes in a moderate oven; try with a straw; if too soft let it remain a few moments longer. Do not open the oven door for at least ten minutes after the cake has been put in. Turn the pans upside down for the cake to cool, and when cold take out, first loosening around the sides with a knife.

ICE CREAM CAKE.

Ingredients.—Two cups of sugar, one cup of sweet milk, whites of eight eggs, four cups of flour, one tea-spoonful of baking powder. Bake in layers.

Mixture to spread between layers.—Three cups of sugar, one cup of water. Boil to a clear thick syrup, and pour boiling over the beaten whites of three eggs. Add a tea-spoonful of citric acid. Flavor with vanilla.

WHITE MOUNTAIN CAKE.

Ingredients.—One pound of flour, one pound of sugar, one-half pound of butter, six eggs, one cup of sweet milk, table-spoonful of baking powder.

Frosting.—One sheet of cooper's isinglass dissolved in a small teacup of boiling water. Stir it into two pounds of powdered sugar. Flavor both cake and icing with vanilla. Bake the cake in layers and put together with this frosting; finally cover the whole with the frosting.

TIPSY CAKE.

Ingredients.—Sponge cake, handful of almonds, white wine, custard.

Bake a sponge cake in a mold. Blanch a handful of almonds, split them into four pieces and stick the cake full of them. Set in a deep dish and turn over as much white wine as the cake will absorb. Let it stand one hour. Turn in as much soft custard as the dish will hold.

PORK CAKE.

Ingredients.—One pound of chopped pork dissolved in one pint of boiling water, two cups of brown sugar, two cups of molasses, two tablespoonfuls of cinnamon, two tablespoonfuls of cloves, two grated nutmegs, one pound of raisins, one spoonful of soda, eight cups of flour, four eggs.

KRAPFEN.

(German Receipt.)

Ingredients.—Two pounds of flour, three table-spoonfuls of yeast, one pint of milk, one-fourth pint of sour cream, two ounces of powdered sugar, four eggs, one-half pound of butter, salt (sufficient), peel of half a lemon (grated), two table-spoonfuls of rose water.

Flour, yeast, milk and cream are mixed and allowed to rise, which takes about an hour and a half. Then the other ingredients are added and the whole is beaten until it is very light. · It is then rolled out to one-half inch thickness, cut in small square pieces and allowed to rise one hour more. Fry in hot lard to a light brown and roll while hot in sugar, to which some powdered cinnamon may be added.

RADANKUCHEN.

(German Receipt.)

Ingredients.—Two pounds of flour, three table-spoonfuls of yeast, one pint of milk, the yolks of four eggs, one-fourth of a pound of sugar, grated peel of one-half a lemon, three-fourths of a pound of butter, one-fourth of a pound of raisins (Sultanas), salt according to taste.

The yeast and half of the milk are poured in the center of a dish which contains the flour, and well stirred, so that a soft dough is formed, which is covered over and allowed to rise. After the dough has risen sufficiently, the other ingredients are gradually added and the whole is beaten with a wooden spoon for half an hour. The dough is then put into a well buttered mold, thickly strewn with small pieces of almond. Then the cake must stand until it has risen to the top of the mold, when it should be baked in a rather quick oven for one and one quarter hours. In putting the dough in the mold care must be taken that it is not over half full. This is a most excellent receipt.

LADIES' CAKE.

Ingredients.—One pound of sugar, six ounces of butter beaten to a cream, the whites of sixteen eggs, the grated rind and juice of one lemon, three-fourths of a pound of flour.

SODA CAKE.

Ingredients.—Two cups of butter, two cups of sugar, three cups of flour, whites of five eggs, three-fourths of a cup of milk, one small tea-spoonful of soda, two small tea-spoonfuls of cream tartar, one cup of raisins, one cup of currants, spice to taste.

GILLET CAKE.

Ingredients.—Two cups of sugar, two cups of butter, two eggs, two tea-spoonfuls of soda, one-half cup of sour cream, flour enough to roll out smoothly.

KATIE'S PLAIN CAKE.

Ingredients.—One cup of butter, two cups of sugar, four eggs, one cup of cold water, three tea-spoonfuls of baking powder, three and one-half cups of flour. Bake immediately.

GLEN COTTAGE CAKE.

Ingredients.—Two cups of sugar, one cup of butter, four cups of flour, one-half cup of sweet milk or cream, the whites of five eggs, one tea-spoonful of soda, two tea-spoonfuls of cream tartar.

HUCKLEBERRY CAKE.

Ingredients.—One cup of sugar, one egg, half a cup of butter, half a cup of milk, one tea-spoonful of soda, two tea-spoonfuls of cream tartar, any essence you prefer, one tea-spoonful; sifted flour to make a stiff batter. Beat thoroughly, add last one pint of dried huckleberries, and bake in a quick oven.

WASHINGTON CAKE.

Ingredients.—Three cups of sugar, two cups of butter, one cup of milk, four cups of flour, five eggs, two tea-spoonfuls of cream tartar, one tea-spoonful of soda, fruit and citron if you like.

CAKE.

NEW YEAR'S CAKE.

Ingredients.—One and one-fourth pounds of sugar, one pound of butter, one-half pint of cold water, two eggs, three and one-fourth pounds of flour, one tea-spoonful of soda dissolved in hot water, four table-spoonfuls caraway seed in the flour.

Chop the butter up in the flour, dissolve the sugar in the water, mix all well with the beaten eggs, then roll and cut in square cakes and bake quickly.

JENNY LIND CAKE.

Ingredients.—Three cups of flour, one and one-half cups of sugar, two eggs, two table-spoonfuls of butter, one cup of sweet milk, one tea-spoonful of soda, two tea-spoonfuls of cream tartar, or a table-spoonful of baking powder.

CUSTARD CAKE.

Ingredients.—One and one-half cups of sugar, two-thirds of a cup of butter, one egg, one cup of milk, three cups of flour, one tea-spoonful of soda, two tea-spoonfuls of cream tartar.

Bake in layers and put boiled custard between.

CIDER SPICED CAKE.

Ingredients.—One-half cup of butter, one and one-half cups of sugar, one cup of cider, one egg, two tea-spoonfuls of cinnamon, two tea-spoonfuls of cloves, one-half a nutmeg, one tea-spoonful of soda, flour enough for a stiff batter.

LOVE CAKE.

Ingredients.—One cup of sugar, one-half cup of butter, one-half cup of milk, two cups of flour, two eggs, full table-spoonful of baking powder.

YELLOW CAKE.

Ingredients.—Whites of two eggs, yolks of seven eggs, one-half pound of sugar, three and one-half ounces of butter, one-half a cup of sour cream, one-half a tea-spoonful of soda, three small cups of flour.

ONE EGG CAKE.

Ingredients.—One-half cup of butter, one cup of sugar, one-half cup of milk, one and one-half cups of flour, one heaping tea-spoonful of baking powder, one egg.

PLAIN CAKE.

(Mrs. John Scott.)

Ingredients.—One-half cup of butter, one cup of sugar, two eggs, one and one-half cups of flour, one-third cup of milk, two tea-spoonfuls of baking powder.

HICKORY NUT CAKE.

Ingredients.—One cup of butter, two cups of sugar, one cup of sour milk, five cups of flour, one large cup of hickory nut meats, four eggs, one tea-spoonful of soda.

SUGAR GINGER BREAD.

Ingredients.—One quart of molasses, one-half pound of sugar, three-fourths of a pound of butter or lard, five eggs, one tea-spoonful of soda dissolved in one-half tea-cupful of milk, flour enough to make it as stiff as pound cake, one small table-spoonful of ginger.

GINGER SNAPS, OR COOKIES.

Ingredients.—Two small cups of molasses, one cup of sugar, one cup of sour milk, three eggs, one tea-spoonful of soda, two table-spoonfuls of ginger, two cups of butter or shortening, flour enough to make a stiff paste.

GINGER BREAD.

Ingredients.—One cup of sugar, one cup of molasses, one cup of butter, one-half cup of sour or buttermilk, four cups of flour, three eggs, one heaping tea-spoonful of ginger, one tea-spoonful of cinnamon, one tea-spoonful of soda. Makes two loaves.

GINGER BREAD.

Ingredients.—One cup of butter, one large cup of molasses, one cup of sugar, three eggs, one tea-spoonful of soda, one table-spoonful of ginger, a cup of raisins, flour enough to make a stiff batter.

GINGER BREAD.

(Delicious.)

Into a coffee cup put one table-spoonful of butter, three table-spoonfuls of boiling water, one tea-spoonful of soda, one tea-spoonful of ginger, one tea-spoonful of cinnamon.

Fill the cup up with molasses. Beat two eggs very light, add the mixture in the cup and one and one-half cups of sifted flour.

GINGER BREAD—WITHOUT EGGS.

Ingredients.—One cup of butter, one cup of sugar, one cup of molasses, one cup of sour milk or coffee, one tea-spoonful of soda dissolved in hot water, one tea-spoonful of cinnamon, two tea-spoonfuls of ginger, five cups of flour, one cup of raisins.

GINGER SNAPS.

Ingredients.—One pint of molasses, one cup of butter, one table-spoonful of ginger, one table-spoonful of soda, flour enough to roll out very thin.

Boil the molasses and butter together, then add the other ingredients.

JACKSON JUMBLES.

Ingredients.—Two cups of sugar, one cup of butter, one cup of cream, a tea-spoonful of soda, two eggs, five cups of flour, and a little nutmeg.

COOKIES.

Ingredients.—One cup of butter, two cups of sugar, one cup of sweet cream, two eggs, one-half tea-spoonful of soda, flour enough to roll, cinnamon or nutmeg.

NEW YEAR'S COOKIES.

Ingredients.—One pound of sugar, one pound of butter, one cup of sour milk, two eggs, one tea-spoonful of soda, flour enough to roll.

SUPERIOR DOUGHNUTS.

Ingredients.—Two cups of sugar, one and one-half cups of sweet milk, five eggs, three spoonfuls of butter, three tea-spoonfuls of baking powder, salt and flavor to suit the taste.

Mix as soft as possible, roll out, cut in proper sizes and drop in hot lard; when removed from the lard and partly cool dip in powdered sugar.

FRIED CAKES.

Ingredients.—One and one-half quarts of flour, two eggs, one cup of sugar, one-half a cup of butter, one coffee cup of sweet milk, three tea-spoonfuls of cream tartar, one and one-half tea-spoonfuls of soda, or a heaping table-spoonful of baking powder.

NUT CAKES.

Ingredients.—One pint of sour cream, three eggs, two cups of sugar, two tea-spoonfuls of soda, two tea-spoonfuls of cream tartar. Flour enough to roll out. Fry in hot lard.

FRIED CAKES.

Ingredients.—Two cups of milk, two cups of sugar, four eggs, one-half a cup of butter, two tea-spoonfuls of cream tartar, one tea-spoonful of soda, flour enough to roll as for biscuit.

DOUGHNUTS WITHOUT EGGS.

Ingredients.—Two cups of sour milk, one and one-fourth cups of sugar, three table-spoonfuls of melted butter, one tea-spoonful of soda, one tea-spoonful of salt, spice to taste. Mix soft.

CREAM CAKE.

Ingredients.—Whites of ten eggs, one goblet of flour, one and one-half goblets of pulverized sugar, one tea-spoonful of cream tartar.

Sift the flour five times, then sift sugar and flour together. Beat the whites on a platter to a stiff froth. Gently stir in the flour and sugar and sifted cream tartar.

Bake in layers and put together with whipped cream prepared as follows: One pint of sweet, thick, *very cold* cream, two table-spoonfuls of powdered sugar, one tea-spoonful of vanilla. Mix together and whip with a Dover egg-beater, or a wire egg whisk, until stiff enough to stand alone like the beaten whites of egg. Keep the cream *very cold.* Therein lies the secret of success.

This is a dainty and elegant cake and well worth the trouble it takes to make it. Heap the whipped cream on the top layer also.

LEMON CAKE.

(Mrs. John Scott.)

Ingredients.—One pint of flour, one pint of sugar, six eggs beaten separately, one heaping table-spoonful of butter, one tea-spoonful of soda, two tea-spoonfuls of cream tartar, four table-spoonfuls of cold water.

Mix according to general directions and add the water the last thing.

Icing.—One pound of coffee sugar, one-fourth of a pound of butter, five eggs, three lemons grated and the juice; boil altogether till thick and spread on the layers.

This makes enough jelly for three entire cakes. Use what is necessary and put the rest away in tumblers like jelly. It will keep for a long time.

ORANGE CAKE.

(From Marian Harland.)

Ingredients.—Three table-spoonfuls of butter, two cups of sugar, yolks of five eggs, whites of three, beaten separately, one cup of ice water, three heaping cups of flour, the juice and half the grated rind of one orange, one heaping table-spoonful of baking powder.

Cream the butter; add the sugar and the yolks of the eggs; beat in the orange, the water, and lastly the whites of the egg, alternately with the flour. Bake in layer cake tins.

Mixture to spread between the layers—Ingredients.—Whites of two eggs beaten stiff, two cups of powdered sugar, the juice and half the grated rind of an orange. Add if necessary a little more sugar for top layer.

DOUGHNUTS.

Ingredients.—One pint of milk, one pint of sugar, one-half cup of lard, two eggs, one cup of yeast, a little salt. Flour enough to roll.

Warm the milk, lard and sugar and pour into the flour; add the other ingredients; set away to rise; when light roll, cut and fry.

LEMON COOKIES.

Ingredients.—Five eggs, two cups of sugar, one cup of butter, five cups of flour, juice and rind of two lemons, one tea-spoonful of soda. Do not knead much. Roll sugar over the top.

GINGER CAKES.

Ingredients.—One-half coffee-cup of butter milk, filled up with molasses, one-half coffee-cup of sugar, two table-spoonfuls of thick sour cream, one egg, one heaping tea-spoonful of soda, one tea-spoonful of ginger, about one coffee-cup of flour.

The cake should be thin. Drop by spoonfuls in a pan, and bake from six to ten minutes in a quick oven.

SPANISH BUNS.

Ingredients.—One and one-half pints of flour, one pint of sugar, four eggs, one cup of butter, one cup of sweet milk, one table-spoonful of cloves, one table-spoonful of cinnamon, two tea-spoonfuls of cream tartar, one tea-spoonful of soda, or one heaping tea-spoonful of baking powder to every cup of flour.

CREAM PIE.

Ingredients.—One cup of sugar, three eggs, one cup of flour, one tea-spoonful of soda, two tea-spoonfuls of cream tartar.

Beat the sugar and eggs together well. Put the soda and cream tartar into the flour and mix well, then put them all together and bake on two plates.

The Custard.—One pint of milk, two eggs, one-half tea-cup of sugar, one-half cup of corn-starch or flour, flavor to suit the taste. When the custard is cold split the cake and put the custard between.

LUNCH LOAF CAKE.

Ingredients.—Two and a half cups of powdered sugar, one and one-half cups of butter, one cup of milk, three eggs, five cups of flour, one glass of wine, one-half pound of raisins, two ounces of citron.

Stir butter and sugar to a cream; add part of the flour with the milk and the well beaten yolks; add the rest of the flour, whites of eggs, wine, spices and fruit, last, also a fresh lemon.

One tea-spoonful baking powder, slightly heaped, to every cup of flour. If wine is sour add a half tea-spoonful of soda.

BOSTON CREAM CAKES.

Boil one-half a cupful of butter in one tumbler of water; stir into the boiling mixture one and one-half tumblers of flour; take from the fire and when cool add five eggs, beating them in, one by one; dissolve one-half a tea-spoonful of soda in one-half a cupful of boiling water; rinse out a baking sheet with this and immediately drop in the batter by spoonfuls.

Bake in a hot oven half an hour; when done split the cakes partly open and fill with custard made as follows:

Custard.—Two tumblers of milk, one and one-half tea-cups of sugar, three-quarters of a tea-cupful of flour, and two eggs. Beat the sugar, eggs, and flour together, flavor with vanilla, and stir into this the boiling milk; return to the stove and let it boil until well thickened, stirring constantly.

MARMALADE CAKES.
(Harper's Bazar.)

Rub together one pound of sugar and one pound of butter until perfectly light; beat the yolks of eight eggs well; add to the butter and sugar; stir into the mixture one tea-spoonful of mixed spices (cinnamon, nutmeg, and mace) and a table-spoonful of rose-water; sift now into this one and one-half pounds of flour; stir the whole well and roll it on the pastry board about one-half an inch thick. Cut round or fancy shaped cakes, and bake till done, which will be in a few minutes; when cold spread with marmalade or preserves; then beat the whites of the eight eggs very light, adding gradually eight large table-spoonfuls of sifted pulverized sugar; flavor with the juice and grated rind of a lemon, and with a spoon put it on each cake, heaping it high in the center. Put the cakes in the oven and brown this mèringue delicately.

These are elegant little cakes. The above receipt makes a great many, and half the quantity is all that will be needed ordinarily.

CHARLOTTE POLONAISE CAKE.

The two following receipts are from Marian Harland's "Breakfast, Luncheon, and Tea." They are both delicious cakes. The amount of filling is more than can be used in either case, and in making them I compound but half the quantity.

Ingredients.—Two cups of powdered sugar, one-half cup of butter, four eggs, whites and yolks beaten separately, one small cup of cream or rich milk, three cups of flour, one table-spoonful of baking powder.

Filling.—Six eggs, whipped very light, two table-spoonfuls of flour, three cups of cream, scalding hot, six table-spoonfuls of grated chocolate, six table-spoonfuls of powdered sugar, one-half pound sweet almonds, blanched and pounded, one-fourth pound chopped citron, one-fourth pound apricots, peaches, or other crystallized fruit, one-half pound macaroons.

Beat the yolks of the eggs very light; stir into the hot cream flour which has been previously wet with a little cold milk; add very carefully the beaten yolks, and keep the mixture at a slow boil, stirring all the time, for five minutes. Take from the fire and divide the custard into three equal portions. Put the grated chocolate, with the macaroons, finely crumbed (rolled or pounded) with one table-spoonful of sugar, into one pan of the mixture, stirring and beating well; boil five minutes, stirring constantly; take from the fire, whip with your egg-beater five minutes more, and set aside to cool.

Pound the blanched almonds, a few at a time, in a wedgewood mortar, adding, now and then, a few drops of rose-water; chop the citron very fine and mix with the almonds, adding three table-spoonfuls of sugar; stir into the second portion of custard; heat to a slow boil; take it off and set by to cool.

Chop the crystallized fruit very small, and put with the third portion of custard; heat to a boil; pour out and cool.

Season the chocolate custard with vanilla; the almond and citron with bitter almond; the fruit will require no flavoring.

When quite cold, lay out four cakes made according to receipt given with this, or bake at the same time a white cake in layers, and alternate with that. This will give you two good loaves. Put the chocolate filling between the first and second cakes; next, the almond and citron; the fruit custard next to the top. (There will be more than enough filling for two loaves.)

Ice the tops with lemon icing made of the whites of the eggs whisked very stiff with powdered sugar and flavored with lemon juice.

A CHARLOTTE À LA PARISIENNE.

Ingredients.—One large stale sponge cake, one cup rich sweet custard, one cup sweet cream, whipped, two table-spoonfuls rose-water, one-half grated cocoanut, one-half pound sweet almonds, blanched and pounded, whites of four eggs, whipped stiff, three table-spoonfuls powdered sugar.

Cut the cake in horizontal slices the whole breadth of the loaf. The slices should be about half an inch thick. Divide the whipped eggs into two portions; into one stir the cocoanut with half the sugar; into the other the almond paste with the rest of the sugar. Spread the slices with these mixtures—half with the cocoanut, half with the almond, and replace them in their original form, laying aside the top crust for a lid. Press all the sliced cake firmly together, that the slices may not slip, and with a sharp knife cut a deep section out of the center down to the bottom slice, which must be left entire. Take out the sections you have cut, leaving walls an inch thick, and soak the part removed in a bowl with the custard. Rub it to a smooth batter and whip it into the frothed cream. The rose-water in the almond paste will flavor it sufficiently. When it is a stiff, rich cream, fill the cavity of the cake with it, put on the lid and ice with the following:

Whites of three eggs, one heaping cup of powdered sugar, juice of one lemon. Beat stiff and cover the sides and top of the cake. Set in a very cold place until needed.

This is a delicious and elegant charlotte.

SWISS ROLL.

Ingredients.—Two eggs, their weight in flour, butter, and sugar, two table-spoonfuls of milk, one tea-spoonful of baking powder.

Bake in a sheet, and spread jam over and roll.

ROCK CAKES.
(English Receipt.)

Ingredients.—One pound of flour, four ounces of dripping or butter, three ounces of sugar, five ounces of currants, grated rind of a lemon, one tea-spoonful of baking powder, one egg, one gill of milk.

7

Rub the shortening into the flour, add the other dry ingredients, stir in the baking powder and bind together with the milk and egg. Drop by spoonfuls on a baking sheet in a rough shape and dredge with sugar. Bake in a quick oven.

GERMAN POUND CAKE.

Ingredients.—One-half pound of sugar, one-half pound of butter, ten ounces of flour, two ounces candied peel (citron, orange, and lemon), four ounces of sultanas, whites of four and yolks of five eggs.

Cream the butter, add the sugar and beat until perfectly soft and smooth; drop two eggs into the mixture and beat well; then add a handful of flour, and then the rest of the eggs; then mix in the remainder of the flour, and add the fruit last. Bake one and one-half hours.

PLAIN CAKE.

(South Kensington Receipt.)

Ingredients.—One pound of flour, five ounces of butter rubbed together, one table-spoonful of baking powder, five ounces sultanas, four ounces of sugar, three eggs, three-fourths of a pint of milk. Bake two hours in a moderate oven.

MADEIRA CAKE.

Ingredients.—One-half pound of flour, seven ounces of butter, one-half pound of sugar, the yolks of six and the whites of four eggs.

Work the sugar and butter well together, drop in two of the eggs and beat well, add a little flour to prevent the batter curdling, then add two more eggs, beat well, then two yolks, then the remainder of the flour.

SPONGE CAKE.

(South Kensington Receipt.)

Ingredients.—One-half pound of loaf sugar, one-half gill of water, melted together in a stew-pan; break into a basin eight yolks and four whites of eggs, whisk lightly, then add a little of the sugar and water, and keep on whisking about two minutes, then place the mixture over a sauce-pan of hot water and add the

' rest of the sugar and water, and keep on beating until the whole is very light (about one-half hour); then add gradually one-half pound of flour.

SHORT BREAD.
(South Kensington Receipt.)

Ingredients—One-half pound of flour, five ounces of butter worked together; three ounces of sugar and one table-spoonful of water melted together, and stirred, while hot, into the flour and butter; mix together with a wooden spoon; take out the spoon, flour the table and the hands and take the mixture out; divide into equal parts and shape lightly into an oval or round form; scatter pieces of candied peel over the top; bake in a moderate oven one-half hour.

FROSTING, OR ICING FOR CAKES.

The whites of eggs do not need beating for plain icing. The sugar should be sifted. Lemon juice not only flavors the icing pleasantly but it also whitens it. Allow one heaping cup of sugar to the white of one egg, and enough lemon juice to make it slightly acid. Beat the whites until they foam a little, add the sugar gradually and put on the cake, if possible, while it is still hot. Dredge the warm loaf with flour, and wipe it quickly off. The icing will then stick to the cake. Have a cup of boiling water and a knife at hand. Put enough of icing in the center of the loaf to cover the top of the cake. Dip the knife in the hot water and smooth it quickly and evenly over the surface.

CHOCOLATE FROSTING.

Ingredients.—One-fourth cake of Baker's chocolate grated, one cup of sugar boiled with three table-spoonfuls of well water; pour over chocolate when it will string; stir until nearly cold, then add the beaten white of an egg.

BOILED ICING.

Ingredients.—One pound of powdered sugar, whites of three eggs; flavor to taste.

Boil the sugar with a little water; when it is nearly ready to candy or will string from the spoon take it off the fire, and while still boiling hot add the whites of eggs well beaten, stirring as fast as possible.

CHAPTER VIII.

PIES AND PUDDINGS.

GENERAL REMARKS.

O make good pastry, light and tender but by no means greasy, requires practice and skill. In the first place everything to be used should be *cold*, the flour must be perfectly dry, the butter free from moisture, and the temperature of the oven just right. The movements of the cook must be quick and delicate, and everything so well timed that the pastry need not wait for the oven, nor the oven for the pastry.

In my receipts, I have given first a plain pie-crust, and have advanced from that to puff paste. I have been most careful to gather the best receipts for this complicated and flaky paste in print, and am able to offer my readers Francatelli's, Soyer's, and Monsieur Ude's instructions on this point. I give also the methods taught in the English National Training School, and therefore am assured that no fuller or more complete set of directions for making puff-paste can be found in any cook-book.

Pie-crust needs a pretty hot oven. It is a good plan to try the heat by putting a small piece of dough on a tin and baking it as a test for the temperature. If by the time it is slightly colored the paste is cooked through, the oven is ready for the pies.

There are a few things to be remembered also in the compounding of puddings to which I call attention.

Suet should be lightly dredged with flour while it is being chopped to prevent sticking.

Raisins and currants must be carefully cleaned before using. Unless sultanas are used, raisins should *always* be stoned for pies or puddings. Currants and sultanas may be cleaned in part by putting them dry on a seive and rubbing flour through them

101

until the stems and dust are rubbed off. Then they must be looked over to make sure they are free from stones or other foreign substances. If they are washed they must be thoroughly dried before being used.

BATTER PUDDINGS should be so mixed as to be entirely free from lumps. It is a good plan to strain them before cooking.

BOILED PUDDINGS should always be put in boiling water, which should continue to boil steadily all the time the pudding is in. If boiled in a cloth, that should be dipped in scalding hot water and slightly dredged with flour before the pudding is put in. When the pudding is taken out, plunge it for a moment in cold water before removing the cloth. This will prevent its sticking.

FOR A MÉRINGUE allow one table-spoonful of sugar to the white of one egg and a few drops of lemon juice. Beat the whites very stiff, add the sugar gradually and lightly, and heap the méringue on the pie or pudding while it is still hot, and then color it slightly in the oven.

PIES.

PLAIN PIE-CRUST.

Ingredients.—Three cups of flour, one cup of lard, or butter (heaping), one tea-spoonful of salt, cold water to mix.

Cut the shortening into the flour to which the salt has been added. Use just enough very cold water to bind the whole together, still mixing with the knife, or, if preferred, the knife can be removed and a spoon used in its place. *Be sure* that the flour is dry, the shortening very cold and hard, and the water also very cold. Handle as little as possible. Take out on to the pastry board just enough to line the pie-tin, and roll it as nearly the size of the tin as possible.

PASTRY.

(*Home Messenger Receipt Book.*)

Ingredients.—One and one-quarter pounds of flour, one pound of shortening and a little salt, all cut together. Sufficient cold water to mix with; no more flour.

Put upon the molding board, roll out and cut into strips; put one upon another, then cut off in squares, roll out and put upon plates.

ROUGH PUFF PASTE.

This, and the short crust for fruit pies which follows, were taught me in the South Kensington School.

Ingredients.—One-half pound of best flour, one-half pound of butter, cold water to mix.

Rub two ounces of the butter into the flour until the mixture is like fine bread crumbs; mix it with cold water to a smooth, rather soft paste; roll thin; shave the rest of the butter into flakes and put in the center; fold the paste over it, the edges just meeting, and smooth it a little with the rolling-pin; then fold the same way again, the long way of the paste, the two sides containing the butter folding over on each other, leaving the ends free from the butter; now roll the ends gently so as to flatten them somewhat and fold one over the upper side one-third, the other on the under side, one-third, and flatten slightly with the rolling-pin; set away to cool; roll four times.

This makes fine vol-au-vents also. I could see very little difference, indeed, between this and the other puff paste.

SHORT CRUST.
(*Excellent.*)

Ingredients.—Six ounces of flour, four ounces of butter, one table-spoonful of sugar, rubbed together, add the yolk of an egg and a few drops of lemon juce, and blend all together with as little cold water as possible.

Fruit tarts or pies are made in England in deep dishes, or "nappies" without a bottom crust. They are delicious. This short crust is used to cover them. The edge of the dish is covered with a strip of the crust, the fruit is put in, and the top crust put on, a few holes are pricked in the top and the whole is slowly baked. Or, the dish is filled with a "dummy," the crust put on, and when baked, carefully removed and the stewed fruit poured in and the crust replaced.

A "dummy" is usually a piece of bread the size of the opening, or a hard crust made by mixing flour and water into a stiff dough and baking it very thoroughly.

PUFF PASTE.

The following is the method taught at "The National Training School of Cookery," at South Kensington, London.

Ingredients.—One-half pound of flour, one-half pound of butter, one good tea-spoonful of lemon juice, the yolk of one egg.

Put the flour in a pile on the pastry-board; make a well in the center; drop in the yolk of the egg and the lemon juice; work the flour and egg and lemon juice with the ends of the fingers of the right hand into a firm paste, using as much very cold water in addition as is necessary; squeeze the whey and butter-milk well out of the butter, make it into a flat cake, put it in the center of the paste (which must previously be rolled into an oblong shape) and fold the edges over so it is completely covered; flatten it gently with the rolling-pin, and let it stand in a cold place, or on ice, until perfectly cold and firm (about ten minutes); then roll it one way, being very particular to keep the edges even and straight; when rolled out into a long even piece, fold one edge exactly to the middle, fold the other over so as to meet it perfectly, make sure that the edges are even and straight, and then turn it and roll in an opposite direction, fold in the same way and leave again until cold; roll six times for pastry, eight times for vol-au-vents.

PUFF PASTE.

(*Francatelli.*)

Ingredients.—One pound of flour, one pound of butter, the yolk of an egg, a tea-spoonful of salt, and about one-half pint of water.

Place the flour on the pastry slab or board, spread it out in the center, so as to form a well, in which place the salt, a small piece of butter, the yolk of an egg, and about two-thirds of the quantity of water required to mix the paste; spread out the fingers of the right hand, and mix the ingredients together gradually with the tips of the fingers, adding a little more water, if necessary; when the whole is thoroughly incorporated together sprinkle a few drops of water over it, and work the paste to and fro on the slab for two minutes, after which it should be rather soft to the touch, and present a perfectly smooth appearance.

The paste, thus far prepared, must now be spread out on the slab with the hands, and after the butter has been pressed in a cloth, to extract any milk it may contain, it should be placed in the center of the paste, and partially spread, by pressing on it with the cloth; the four sides should then be folded over so as to entirely cover the butter; a little flour must next be shaken over and under it, and the paste should be shaped in a square form, measuring about ten inches each way, by pressing it out with the hand; it should then be placed on a clean baking sheet, laid on some pounded ice, and a deep pan also filled with ice should be placed upon it. By these means the paste will be kept cool and firm. About ten minutes after the paste has been made, take it from the ice, shake a little flour over and under it, and then roll it out about two feet long and ten inches wide, observing that the paste must be kept square at both ends, as much of the success depends on due attention being paid to the turning and folding. The paste should then be laid in three equal folds, and after these have been rolled over to cause them to adhere together, the paste must next be turned round in the opposite direction, and rolled out again in the same manner as before; it should then be put back on the ice, and after allowing it to rest for about ten minutes or a quarter of an hour, roll it out again, or, as it is technically termed, give it two more turns; the paste must now be put back on the ice, and again rolled twice or three times, as the case may require, preparatory to its being cut out for whatever purpose it may be intended.

In the summer season it is impossible to secure success in making puff paste, unless ice be used to further that end, it being a matter of the first necessity that it should be kept cool and firm; two requisites that tend materially to facilitate the working of the paste, and also contribute very materially to give to it that extraordinary degree of elasticity so well known to experienced pastry cooks. A piece of puff paste, a quarter of an inch thick, when baked, will rise to the height of two inches, thus increasing the volume eight times. To effect this properly, it is necessary to procure three oblong tin pans, of the following dimensions: the first should measure twenty inches by sixteen, depth three inches; the second, eighteen inches by four, depth two inches; and the third, sixteen inches by twelve, depth three inches. Place some pounded ice in the largest, then set the second sized tin on this, with the puff paste in it; lastly, put the smallest pan, also filled with ice, on the top of the paste. By this method puff paste may easily be made to perfection during the hottest days of summer.

In winter the use of ice may, of course, be dispensed with. In extreme cold weather when the butter is very hard, it will be necessary to press it in a cloth or on the slab, to give it more expansion, and thus facilitate its incorporation with the paste. Care must be taken, in mixing the paste, not to make it too stiff, especially in summer, as, in that case, it becomes not only troublesome to work, but it also affects its elasticity in baking.

PUFF PASTE.
(Soyer's Receipt.)

Ingredients.—To every pound of flour allow the yolk of one egg, the juice of one lemon, one-half salt-spoonful of salt, cold water, one pound of fresh butter.

Put the flour on to the paste board; make a hole in the center, into which put the yolk of the egg, the lemon juice, and salt; mix the whole with cold water (this should be iced in summer) into a soft flexible paste, with the right hand, and handle it as little as possible; then squeeze all the butter-milk from the butter, wring it in a cloth, and roll out the paste; place the butter on this, and fold the edges of the paste over, so as to hide it; roll it out again to the thickness of one-fourth of an inch; fold over one-third, over which again pass the rolling-pin; then fold over the other third, thus forming a square; place it with the ends, top, and bottom before you, shaking a little flour both under and over, and repeat the rolls and turns twice again as before. Flour a baking sheet, put the paste on this, and let it remain on ice or in some cool place for one-half hour; then roll twice more, turning it as before; place it again upon the ice for one-fourth hour, give it two more rolls, making seven in all, and it is ready for use.

PUFF PASTE.
(M. Ude's Receipt.)

Ingredients.—Equal quantities of flour and butter, say one pound of each, one-half salt-spoonful of salt, the yolks of two eggs, rather more than one-fourth of a pint of water.

Weigh the flour, ascertain that it is perfectly dry, and sift it; squeeze all the water from the butter, and wring it in a clean cloth till there is no moisture remaining. Put the flour on the paste board, work lightly into it two ounces of the butter, and then make a hole in the center; into this well put the yolks of two eggs, the salt, and about one-fourth pint of water (the quantity of this latter ingredient must be regulated by the cook, as it is impossible to give the exact proportion of it); knead up the paste quickly and lightly, and, when quite smooth, roll it out square to the thickness of about one-half inch. Presuming that the butter is perfectly free from moisture, and as cool as possible, roll it into a ball, and place this ball of butter on the paste; fold the paste over the butter all round and secure it by wrapping well all over. Flatten the paste by rolling it lightly with the rolling pin until it is quite thin, but not thin enough to allow the butter to break through, and keep the board and paste dredged lightly with flour during the process of making it. This rolling gives it the *first* turn. Now fold the paste in three, and roll it out again, and, should the weather be very warm, put it in a cold place to cool between the several turns, for, unless this is particularly attended to, the paste will be spoiled. Roll out the paste again *twice*, put it by to cool, then roll it out *twice* more, which will make *six turnings* in all. Now fold the paste in two, and it will be ready for use. If properly baked and well made, this crust will be delicious, and should rise in the oven several inches. The paste should be made rather firm in the first instance as the ball of butter is liable to break through. Great attention must also be paid to keeping the butter very cool, as, if this is in a liquid and soft state, the paste will not answer at all.

GREEN APPLE PIES.

Grate raw six sour apples, add a cup of sugar, three table-spoonfuls of melted butter, four eggs, one table-spoonful of lemon juice, two table-spoonfuls of chopped almonds (blanched), a few Zantee currants. Line a pie plate with paste, fill and bake without an upper crust. Cover with a méringue if desired.

GREEN APPLE PIE.

Line a rather deep pie plate with pastry; slice tender, sour apples to fill the plate; season with sugar, little lumps of butter and nutmeg or cinnamon; add a very little water, cover and bake.

GREEN APPLE PIE.

Proceed as above, omitting all seasoning until baked; then carefully remove the upper crust, mash the apple gently with a spoon, season to taste, and replace the cover.

GREEN APPLE PIE.

Stew tender sour apples; press them through a sieve; add the yolks of three eggs, half a cup of milk, and half a cup of sugar to a quantity sufficient for one pie. Bake without an upper crust; make a méringue of the whites of the eggs, three table-spoonfuls of sugar and a tea-spoonful of lemon juice for the top of each pie; spread on while the pie is still hot and color a light brown in the oven.

DRIED APPLE PIE.

Pass the stewed apple through a cullender; if the apples are not tart add the juice and grated rind of a lemon; sweeten to taste; to a quantity sufficient for one pie add the yolks of four eggs and half a cupful of sweet milk. Bake with one crust, and when the pastry is done, make a méringue for the top with the whites of the eggs and four table-spoonfuls of powdered sugar.

DRIED PEACH PIE.

This can be made in the same way, or the eggs and milk may be omitted, and the pie filled simply with the peach pulp. Cover with a méringue.

PIE PLANT PIE.

Line a pie tin with pastry, cut the pie plant, after taking off the skin, in inch lengths; fill the pie very full, allow a good tea-cupful of sugar to one pie; dot with little lumps of butter (about a tea-spoonful in all), cover, and bake in a rather slow oven.

PIE PLANT PIE.

Stew the pie plant as for sauce, sweeten well, press through a cullender or sieve, add to a quantity sufficient for one pie the yolks of three eggs and half a tea-cupful of milk; bake with one crust and cover with a méringue.

This can scarcely be told from a lemon pie.

PIE PLANT PIE.

Cut the pie plant in inch lengths, fill a deep dish, sweeten, add a very little water (a table-spoonful) and bake with a top cover, made after the receipt for short crust.

LEMON PIE.

Ingredients.—Grate the rind and squeeze the juice of two lemons; beat the yolks of three eggs with eight table-spoonfuls of coffee sugar, half a cup of water and two table-spoonfuls of flour.

Stir the flour into the well beaten yolks and sugar, then add water, juice and rind; bake with an under crust; have ready, when it comes from the oven, the whites beaten to a stiff froth, with four table-spoonfuls of pulverized sugar; put on, set in the oven and brown as quickly as possible to avoid its being leathery.

LEMON PIES.

Ingredients.—Two lemons, grated rind and juice, two cups of sugar, yolks of six eggs, two table-spoonfuls of corn starch, one and one-half cups of sweet milk.

Bake till crust is done. Beat the whites of six eggs with eight table-spoonfuls of sugar. Frost the pies and bake to a very light brown. Makes two pies.

LEMON PIE.

Ingredients.—One cup of white sugar, one table-spoonful of corn starch, one lemon (grate off the outside rind and squeeze out the juice), one egg, one cup boiling water, a dessert-spoonful of butter.

Put the corn starch in a tea-cup and wet it with cold water and fill the cup with boiling water; add butter. When a little cold add the egg and lemon. Make two crusts and bake.

LEMON PIE.

Ingredients.—Grated peel and juice of one lemon, yolks of four eggs, six table-spoonfuls of sugar, one tumbler of cold water, piece of butter the size of a butternut, one table-spoonful of flour.

The whites of the eggs and four table-spoonfuls of powdered sugar make the méringue.

LEMON PIE.

Ingredients.—Three cups of sugar, one and one-half cups of sweet milk, five eggs, three lemons, whites of six eggs, six table-spoonfuls of sugar. Makes two pies.

Use the whites of the eggs and the six table-spoonfuls of sugar for a méringue for the top.

LEMON PIE.

Ingredients.—One large sour apple, chopped fine, grated rind and juice of one lemon, one egg, one cup of sugar, one teaspoonful of butter.

Bake with two crusts or with a méringue and one crust.

MINCE MEAT.

Ingredients.—Four pounds of beef, three pounds of suet, eight pounds of apples, three pounds of currants, three pounds of raisins, six pounds of sugar, spice, wine and cider to taste.

RICH MINCE MEAT.

(*Home Messenger Receipt Book.*)

Ingredients.—Three pounds of beef, one fresh beef's tongue, four or six pounds of suet, three and a half pounds of raisins, three pounds of currants, three-quarters of a pound of citron, eight pounds of chopped apples, four and a half pounds of sugar, three pints of molasses, three ounces of cinnamon, two ounces of cloves, a nutmeg, one tea-cupful of mace compound, one and one-fourth ounces of salt, half an ounce of pepper, one and one-half gallons of sweet cider.

When mixed, put into a kettle and scald, stirring it all the time. Put it hot into Hero or Mason jars—two quarts or gallon jars—and the longer you keep it the nicer it will be.

CUSTARD PIE.

To one pint of milk allow three whole eggs or the yolks of five, one-half cup of sugar, a pinch of salt, and flavoring to taste. If the yolks only are used, cover the pie with a méringue made with the whites.

PUMPKIN PIE.

To one quart of stewed pumpkin mashed and free from lumps, add one quart of milk, three or four eggs well beaten, a small cup of sugar, one tea-spoonful of salt, one table-spoonful of ginger.

Bake in a very hot oven.

SQUASH PIE.

(Miss Parloa.)

Pare, boil, and sift a good dry squash. To one quart of the squash pour on two of boiling milk, and then stir in two cups of sugar, two spoonfuls of salt, one of cinnamon, one grated nutmeg, and five well beaten eggs.

PEACH COBBLER

Fill a pudding dish with *whole* pared peaches, having first placed a small cup in the center of the dish; add a good half tea-cupful of sugar, and a half tea-cupful of water, and cover with rich pie-crust. Bake half an hour.

BERRY PIE.

Use a deep pie plate for all berry pies. Cherries and currants do not require any water; for other small fruits allow about two table-spoonfuls of water and three table-spoonfuls of sugar to a pie. Use the same amount of sugar for cherries and currants. Bake with two crusts.

CREAM PIE.

Ingredients.—One pint of rich cream, one scant tea-cup of sugar, the whites of four eggs whipped to a stiff froth.

Beat all together and pour into a pie plate lined with paste. Bake as you would custard pie and eat very cold.

CREAM PIE.

Ingredients.—Three pints of rich cream, five eggs, and one cup of sugar, the grated rind of a lemon, or a tea-spoonful of vanilla.

Beat eggs and sugar together; and the milk and flavoring, and bake like custard.

The quantity given above makes two pies.

COCOANUT PIES.

Ingredients.—One quart of milk, four eggs, eight table-spoonfuls of prepared cocoanut. Sweeten to taste. Two pies.

MOCK MINCE PIES.

Ingredients.—Two cups of warm water, one-half cup of butter, two-thirds of a cup of vinegar, one cup of raisins, one cup of bread crumbs, one cup of sugar, one cup of molasses, spice to taste.

CHEESE CAKES.

Ingredients.—One and one-half ounces of butter, one and one-half ounces of sugar, one egg, five drops of almond essence, grated rind of a lemon, a sprinkle of nutmeg; one ounce of cracker crumbs, four table-spoonfuls of milk.

Bake in patty-pans lined with puff paste.

POTATO CHEESE CAKES.

Ingredients.—One pound of mashed potatoes, one-quarter of a pound of Zantec currants, one-quarter of a pound each of sugar and butter, four eggs, and the grated rind of one lemon.

Mix all together with a little cold milk or water, and bake in patty pans lined with puff paste.

POTATO CHEESE CAKES.

Ingredients.—Six ounces of mashed potatoes, four ounces of lemon peel, four ounces of sugar, four ounces of butter, a little cream.

Bake in puff paste, and before putting them in the oven sift a little loaf sugar over them.

PUDDINGS.

PLUM PUDDING.
(Francatelli.)

Ingredients.—Three-quarters of a pound of raisins, three-quarters of a pound of currants, half a pound each of candied orange, lemon, and citron, one and one-fourth pounds of chopped beef suet, one pound of flour, three-quarters of a pound of moist sugar, four eggs, about three gills of milk, the grated rind of two lemons, half an ounce each of ground mustard, cinnamon, and cloves, a glass of brandy, and a very little salt.

Mix the above ingredients thoroughly together in a large basin several hours before the pudding is to be boiled; pour them into a mold spread with butter, which should be tied up in a cloth. The pudding must then be boiled four hours and a half; when done, dish it up with a German custard-sauce spread over it.

GERMAN CUSTARD SAUCE.

(Francatelli.)

Put four yolks of eggs into a stew-pan, together with two ounces of pounded sugar, a glass of sherry, some orange or lemon peel (rubbed on loaf sugar), and a very little salt. Whisk this sharply over a very slow fire, until it assumes the appearance of a light, frothy custard.

PLUM PUDDING.

Ingredients.—One cup of suet chopped fine, one cup of molasses, one cup of raisins, one cup of sweet milk, one egg, one tea-spoonful of soda, a little salt, enough flour to make the batter as stiff as for cake.

Boil or steam two or three hours.

PLAIN PLUM PUDDING.

Ingredients.—One cup of molasses, one cup of sweet milk, one half a cup of butter, one nutmeg, one tea-spoonful of allspice, one-half tea-spoonful of cloves, one tea-spoonful of soda, one-half pound of raisins, one-half pound of currants, one-fourth pound of citron.

Boil one hour; serve with wine sauce.

POOR MAN'S PUDDING.

Ingredients.—Two cups of raisins chopped fine, two cups of molasses, one cup of butter, one cup of sweet milk, one tea-spoonful of soda, two tea-spoonfuls of cream tartar, flour enough to make it as stiff as plum pudding.

Boil three hours.

8

PUDDING À LÁ FRANCAISE.

(South Kensington School.)

Ingredients.—Twelve ounces of suet, eight ounces of flour, eight ounces of apricot jam, four ounces or chopped apple, six ounces candied cherries, six ounces of candied peel, four ounces of sugar, one tea-spoonful mixed spices (cinnamon, cloves, nutmeg), the grated peel of two lemons, five eggs, one glass of sherry, one-half pint of cream.

Mix and boil four hours. This is an expensive and elegant pudding, and the quantity made from the above ingredients is sufficient for a dinner party of twelve or fourteen guests.

VIENNOISE PUDDING.

(South Kensington School.)

Ingredients.—Five ounces crumb of bread, two ounces candied peel, three ounces granulated sugar, one ounce lump sugar, grated rind of one lemon, two eggs, one-half pint of milk, one gill of cream, three ounces sultanas, one wine-glass of sherry.

Cut the bread in dice, add the three ounces of granulated sugar, the raisins, lemon rind, and chopped candied peel, and sherry; now put the lump sugar, in a saucepan, over the fire, to brown; when it is a dark brown, add the milk and stir until the milk is evenly and thoroughly colored; break the eggs in a basin, beat, and add the colored milk, stirring all the time; pour this custard over the other ingredients; add the cream; steam in a well buttered mold one and one-half hours. Eat with sauce.

COLD APPLE PUDDING.

Ingredients.—Six good sized sour apples, five ounces of sugar, two table-spoonfuls of water, one-fourth pound of macaroons, one-half pint of milk, yolks of four eggs, one-half ounce of gelatine, two dozen pistachio or almond kernels.

Stew the apples with three ounces of sugar and two table-spoonfuls of water; when tender pass them through a sieve (there should be one-half pound after they are sifted); pound and sift the macaroons; make a boiled custard with the milk, eggs, and two ounces of sugar, add to it the macaroons and one-fourth ounce of gelatine previously dissolved; add one-fourth ounce dissolved gelatine to the apple also; blanch, dry, and chop fine the nuts; wet the bottom of the mold with a little gelatine dissolved and sweetened; when it is nearly set strew the nuts thickly over it; when firm, wet the sides of the mold also with the gelatine and cover thickly with grated cocoanut; when firm pour a layer of the custard in and leave it to become solid; then put in a layer of the apple and let it set; then another of custard, and so on until the mold is filled. When firm, turn out and serve.

COLD PINE-APPLE PUDDING.

Ingredients.—One can of pine-apple, two ounces macaroons, two dozen almonds, one-half ounce gelatine.

Pound the pine-apple and pass it through a hair sieve; put the juice in a stew pan over the fire and simmer until reduced to half the quantity; pound and sift the macaroons; blanch and chop the almonds; pour the reduced juice on the pine-apple pulp, add the gelatine, previously dissolved, and the macaroons, and almonds; decorate the bottom of the mold with gelatine, dissolved and sweetened, and colored a bright red with extract of cochineal; when it is set pour some clear gelatine over the sides and decorate with fancy pieces of angelica or citron; when firm fill the mold with the pine-apple and leave to become solid.

APPLE AMBER PUDDING.

Ingredients.—Six ounces bread crumbs, two ounces flour, four ounces suet, three-fourths pound chopped apple, two ounces granulated sugar, one lemon, a little nutmeg, three eggs, one-half ounce of butter.

Boil in a mold well buttered, two and one-half hours.

BROWN BETTY.

Butter and strew thickly with fine bread crumbs a deep pie dish, and fill it with alternate layers of sliced sour apple seasoned with sugar, bits of butter, and either cinnamon or nutmeg, and bread crumbs, having the top layer of bread crumbs stuck with lumps of butter; pour over the whole a few table-spoonfuls of cold water; press a plate over the top and keep covered while baking. Bake three-quarters of an hour. Eat with sweet cream.

APPLE PUDDING.

Stew some tender juicy apples in a very little water; when cooked mash them fine and whilst hot add to one pound of the apple one-quarter of a pound of butter, sugar and spice to taste. When cold add four well beaten eggs. Butter well a large pudding dish, strew the bottom well with bread crumbs. Either bake or steam and when done sift sugar over it.

ANOTHER APPLE PUDDING.

Prepare the apples the same as above, or grate sweet apples instead of stewing sour ones. Take three cups of rich sweet milk, four well beaten eggs, a pinch of salt, and flour sufficient to make a batter. Butter well the pudding dish, pour half the batter in, then the apple, then the balance of the batter. This can be either baked or steamed.

Both puddings are nice eaten with rich milk, or cream and sugar, or other sauce.

BAKED APPLE PUDDING.

Stew nicely four large sour apples, with the rind of a lemon grated, one tea-cup of sugar, six table-spoonfuls of melted butter, two slices of bread crumbed, whites of two and yolks of five eggs.

Line the dish with pastry; bake half an hour. Beat the remaining whites with twelve table-spoonfuls of sugar, spread on the top and bake a light brown.

APPLE PUDDING.

Pare and chop six good sour apples; butter a pudding dish and put in a layer of grated bread half an inch thick. Add small bits of butter, put in a layer of chopped apple with sugar and grated lemon peel, and another layer of bread crumbs, until the dish is full, having grated bread at the top. Pour on one cup of cold water, and bake thirty minutes.

APPLE OMELET.

Pare, core, and stew six large tart apples. Beat them very smooth while hot, adding one spoonful of butter, six spoonfuls of sugar, and a little nutmeg. When perfectly cold add three eggs, yolks and whites beaten separately. Pour this into a deep buttered baking dish and bake to a delicate brown.

APPLE BATTER PUDDING.

Core and pare eight apples, put in a pudding dish, fill the places from which the cores have been taken with sugar, cover and bake until tender. Beat the yolks of four eggs light, add two tea-cups of flour with three even tea-spoonfuls of baking powder sifted with it, one pint of milk, a tea-spoonful of salt, and the beaten whites of the eggs. Pour this over the apples and bake half an hour.

BOILED APPLE OR FRUIT PUDDING.

Ingredients.—Two eggs, one pint of milk, one-half tea-spoonful of baking powder, sliced apples.

Make a batter thicker than for waffles; fill a pudding dish with alternate layers of batter and sliced apple, and steam one and one-half hours.

SUET PUDDING.

Ingredients.—One-half pound of suet, one pound of fruit, two pounds of flour, enough cold water for a stiff paste. Boil three hours.

DARK PUDDING.

Ingredients.—One cup of molasses, one cup of milk, one cup of suet, one and one-half cups of raisins, chopped fine, three and one-half cups of flour, one-fourth tea-spoonful of nutmeg, one-half tea-spoonful each of cinnamon and soda, one tea-spoonful of salt. Steam four hours.

JELLY PUDDING.

("'76.")

Ingredients.—Two cups of sugar, two cups of flour, six eggs, a half cup of milk, one tea-spoonful of soda, and two tea-spoonfuls of cream tartar.

Bake in a long tin; when done spread with jelly and roll up. Serve with boiled sauce.

COTTAGE PUDDING.

Ingredients.—One egg, one pint of flour, one cup of milk, three table-spoonfuls of melted butter, one tea-spoonful of soda, two tea-spoonfuls of cream tartar.

Mix the cream tartar in the flour and the soda in the milk. Can be made in twenty minutes. Bake quickly and eat with sauce. Square, shallow pans are best to bake in. Two tea-spoonfuls of baking powder can be used.

FIG PUDDING.

Ingredients.—Three-quarters of a pound of grated bread crumbs, six ounces of suet chopped fine, half a pound of figs, also chopped, six ounces of sugar, a little nutmeg, a tea-cupful of milk and one egg.

Mix the bread and suet first, then the figs, sugar, nutmeg, and egg, and add the milk lastly. Boil in a pudding mold four hours.

BLACK PUDDING.

Ingredients.—Eight eggs, one pint of molasses, one cup of butter, one cup of sugar, one cup of milk, two cups of flour, one table-spoonful of soda.

Sauce for same.—Two cups of sugar, one table-spoonful of butter, one and one-half cups of boiling water, one lemon, squeeze in the juice and grate the peel. Bake one hour.

STEAM PUDDING.

Ingredients.—One tea-cup of beef suet, one tea-cup of raisins, one tea-cup of molasses, one tea-cup of sweet milk, one tea-spoonful of cream tartar, one-half tea-spoonful of soda, flour enough to make a stiff batter.

CHRISTMAS PUDDING.

Ingredients.—One pound of flour, two pounds of suet, one pound of currants, one pound of raisins, eight eggs, two ounces of candied peel, almonds, and spice to your taste. Boil gently for seven hours.

POTATO PUDDING.

Ingredients.—One pound of mashed potatoes, one-fourth of a pound of butter, the yolks of six eggs, sweeten to taste, a little lemon, a few blanched and pounded almonds, a small tea-cup of sweet cream, one nutmeg.

Beat it well and bake half an hour.

BATTER PUDDING.

(German Receipt.)

Ingredients.—One dozen eggs, one quart of sweet milk, one table-spoonful of sugar, one cup of flour, one-half a cup of butter.

Put the milk in a basin set in boiling water, reserving enough to wet the flour just as you would prepare a thickening for gravy. When the milk is scalding hot, pour in the flour, stirring it smooth. Add the butter and sugar. When this mixture is cool enough, add the yolks of the eggs well beaten; after that the beaten whites; then pour the whole through a flour sieve into the baking dish (there will always be a few lumps in the flour paste). The pudding pan must then be placed in a larger one, the outside pan being filled with boiling water as you put it in the oven. Bake one hour.

Sauce for same.—One cup of pulverized sugar, one-half cup of butter stirred to a cream. Add two eggs, yolks and whites beaten separately; stir well and add the juice of a lemon or wine.

BOILED GINGER PUDDING.

Ingredients.—One cup of molasses, one cup of sweet milk, one cup of stoned raisins, three cups of flour, two eggs, one tea-spoonful of soda, a little salt, ginger, cinnamon, and cloves, butter size of a small egg.

Boil or steam two and one-half hours.

Sauce.—Pour a cup of sweet milk on a cup of sugar, and one-half cup of butter beaten to a cream.

GINGER PUDDING.

Ingredients.—Six ounces of flour, six ounces of sugar, six eggs, eight ounces of preserved ginger, a pint of cream, six ounces of butter, a litle salt.

Put the cream, sugar, butter, and salt in a stew-pan on the fire, and as soon as these begin to simmer, take off the stew-pan, throw in the flour and stir the whole together quickly; then put this paste back again on the fire, and continue stirring it for about five minutes; it must then be withdrawn, and the six eggs mixed in gradually with it. The ginger, cut into small pieces, must now be added to the preparation, which must then be poured into the mold, previously spread with butter. Steam it for an hour and a half, and when done dish up the pudding with a custard sauce made with the syrup from the ginger.

PINE-APPLE PUDDING.

Made in the same way, substituting pine-apple for ginger.

BERRY PUDDING.

One pint of molasses, one tea-spoonful of soda, stirred until very light, then add a little salt, one tea-spoon of cloves, one tea-spoon of cinnamon, and flour to make a very stiff batter; stir in one quart of berries (huckleberries are best) and steam three hours. This makes a very large pudding.

CARAMEL PUDDING.

Put a handful of loaf sugar to boil with quarter of a pint of water until the syrup becomes a deep brown. Warm a small basin, pour the syrup in it and keep turning the basin in your hand until the inside is completely coated with the syrup, which will, by that time, have set. Strain the yolks of eight eggs from the whites, and mix them gradually and thoroughly with a pint of milk. Pour this mixture into the prepared mold. Lay a piece of paper on the top; set it in a sauce-pan full of cold water, taking care that the water does not come over the top of the mold, put on the cover and let it boil gently by the side of the fire one hour. Remove the sauce-pan to a cool place, and when the water is quite cold take out the mold and turn out the pudding very carefully.

By using a portion of the whites as well as the yolks, the risk of the pudding breaking is avoided, but it will not be as delicate as the one made with yolks alone.

SUNDERLAND PUDDING.

Ingredients.—One quart of milk, eight large table-spoonfuls of flour, eight eggs and a little salt.

Bake in pudding cups and serve with fairy butter.

THE QUEEN OF PUDDINGS.

Ingredients.—One pint of fine bread crumbs to one quart of milk, one cup of sugar, the beaten yolks of four eggs, the grated rind of one lemon, a piece of butter the size of an egg. Bake until done but not watery.

Whip the whites of the eggs stiff and beat in a cup of sugar, in which has been stirred the juice of one lemon. Spread on the pudding a layer of jelly or any sweetmeats you prefer. Pour the whites of the eggs over this and replace in the oven and bake lightly. To be eaten with cold cream. It is second only to ice cream, and in some seasons better.

GREEN CORN PUDDING.

Ingredients.—Three pints of milk, two eggs, a heaping table-spoonful of sugar, four ears of sweet corn.

Beat the eggs and sugar together and add the milk. Grate the raw corn from the ears and add that. Bake in a brisk oven until it is thoroughly cooked.

MOLASSES PUDDING—STEAMED.

Ingredients.—One cup of sugar, one cup of molasses, butter the size of an egg, one and one-half cups of water, two eggs, five cups of flour, three table-spoonfuls of baking powder.

Steam three hours. Eat with sauce.

PUFFS.

Ingredients.—Six table-spoonfuls of flour, one pint of milk, two eggs.

Bake in cups not quite half full or in gem pans. Serve immediately with cream and sugar or sweet sauce.

QUICK PUDDING.

Ingredients.—One egg, one cup of sugar, one table-spoonful of melted butter, one cup of sweet milk, one table-spoonful of baking powder, three cups of flour. Bake one hour.

POP PUDDING.

Ingredients.—One pint of milk, three eggs, ten table-spoonfuls of flour, a little salt, one table-spoonful of butter. Bake one-half hour. To be eaten with "Fairy Butter."

MILK CRACKER PUDDING.

Twelve milk crackers, three eggs, one quart of milk. Sweeten and flavor to suit the taste. Break the crackers fine, heat the milk to boiling and stir in the eggs, sugar, and flavoring; immediately pour over the broken crackers and let stand a few minutes, then set upon the ice until cold. Eat cold.

CREAM PUDDING.

Ingredients.—One and one-half cups of sour milk, one and one-half cups of sour cream, four eggs, one-half table-spoonful of soda, six heaping table-spoonfuls of flour.

Bake from a half to three-quarters of an hour. Eat with sweet cream.

CREAM PUDDING.

Ingredients.—One quart of milk, four eggs, four full table-spoonfuls of flour. Beat the eggs and flour together with a little cold milk, and stir into the quart of milk while warming; stir and boil until thick; flavor with lemon or vanilla; pour into a dish for the table; spread over the top a cup of sugar. To be eaten cold.

DELMONICO PUDDING.

Ingredients.—One quart of milk, four table-spoonfuls of sugar, three table-spoonfuls of corn starch or mazena, yolks of four eggs.

Scald the milk, beat the eggs, sugar, and corn starch or mazena together, and stir into the boiling milk. Flavor with one tea-spoonful of vanilla and half tea-spoonful of lemon; pour into a dish; beat the whites of the eggs and one cup of sugar and pour over the top. Set it in the oven and let it brown over. *Eat cold.*

If mazena be used in place of corn starch, stir it with a little cold milk instead of beating with eggs and sugar.

HOW TO COOK RICE.

To cook rice, only just enough water should be poured on to prevent the rice from burning at the bottom of the pot, which should have a close fitting cover, and with a moderate fire the rice is steamed rather than boiled until it is nearly done; then the cover is taken off, the surplus steam and moisture allowed to escape, and the rice turns out a mass of snow white kernels, each separate from the other and as much superior to the usual soggy mass, as a fine mealy potato is superior to the water soaked article.

RICE PUDDING.

Ingredients.—One cup of boiled rice (the rice is measured *after* boiling), yolks of five eggs, grated peel of one lemon, one pint of cold milk. Stir all together, add a little salt and bake it.

Take the whites of the eggs, one pound of sugar, the juice of the lemon, make a frosting. When the pudding is done cover it over with the frosting and set it in the oven until it is a nice brown.

RICE PUDDING.

Put one-half cup of rice in one and one-half cups of cold water, let it swell on the stove, then put in one pint of milk and let it come to a jelly, but not cook down too much. Beat the yolks of three eggs with five spoonfuls of sugar, stir it while boiling. Put in a pudding dish and bake, then beat the whites of three eggs to a froth with five spoonfuls of sugar, spread it on the top and set it in the oven to brown lightly. Put in raisins if desired.

TAPIOCA PUDDING.

Six table-spoonfuls of tapioca, soaked over night in a pint of water; scald a quart of milk; stir in the tapioca and let it come to a boil; add a little salt, beat the yolks of three eggs and a cup of white sugar together and stir into the mixture. Boil like custard; flavor with lemon or vanilla, beat the whites and stir quietly into the mixture. To be eaten cold.

TAPIOCA PUDDING.

Pare seven nice tart apples, remove the cores, and lay them in a buttered dish. Take one cup of tapioca (or sago) and pour over it one quart of boiling water, let it stand a few minutes; add two cups of sugar, one lemon, grate the peel and add the juice. Pour over the apples and bake one hour.

CHOCOLATE PUDDING.

One cup of fine bread crumbs, three-fourths of a cup of chocolate wet together with a little milk; add one quart of milk and let it come to a boil. When cool add the yolks of four eggs and one cup of sugar; then bake slowly. When done ice with the whites of the eggs, well beaten, with a little sugar and flavored with vanilla.

CHOCOLATE PUDDING.

(German Receipt.)

Ingredients.—Three ounces of grated chocolate, two and one-half ounces of butter, two and one-half ounces of butter crackers, three table-spoonfuls of sugar, five eggs.

The butter is rubbed to cream, the yolks, sugar, chocolate, and crackers are added and well stirred together until smooth. Then the froth of the whites is added and the mass is poured into a well buttered pudding mold and baked twenty-five minutes. Serve up hot with fruit or red wine sauce.

CORN STARCH PUDDING.

(Mrs. Henderson.)

Ingredients.—One pint of rich milk, two table-spoonfuls of corn starch, a scant half-cupful of sugar, whites of three or four eggs.

Beat the eggs to a stiff froth; dissolve the corn starch in a little of the milk; stir the sugar into the remainder of the milk, which place on the fire. When it begins to boil add the dissolved corn starch; stir constantly for a few moments, when it will become a smooth paste; now stir in the beaten whites of the eggs, and let it remain a little longer to cook the whites of the eggs. It can be flavored with vanilla and put into a form; yet it is still better as a

COCOANUT PUDDING.

When the preceding pudding is just finished, add half a cocoanut grated; put it in a mold, serve with whipped cream around it, or a sauce of boiled custard made with the yolks of the eggs. The same receipt can also be used for a

CHOCOLATE PUDDING.

When cooked, first flavor the whole with vanilla; now take out a third of the pudding; flavor the remainder in the kettle with a bar of chocolate, softened, mashed, and dissolved with a little milk. Put half of the chocolate pudding in the bottom of a plain mold, which has been wet in cold water; smooth the top; next make a layer with the white part taken out; smooth it also; next the remainder of the chocolate pudding. Serve with whipped cream, or a boiled custard, made with the yolks of the eggs and flavored with vanilla, around it; or the one-third portion of pudding may be flavored with half a bar of chocolate, and placed in the center of the two layers of white; or one can use the same receipt for a corn starch pudding and flavor it with chopped pine-apple, strawberries, or, in winter, with dried cherries swollen in water; or it may be flavored with chocolate, with the white center part flavored with cocoanut.

ORANGE PUDDING.

Ingredients.—Four sweet oranges, two cups of sugar, one quart of milk, three eggs, two dessert-spoonfuls of corn starch, one-half cup of powdered sugar.

Peel the oranges, making sure that every particle of the white rind is removed. Cut in thin slices, remove the seeds, lay the slices in the bottom of a deep pudding dish and cover with one cup of sugar; make a custard of the milk, the yolks of the eggs, the corn starch, and the other cup of sugar. Pour it over the oranges; beat the whites to a stiff froth, add half a cup of powdered sugar, put it over the pudding and brown it lightly in the oven.

LEMON PUDDING.

Ingredients.—The juice and grated rind (rubbed on sugar) of three lemons, half a pint of cream, three ounces of bruised macaroons, six yolks and the whites of two eggs, whipped, one-fourth of a nutmeg, grated, a little cinnamon powder, six ounces of pounded sugar, and a very little salt.

Mix the above all together in a large basin, and work the ingredients together with a whisk for about ten minutes. Next, put a border of puff paste around the edge of a pudding dish, spread the dish with butter, pour the batter into it, strew some shred pistachio kernals or almonds on the top, and bake it for about half an hour (at moderate heat). When done, shake some sifted sugar over it, and serve.

ORANGE PUDDING.

This is made as the above; double the quantity of oranges may be used for this purpose, owing to their not containing so much acid as lemons; but the rind of one and a half will suffice for the zest.

LEMON PUDDING.

Ingredients.—One quart of milk, four eggs, three table-spoonfuls of corn starch, one lemon, five table-spoonfuls of sugar.

Cook the milk, starch, and three table-spoonfuls of sugar together; beat the yolks and add them and the grated rind and juice of the lemon. Add two table-spoonfuls of powdered sugar to the whites of the eggs, well beaten, and put over the pudding. Let it brown nicely and put on the table.

LEMON PUDDING.

Mix three table-spoonfuls of corn starch in water, very thin; pour in three coffee-cups of boiling water; stir constantly until it thickens; add two coffee-cups of sugar, the grated rind and juice of two lemons, two eggs well beaten, and a little salt; bake twenty minutes. Eat cold.

BAKED INDIAN PUDDING.

Boil one quart of sweet milk and turn it on one pint of sifted meal; stir it well; add three table-spoonfuls of wheat flour and one pint of cold milk. Beat three eggs with three table-spoonfuls of sugar, stir into the pudding, add two tea-spoonfuls of salt, and two tea-spoonfuls each of cinnamon or grated nutmeg and butter or suet. If the pudding is liked very rich let it bake six minutes, then stir in one-half pound of raisins and a tea-cup of milk or cream.

BAKED INDIAN PUDDING.

Ingredients.—One pint of sweet milk, one-half pint of Indian meal, one pint of molasses, one-half a cup of butter, three eggs, well beaten, a cup of cold sweet milk.

Boil the milk in a double kettle and stir in the meal; let it stand on the back part of the stove an hour; melt the butter and molasses together and add to the hot mixture and allow it to stand a half hour. The eggs and milk are added just before baking. Bake three-fourths of an hour.

BOILED INDIAN PUDDING.

Ingredients.—One pint of sour milk, made into a very thin batter with Indian meal and allowed to stand one hour. Then add one tea-spoonful of soda, one-half cup of molasses, one-half a cup of beef suet chopped fine, one beaten egg and salt. Boil three hours.

BOILED INDIAN PUDDING.

Ingredients.—One cup each of corn meal, flour, sweet milk, chopped raisins, suet, molasses; one tea-spoonful of soda, one tea-spoonful of salt, spice to taste. Steam three hours.

CABINET PUDDING.

Spread the inside of a plain mold with butter, and ornament the sides with dried cherries and candied citron; fill the mold with alternate layers of slices of sponge cake and macaroons; then fill up a mold with lemon custard made with yolks of six eggs, a pint of milk or cream, six ounces of sugar, and the grated rind of a lemon. This custard must not be set, but merely mixed up. Steam the pudding in the usual way for about an hour and a half, and when done, dish it up with a custard.

SNOW PUDDING.

Dissolve three table-spoonfuls of corn starch in a little cold water; pour one pint of boiling water over this, stirring all the time; stir in the stiffly beaten whites of three eggs, and steam ten minutes. Before steaming add a little salt, and flavor to taste.

Serve with sauce made as follows: Yolks of three eggs, one cup of sugar, one cup of milk, and a piece of butter the size of a walnut; boil and flavor.

CHAPTER IX.

SWEET SAUCES.

PUDDING SAUCE.

Ingredients.—Three table-spoonfuls of white sugar, one even of flour, a piece of butter the size of a hen's egg, stirred to a cream, two table-spoonfuls of mace compound, a cup of boiling water.

Mix the sugar, flour, and butter, stir in the mace compound and add the water; set into a kettle of boiling water, stirring it constantly, until the flour is cooked.

SAUCES FOR PLUM PUDDING.

1. Foam Sauce.—One cup of white sugar, three cups of butter, one table-spoonful of flour. Beat to a cream, put it on the stove, add a wine-glass of sherry or half a wine-glass of brandy; stir quickly until it is all foam.

2. Hard Sauce.—Four ounces of butter, five ounces of sugar, beaten to a cream; pile it on the dish. You can add a scrape of nutmeg or a little lemon juice when beating it, or brandy, as you like—not enough to thin it, only to flavor.

FAIRY OR NUN'S BUTTER.

Ingredients.—One table-spoonful of butter and three table-spoonfuls of powdered sugar stirred together until very light, one lemon.

Cover the top with the grated rind of a lemon and squeeze over the whole the juice of a lemon.

CARAMEL SAUCE.
(New York Cooking School.)

Dissolve six ounces of cut loaf sugar in half a pint of boiling water; add a stick of cinnamon, a little lemon-zest, and two

cloves, and boil it ten minutes. Next put two ounces of loaf
sugar, dissolved in a table-spoonful of boiling water, on a moderate fire, and stir it until it assumes a light brown color; pour the
other boiled sugar over this; give it one boil, remove it from the
fire, and add two or three table-spoonfuls of sherry.

FOAMING SAUCE.

Ingredients—One cup of sugar, one cup of butter, two eggs,
juice and grated rind of one lemon.

Beat the yolks with the sugar and rind and juice of the lemon;
beat the whites by themselves and when stiff mix with the sugar
and yolks. The *minute before* it is sent to the table stir in rapidly a tea-cup of boiling water.

GERMAN SAUCE.

Beat together the yolks of two eggs, one table-spoonful of
sugar, and one-half gill of sherry. Put over the fire in a saucepan and beat rapidly with an egg whisk until it thickens. Do
not let it boil or it will curdle.

SABYLLON.

Mrs. Henderson.)

Put two yolks and one whole egg, also a scant half tea-cupful
of sugar into a little stew-pan; beat them well for a few minutes. Then put the sauce-pan into another, containing boiling
water, over the fire; beat the eggs and sugar briskly with an egg
whisk, while you gradually pour in a scant half tea-cupful of
sherry; when the sherry is all in the egg will begin to thicken;
then take it from the fire and add the juice of a quarter of a
small lemon. (Quantity sufficient for six persons.)

MACE COMPOUND.

(Home Messenger Receipt Book.)

To take the place of "sherry wine" in puddings and sauces.

Soak half an ounce of mace eight hours in one tea-cup of lemon
juice, add half a tea-cup of boiling water and scald twenty
minutes.

CHAPTER X.

CUSTARDS, CREAMS. AND SOUFFLEES.

CUSTARDS.

IT is so easy a thing to make a smooth, velvety, rich custard, it is a wonder any one ever fails. It requires attention, of course, but the ingredients are few in number, the *modus operandi* exceedingly simple, and the result sure.

Everything should be of the best quality, the eggs fresh, the milk sweet and rich, and the sugar as good as the market affords; then proceed as follows: put the milk over the fire in a double kettle; while it is heating beat the eggs with the sugar until light and creamy; when the milk boils, pour it slowly over the sugar, stirring all the while; then strain it back into the double kettle and return to the stove to thicken. Now comes "the tug of war." If the custard heats too much it will curdle—if not enough it will be thin and unsatisfactory. Watch it closely and stir constantly until you feel it thickening (it will take a minute and a half or two minutes); as soon as it thickens take it off the stove and pour at once into a cool dish; stir still a moment longer and then put away to cool; flavor when cool. Always add a pinch of salt to all custards.

CREAMS.

When you are able to make a smooth, rich custard you have mastered one step in the preparation of most creams; the next is to know how to prepare the gelatine, and the final one how to combine the custard, gelatine, and whipped cream. The gelatine should soak at least an hour in cold water before hot water is added to it. Use just enough water to cover it, about a half teacupful to a half ounce, and after it has soaked an hour add two or three table-spoonfuls of boiling water, then *strain* into the hot custard; stir until the gelatine is perfectly blended with the custard and then set the whole away to cool. Now whip the cream; use a Dover egg-beater or a large egg-whisk, and be sure that the cream is almost ice cold. Allow two table-spoonfuls of powdered sugar to a pint of cream, flavor to taste, and then whisk it quickly and steadily until like the beaten whites of eggs. When the custard is perfectly cold and is beginning to " set " or jelly, stir it briskly for a few moments to even it, then blend delicately with the whipped cream. If these directions are followed the result must be a success.

SOUFFLÈES.

These depend a good deal on the thoroughness with which the eggs are beaten, the quickness with which the materials are combined and the care taken in cooking them. They should be served *immediately* upon being done.

If nut meats are to be blanched, boiling water should be poured over them and they should remain in the hot water until the skin will easily slip off. Then turn them into cold water, remove the skins and dry the meats before pounding or chopping. It is always best to add a few drops of rose-water occasionally to almonds while pounding them.

Always, in preparing oranges for soufflées or creams, be particular to remove every particle of the white coat that lies under the skin, otherwise the cream or soufflée will be bitter.

BOILED CUSTARD.

Allow five whole eggs, the yolks of four and the whites of two, or eight yolks to a quart of milk, one tea-cupful of sugar, a pinch of salt, and one tea-spoonful of flavoring. Then proceed according to directions. The yolks of eggs make a more delicate custard than when both yolks and whites are used.

FOR CHOCOLATE CUSTARD,

allow two table-spoonfuls of chocolate to a quart of milk and four eggs.

BAKED CUSTARD.

This is made with the same ingredients as boiled custard, but baked instead of boiled. My way is to heat the milk and proceed exactly as for boiled custard until I come to strain the mixed milk, sugar, and eggs. I strain this into a deep dish, put this in a pan partly filled with boiling water, and place the whole in the oven to remain until the custard is firm but not watery. It can be baked in custard cups in the same way.

A delicate way to flavor custards is to rub the loaf sugar with which they are sweetened on the rind of the lemon until the sugar has absorbed the oil that gives the rind color and flavor. This yellow rind may also be pared off, very thin, so as not to include any of the white underneath it, and boiled in the milk until it imparts the desired flavor.

One or two pieces of stick-cinnamon boiled in the milk gives an agreeable flavor. In the spring, a few tender, fresh peach leaves boiled in the milk flavor it delightfully.

RENNET CUSTARD, OR CURDS AND WHEY.
(Detroit Free Press.)

Take a piece of rennet an inch long, or a tea-spoonful of spirits in which rennet has been kept, or a tea-spoonful of liquid rennet (such as is kept by druggists and is apt to be weak), to each quart of milk. Season with vanilla or lemon and a table-spoonful of sugar to each quart. Set in a warm place near the fire, closely covered. Draw a spoon through gently from side to side and down to the bottom of the dish, for half a minute or more before covering. Look at it from time to time, and if in the course of an hour there are no signs of stiffening, add more rennet. When it is firm like *blanc mange*, and before the whey separates from the curd, remove the rennet, if you have not used it in liquid form, and set in a cold place until wanted. Grate nutmeg over the dish, and serve with powdered sugar and cream.

The nicest rennet is home-made. Buy a calf's stomach from your butcher, having him first scour it thoroughly inside and out with salt. Tack it upon a frame and dry in the sun a day or two. Cut in squares, put them in a bottle and fill with alcohol, or pack down with salt, in which case the rennet to be used must be soaked half an hour in water, washed well and tied to a string, that it may be easily removed from the curd before using.

The dried or salted rennet may sometimes be bought of the druggists, or in the markets. Not to be omitted in a list of the virtues of curds and whey is its economy and also the ease with which it is prepared.   ‽

This is so delicate and delicious, as well as so easily prepared, that I recommend it heartily to all my readers.

TO MAKE SLIP.

Make a quart of rich milk moderately warm; then stir into it one large spoonful of liquid rennet, set it by, and when cold it will be as stiff as jelly. It should be made only a few hours before it is used or it will be tough and watery; in summer set the dish on ice after it has jellied. Eat with powdered sugar, cream, and a sprinkle of nutmeg.

CURDS AND CREAM.

Prepare one quart of milk as for the slip, and let it stand until just before it is to be served; then take the curd up carefully with a skimmer and lay it on a sieve; when the whey has drained off, put the curds in a dish and surround them with cream, and cover with powdered sugar.

APPLE CUSTARD.

Put one pound of loaf sugar in a stew-pan with one pint of water and twelve cloves; boil and skim it; then put in twelve good sized tart apples pared, cored, and sliced, and stew them till clear· and but little of the syrup remains; lay them in a deep dish, remove the cloves, and when they are cool pour in a quart of rich boiled custard; set the dish in a pan partly filled with hot water, and put in the oven until the custard is firm.

APRICOT CREAM.

Ingredients.—One pint of sweet cream, one table-spoonful of sugar, one-half can of apricots, one-half ounce of gelatine, the juice of one lemon.

Whip the cream and sugar to a stiff froth; press the apricots. leaving out the syrup, through a hair sieve; put the syrup over the fire in a stew-pan and simmer until it is reduced to half the quantity; add the pulp, reduced syrup, lemon juice, and dissolved gelatine to the whipped cream.

If it is desired to ornament the mold, pour a little dissolved gelatine into it and let it run over the bottom and sides; when partly set, stick into it candied cherries, citron cut in ornamental shapes, angelica, pistachio nuts, or whatever suits the fancy; fill the mold with the cream and set in a cold place until firm.

PINE-APPLE CREAM.

This is made in the same way except that the pine-apple is cut in small dice instead of being pressed through a sieve. No lemon juice is added.

HAMBURG CREAM.

Stir together the juice and rind of two large lemons and one cup of sugar; add the well beaten yolks of eight eggs, put all in a tin pail and set in a pot of boiling water (if you have not a double boiler); stir for three minutes, take from the fire, add the well beaten whites of the eggs, and serve, when cold, in custard glasses.

COFFEE CREAM.

Roast four ounces of Mocha coffee berries in a small stew-pan over a fire, stirring it the whole time with a wooden spoon until it assumes a light brown color; then blow away the small burnt particles, and throw the roasted coffee into a stew-pan containing half a pint of boiling milk or cream, put the lid on the stew-pan and set it aside to allow the infusion to draw out the flavor of the coffee. Next strain this through a napkin into a stew-pan containing four yolks of eggs and six ounces of sugar, and a very small pinch of salt, stir the cream over the fire until it begins to thicken, then quicken the motions of the spoon, and when the yolks of eggs are sufficiently set, strain the cream through a sieve into a large basin. Mix a gill of whipped cream and three-fourths of an ounce of Cox's gelatine in with this, pour the whole into a mold ready set in ice for the purpose, and when the cream has become firm, dip the mold in warm water and turn the cream out on a dish.

• CHOCOLATE CREAM.

Grate four ounces of vanilla chocolate, put this into a stew-pan with four ounces of sugar, four yolks of eggs, and a half pint of cream; stir the whole over a fire until it begins to thicken, and the yolks of eggs are sufficiently set without allowing them to curdle; strain through a hair sieve, with pressure, into a basin; add a gill of whipped cream, and three-quarters of an ounce of Cox's gelatine; mix the whole well together, and pour into a mold previously imbedded in ice to receive it.

LEMON CREAM.

To be eaten cold and served in custard cups or glasses.—Pare the rind very thin from four fresh lemons; squeeze the juice and strain it; put both into a quart of water, sweeten to taste, add the whites of six eggs, beaten stiff; set it over the fire and stir until it thickens, but do not let it boil; then pour it into a bowl, let it cool, strain, return to the fire and add the beaten yolks of the six eggs; stir till quite thick.

Orange cream is made in the same way, but requires more juice to flavor it well.

GOOSEBERRY CREAM.

Clean two quarts of green gooseberries; put them in a stewpan with their weight in loaf sugar, and a very little water; when sufficiently stewed, pass the pulp through a sieve; when cold add enough rich boiled custard to make the mixture like thick cream; put it in a glass dish, and heap whipped cream on the top.

BAVARIAN CREAMS.

The following Bavarian creams are taken from "Practical Cooking, and Dinner Giving," Mrs. Mary F. Henderson's valuable Cook Book.

BAVARIAN CREAM WITH VANILLA.

Whip one pint of cream to a stiff froth. Boil another pint of cream or rich milk, with a vanilla bean, and two table-spoonfuls of sugar, until it is well flavored; then take it off the fire and add half a box of Nelson's or Cox's gelatine soaked for an hour in half a cupful of water, in a warm place near the range; when slightly cooled stir in the yolks of four eggs, well beaten. When it has become quite cold, and begins to thicken, stir it without ceasing a few minutes, until it is very smooth, then stir in the whipped cream lightly until it is well mixed. Put it into a mold or molds, and set on the ice, or in some cool place.

BAVARIAN CREAM WITH CHOCOLATE.

is made as the preceding cream, adding two sticks of chocolate, soaked and smoothed, to the yolks of the eggs.

BAVARIAN CREAM WITH STRAWBERRIES.

After picking two pounds and a half of strawberries, squeeze them through a colander, and add six ounces of sugar to the juice; when the sugar is dissolved, add half a box of gelatine soaked as before described. Place it on the ice, stir it smooth when it begins to set, then stir in a pint of whipped cream; put it into a mold or molds, and serve with fresh strawberries around it.

BAVARIAN CREAM WITH ALMONDS.

Take three ounces of sweet and one ounce of bitter almonds, blanch and skin them, and put them into a pan on a moderate fire, stirring them continually. As soon as they have acquired a fine yellow color, take them off the fire, and when cold pound them into fine pieces. Then add a pint of cream or rich milk (nearly boiling) and two or three table-spoonfuls of sugar, and half a package of gelatine, which has been soaked as before described. Put it upon the ice, and when about to thicken, stir it until it is very smooth, then stir in lightly a pint of whipped cream, and put it into a mold.

CARAMEL CREAM.

Boil two quarts of rich new milk and mix in some caramel as below. Beat up three yolks and one whole egg together and add to the milk. Pass the whole through a fine hair sieve, and putting it in a basin in a sauce-pan of boiling water, cook until it thickens. This cream is served in glasses like custard. For caramel take four ounces of sugar and stir over a good fire with a spoonful of water, until it becomes a rich golden brown.

BURNT CREAM.

(Francatelli.)

Put an ounce of pounded sugar into a stew-pan, with the grated rind of one lemon; stir these with a wooden spoon over a slow fire until the sugar begins to assume a rather light brown color; then pour in half a pint of cream, add to this four ounces of sugar, four yolks of eggs, a little salt, and stir the whole over a fire until the eggs are set; then strain the cream through a hair sieve into a large basin, and mix it with a gill of whipped cream and three-fourths of an ounce of Cox's gelatine.   Pour the cream into a mold imbedded in rough ice.

CARAMEL CUSTARD.

Put one quart of milk over the fire in a custard kettle.   Beat five eggs with a small cup of sugar till light; when the milk boils pour it over the beaten eggs and sugar, stirring carefully all the time.   Return to the fire for a moment until the custard thickens, when it should be at once removed and put in a cool place.

For flavoring put half a cup of loaf sugar over the fire in a small sauce-pan.   Watch it carefully, and when it melts stir it constantly so it may brown evenly.   When it is a dark rich color add enough boiling water to make a thick syrup.   Flavor the custard to taste with this syrup, pour into custard cups and set in a moderate oven till firm in the center.   This amount of caramel is about right for a quart of custard.

FLUMMERY.

One measure of jelly, one measure of cream, and half a measure of wine; boil fifteeen minutes, stirring all the time; sweeten and add a spoonful of rose-water; pour into a mold, and when set, turn on to a platter, and surround it with whipped cream.

BLANC MANGE.

(Detroit—Old fashioned and genuine.)

Take four ounces of sweet almonds, blanched, and half an ounce of bitter almonds; pound them in a wedge-wood mortar, moistening them gradually with orange flower water; mix this with one quart of fresh cream.   Have the largest half of a box of Cox's gelatine soaking in half a cup of cold water one hour. Set your cream and almonds on the fire, stirring constantly; when it comes to a scald, pour in the gelatine and stir till it dissolves.   Put in molds.

BLANC MANGE.

Break an ounce of isinglass and pour on it one pint of boiling water; let it stand all night, and add the next morning one quart of rich milk or cream; boil until the isinglass is completely dissolved; strain it; put in two ounces of sweet almonds, blanched and pounded; sweeten it and pour into a mold. Serve with raspberry cream or whipped cream.

TO MAKE A HEN'S NEST.

Get five even sized eggs; make a hole at one end, empty them, and fill the shells with blanc mange; when cold and stiff, break off the shells. Pare the yellow rind, very thin and in narrow strips, from six lemons; boil these in water until tender, then drop for a few moments in a hot syrup of sugar and water; drain them and then fill a small, oval dish, half full of jelly; put the straw on in the shape of a nest and lay the eggs in it. A delicious dessert for Easter Sunday.

CHARLOTTE RUSSE.
(For a pint mold.)

Ingredients.—Sponge cake, thick, sweet cream one-half pint, three tea-spoonfuls of powdered sugar, one-fourth ounce of gelatine.

Line a *charlotte* mold with sponge cake, fitting the pieces carefully together. Whisk the cream to a stiff froth with the previously melted gelatine, the sugar, and a few drops of vanilla; pour this mixture into the mold, covering it with a slice of sponge cake the size of the mold; place the mold over it to become cold and firm. Turn out when ready to serve.

Simple whipped cream, with the whites of three eggs beaten stiff and delicately stirred in makes as good a Charlotte Russe as one could wish.

A stale loaf of sponge cake is better than a mold. Cut off the top slice and lay it one side; scoop out the center of the loaf; fill with whipped cream; replace the top, and set the loaf away in the ice-chest till needed.

APPLE CHARLOTTE.

First of all, some apple marmalade must be prepared as follows: Let two or three dozen apples be pared, cored, sliced up, and placed in a stew-pan with one pound of sugar, two ounces of butter, and some lemon peel and cinnamon tied up togther; moisten with half a pint of water, place the lid on the stew-pan, and set the apples to boil sharply over a quick fire until they are melted; then remove the lid and with a wooden spoon continue stirring the marmalade over a brisk fire until it is reduced to a rather stiff consistency.

A plain round *charlotte* mold must now be lined at the bottom with small thin circular pieces of bread, dipped in clarified butter and placed so as to overlap each other until the bottom of the mold is well covered. Next cut some oblong squares of thin bread, also dipped in clarified butter, and set these up the sides of the mold over lapping each other, in order that they may thus be enabled to hold firmly to the sides of the mold. Fill the cavity with the apple marmalade, cover in the top with a thin circular piece of bread dipped in butter, place the *charlotte* on a baking sheet, and bake it in a rather brisk oven, of a light color; and when done, turn it out on a dish, glaze it on the top with sifted sugar, pour some diluted apricot jam, or any other fruit jam, around the base, and serve.

LEMON SOUFFLÉE.

Ingredients..—Two ounces of flour, one ounce of butter, one ounce of sugar, one-half pint of milk, grated rind of two lemons, two eggs.

Mix the flour and milk together perfectly smooth; add the sugar and butter and put in a sauce-pan over the fire; stir constantly until it boils when it should be quite thick; now take it off the stove and stir in the yolks of the two eggs and the grated lemon peel; beat the whites to a stiff froth and add gradually and very gently to the mixture. Put in a well buttered mold and steam one-half to three-quarters of an hour.

To be eaten with boiled custard flavored with lemon.

APPLE SOUFFLÉE.

Ingredients.—Six good sized apples, two ounces of sugar, a table-spoonful of water, one and one-half ounces of flour, grated rind of two lemons, one ounce of butter, one-half gill of milk, three eggs.

Pare and core the apples and stew them until tender with the sugar and water; then rub them through a sieve (there should be one-half pound of the pulp); work into this pulp the flour, the grated rind of lemon, the butter and the milk; stir over the fire until it thickens; then add the yolks of two of the eggs and one whole egg to the hot mixture; whip the whites of the two eggs to a stiff froth and add gently. Steam in a well buttered mold one-half hour. Eat with cream or boiled custard.

BAKED OMELETTE SOUFFLÉE.

Ingredients.—Whites of six eggs, yolks of four, three ounces of sugar, one-half ounce of flour, one teaspoonful extract of vanilla.

Stir the yolks and sugar together for ten minutes; beat the whites to a stiff froth; add the flour very lightly to the yolks and sugar at the end of the ten minutes' beating; stir in the vanilla; blend the beaten whites with the mixture, quickly and delicately; bake ten minutes in a hot oven. To be served immediately.

OMELETTE SOUFFLÉE.

Ingredients.—The yolks of four and whites of six eggs, five tablespoonfuls of powdered sugar, vanilla or grated peel of one-half a lemon.

Yolks of eggs, sugar and seasoning are well stirred until very stiff; then the stiff froth of the whites is added and carefully mixed in. The mass is then poured on to a flat round baking dish, which must be well warmed before buttering. Place in a quick oven and bake fifteen minutes.

ORANGE SOUFFLÉE.

Make a soft custard with one pint of milk, the yolks of five eggs, and half a tea-cupful of sugar. Grate the rind of one orange and flavor the custard with it. Pare four large oranges, making *sure* to take *every bit* of the white rind off; slice thin, take out the seeds, put in the bottom of a pudding dish, and pour over them the hot custard. Beat the whites of the eggs to a stiff froth, add seven table-spoonfuls of powdered sugar, put over the top of the custard and orange, and bake a light brown. Serve cold.

SOUFFLÉE OF RICE.

Ingredients.—Three ounces of rice, five ounces of sugar, two ounces of butter, five eggs, one lemon, a pint of milk, and a little salt.

Wash the rice and parboil it in water for five minutes; then put in a stew-pan with the sugar, butter, milk and salt, and set this to simmer very gently on a slow fire for about an hour, by which time the grains of the rice will have become quite soft; the whole should now be well worked with a wooden spoon, and the five yolks of eggs, with the rind of the lemon rubbed on sugar, should then be added, and if the rice be too firm, a little cream also. The five whites of eggs must be whipped very firm, then lightly mixed in with the preparation, and poured into the *soufflée* or any plain mold; baked for about three-quarters of an hour, and served immediately

CHAPTER XI.

ICES.

O get ready to freeze your cream is half the battle. The ice should be broken fine, the salt should be coarse and well mixed with the ice, the proportion being about one third salt to two-thirds ice. It greatly facilitates freezing to have the cream or custard well chilled by having it on the ice for two hours, before you begin to freeze. Put the freezer into a tub, and fill the wooden bucket in which it turns with the pounded ice and salt; then fill in the cream and turn steadily until it becomes stiff. It is really better not to drain the water off while freezing, as the ice cold water and ice together make a more complete surrounding for the freezer than the ice and salt unmelted. When the cream is frozen, carefully remove the cover, take out the dasher, replace the cover, stop the hole, cover with a clean cloth, and pack well with ice and salt.

In making water ices, it is better to boil the sugar and water, making a thin syrup, and then add the lemon juice, or fruit juice. It does not take nearly so many eggs to make the ice smooth when mixed in this way.

ICE CREAM.

To one quart of rich cream take four table-spoonfuls of sugar; beat the yolks of two eggs to a creamy froth; stir them into the cream; strain the cream into the freezer, and add the whites of the eggs beaten very light with three tablespoonfuls of powdered sugar.

This cream cannot be surpassed. Flavor, if possible, by boiling a vanilla bean in a little milk, and adding it when cold. Burnet's extract of vanilla comes next. Flavor somewhat more heavily than for custard.

143

ICE CREAM.

Make a rich boiled custard, flavor to taste, cool thoroughly and freeze.

ICE CREAM.

(Home Messenger Receipt Book.)

Boil two quarts of milk, into which stir a pint of cold milk that has had four level table-spoonfuls of arrow root mixed smoothly in it, then scald, but not boil; when cold add two quarts of cream, a table-spoonful of vanilla or other flavoring, and two pints of sugar; put in the freezer and turn until well chilled, then add the whites of six eggs beaten to a stiff froth.

RASPBERRY ICE CREAM.

Make a quart of rich boiled custard; when cold pour it on a quart of ripe red raspberries; mash them in the custard, pass through a sieve, sweeten, and freeze.

STRAWBERRY ICE CREAM.

This is made in the same way.

CHOCOLATE CREAM.

Scrape a quarter of a pound of chocolate fine, put it in a quart of milk, with one-half pound of sugar; boil it until the chocolate is dissolved, stirring it continually; make a custard of this with six eggs; flavor with vanilla; cool and freeze.

COFFEE CREAM.

Roast half a pint of coffee a rich even brown, being careful not to burn a single grain; pour over while still hot a quart of rich sweet milk; cover closely and leave one hour; then sweeten to taste, put over the fire, and when scalding hot stir it into the beaten yolks of eight eggs; strain, return to the fire to thicken, cool and freeze.

ALMOND CREAM.

Blanch and dry one pound of sweet almonds; pound them to a paste in a wedge-wood mortar, using a few drops of rose-water to facilitate the progress; mix into this paste one quart of rich cream and one cupful of sugar. Freeze.

The kernels of the common black walnut, prepared the same way, make an excellent cream.

LEMON ICE.

(Home Messenger Receipt Book.)

Take the juice of four lemons, add about three pints of thin syrup made with about one pint of sugar. Into every quart, when it begins to freeze, stir the whites of two eggs beaten very light, with a little powdered sugar. This will make it smooth.

Any kind of water ice may be made in this way, by mixing the strained juice of the fruit, currant, raspberry, strawberry, etc., with syrup flavored to taste, and add the whites of eggs when it begins to freeze.

LEMON ICE.

Make a quart of rich lemonade; whip the whites of six eggs to a stiff froth; mix them well with the lemonade, and freeze.

The juice of cherries, or of currants, mixed with water and sugar, and prepared in the same way, makes a very delicate water ice.

10

CHAPTER III.

SOUPS, MEATS, POULTRY, AND GAME.

GENERAL REMARKS.

F we cut a piece of meat in thin strips, and wash it in several waters, we shall discover that we have left a bundle of almost colorless fibres. Upon examining the waters in which it is washed, you will find the extractive juices of the flesh, blood, and all the materials soluble in cold water. Take now the bundle of fibres and plunge it into boiling water. It will contract and shrivel at the ends and if left boiling long enough, will shrink and toughen the whole length. Heat now the water in which the meat was washed, and as it approaches the the boiling point a thick scum will be seen floating in the water or gathering on the surface. This is chiefly one form of albumen, a most valuable ingredient in the meat.

By this simple experiment you may learn several things:

1. The juices of the meat which give it flavor, and add so much to its nutritive power, as well as give it its peculiar color, a portion of the albumen and such salts as are soluble in cold water, have been washed out. Meat, therefore, soaked in water, loses a large portion of that which gives it value as food.

2. Upon heating the water containing the juices, etc., extracted from the beef, the albumen it contains is hardened, or coagulated.

3. By applying heat to the fibres they are made to contract, and become hard and tough, but by leaving them in water something lower in temperature than boiling, they are softened and made tender.

All this knowledge can be directly applied in our methods of cooking meats.

147

Stock is simply a strong, highly-flavored extract of meat. How shall we prepare it? By putting the meat, of course, into cold water and heating it very gradually to near the boiling point, thus allowing the water to reach every portion of the fibre which gives it shape. To do this most effectually you should cut the meat into small pieces. Break up the bones also, and add them to the meat and cold water. They will add something, both of flavor and actual value, to the stock. If instead of stock I desire to prepare a piece of boiled meat for the table, how shall I proceed? By plunging the meat at once into boiling water. And why? Because by so doing the ends of the fibres will contract, and the albumen distributed over the surface will coagulate, both serving to prevent the escape of the juices and sealing them up in the interior of the meat. Shall I continue to boil the meat rapidly until thoroughly cooked? No, because so great a degree of heat will shrivel the fibre its entire length, and make the meat tough and leathery. It should therefore be subjected to a fierce heat only long enough to seal the ends of the fibres, and then simmer gently until done. The same philosophy applies to roasting and broiling. A strong heat at first, and then a more moderate temperature until the process is completed. When meat is cooked for the table by any method whatever, the whole aim should be to preserve the juices in the interior of the cut, and then to apply an even and gentle heat until ready to serve. Beefsteak should never be pounded, since then the fibres are so torn and lacerated as to afford ready escape to all the juices. For the same reason a roast should not be skewered to keep it in shape, but tied rather. Never stick a fork into a roast, steak, or boiling piece. If necessary to turn it, use a spoon or wooden ladle. The general theory as to the cooking of meats, is that all red meats should be underdone, or rare, and all white meats well done. We have beef as an example in the first class, and veal or pork in the second.

Game birds, and game in general, will, as a rule, come under the first class—domestic fowls under the second.

SOUP.

GENERAL REMARKS.

The pieces of meat for soup are portions of either the shank, the shin, or the neck. The two last named are to be preferred, as containing proportionately more gelatine. The meat should either be cut in small pieces or gashed many times, and the bone should be broken. Every particle of fat should be removed. Greasy soup is an abomination, and no greasy food is either good or wholesome. The advantage of making stock for soup the day before it is served is, that when perfectly cold the grease will collect in a cake on the top, and can then be entirely removed. The water in which stock is made should never boil rapidly or irregularly, but should simmer slowly and evenly. If it gets to boiling too fast, pour in a little cold water to reduce the temperature. This will also aid the scum to rise to the surface. It will be noticed that as the water approaches the boiling point a thick scum will appear. If a clear stock or soup is required, this must be carefully skimmed off. It is, however, nothing unclean, or unfit for food, but on the contrary is a most valuable and nutritious element, being albumen. If the stock is intended for immediate use, add carrot, turnip, an onion stuck with cloves, and a bouquet of herbs; namely, parsley, marjoram, thyme, and a bay leaf. If, however, it is desired to keep the stock for several days, and use from it gradually, do not add the vegetables until the day the soup is to be served, as they are apt to make the stock sour.

A little salt is used, as it also aids the scum to rise, but it is better to defer the full seasoning until the soup is prepared for the table. Use pepper corns, whole spices, and herbs in the sprig, for seasoning soups, as they do not cloud and discolor them, and they can be strained out easily when the soup is served. When the stock has simmered the full time, strain through a colander into an earthen vessel. It should never be left to cool in the kettle in which it was cooked.

RICH STOCK.

Cut the meat from the bones and divide it into rather small pieces of even size; remove all fat; break the bones, and take out the marrow, as this will make the stock greasy. Use one pint of cold water to one pound of meat and bone, and an extra pint to every four pounds of meat and bone, to allow for evaporation; add a half tea-spoonful of salt to aid the scum in rising. Put over the fire in a covered pot and bring it quickly to a boil; skim occasionally, and pour in from time to time a half tea-cup of cold water, which will also help the scum to rise.

Scrape two carrots, pare one turnip, one large onion, which should be stuck with two or three cloves; wash half a head of celery if it can be obtained, and put all in the stock pot. Tie together a few sprigs of parsley, marjoram, thyme, and a bay leaf, and put these also in the stock pot; add a few pepper corns. Let the stock simmer one hour for every pound of meat and bone. When it has simmered the requisite time take the stock pot off the fire; have a sieve ready over the jar large enough to contain the stock, put a clean cloth in the sieve, and pour the contents of the stock pot through it. Set it away to cool. When cool, remove all the fat which will have collected at the top in a cake; wring a cloth out of hot water and wipe off the top, so as to remove every particle of fat. When replaced in the soup kettle to heat, be careful to remove the settlings at the bottom of the jelly.

If made of beef this will produce brown stock. Veal treated in a similar manner makes white stock.

The bones from roast beef, bits of ham, the carcases of fowls, and any bits of cold meat, make good additions to the stock pot.

If the stock is to be kept any length of time, it is better not to add the vegetables until the soup is wanted for use, as they cause the stock to sour sooner than if made without them.

Browning the vegetables in a little hot fat before putting into the stock, brings out their flavor better.

Macaroni, vermicelli, pearl barley, sago, tapioca, rice, and oat-meal, are all used for flavoring soups, the proportion being two or three table-spoonfuls to the quart. Thick soups are made from split peas, beans, etc., one-half a tea-cupful of either being sufficient to thicken one quart of soup. If after straining these the soup is unevenly thickened, the meal of the peas or beans sinking to the bottom of the kettle, it may be held in suspension by mixing together, dry, a table-spoonful of butter and flour, and stirring it into the soup.

TO CLARIFY STOCK.

To every quart of stock allow the white and shell of one egg. Beat these to a froth; add a few table-spoonfuls of the cold stock, then mix the whole with the stock to be clarified. Set on the stove and stir pretty constantly until it comes to a boil. Let it boil a few moments, then remove it from the stove and let it stand until the bubbling has entirely ceased. Skim off the egg, etc., that has risen to the top, taking great pains not to disturb the contents of the kettle more than is necessary. Strain through a fine hair sieve, a flannel bag, or a coarse cloth laid in the colander. The broth should be clear and sparkling.

If expense is not to be considered, it adds much to the value of the stock, and helps also to make it beautifully clear and bright, to add with the egg one pound of very finely chopped beef to every five pounds of meat used in making the stock.

Chop the meat as fine as possible, put it with the whites and shells of the eggs as you put them in the stock; stir constantly until the whole boils; let it boil half an hour, then strain as before. If it does not run clear at first, pass it through the sieve again and again until perfectly clear.

CLEAR SOUP, OR CONSOMMÉ.

This is simply the clarified stock heated and seasoned with salt. It may be served in various ways. Thin slices of lemon, at least one slice to a person, are often added just before it is sent to the table, or one poached egg for each person, is served with it, or a little grated cheese may be handed round and each person add a spoonful to the soup served him.

The soup plates, the turreen, and even the ladle should be hot. Lukewarm soup is an abomination.

CONSOMMÉ À LA ROYALE, OR CLEAR SOUP WITH ROYAL CUSTARD.

Consommé à la Royale is clear soup in which custard à la Royale is served. This is prepared as follows:

CUSTARD À LA ROYALE.

Take the yolks of four eggs and the whites of two; add one-half pint of clear soup and a half a salt-spoonful of salt, and a very little nutmeg. Whisk the eggs and stock well together. Butter a shallow pan and put the custard in it. Place this in another pan containing boiling water. Put the whole in the oven or on the stove, and let it simmer until the custard is firm. When done turn it out on a plate to cool. Cut in dice, or fancy shaped pieces, and just before serving add it to the soup.

TOMATO SOUP.

This is made from beef stock by adding one pint of tomatoes, freed from seeds by straining, to two quarts of stock; add three table-spoonfuls of rice, salt to taste, and boil until the rice is tender.

TOMATO SOUP WITHOUT STOCK.

Fry half a medium sized onion, cut in slices, in a little butter; add a quart can of tomatoes, and, if possible, two sprigs of parsley. Let it cook fifteen minutes and then pass through a sieve. Put into a sauce-pan a tea-spoonful of butter, and when it bubbles, add a tea-spoonful of flour; stir until perfectly smooth, and when it begins to boil, stir in the tomato pulp and season with pepper and salt; add one-half pint of boiling water, and a cupful of fresh boiled rice, and a small half tea-spoonful of soda dissolved perfectly in a little boiling water.

JULIENNE SOUP.

After clarifying the stock as previously described, add to it two carrots, one turnip, and two or three cabbage leaves, or leaves of lettuce, cut into long, narrow strips, or shred. These vegetables must have been previously boiled until tender, each in separate water well salted, so that the color may be perfectly preserved. If they are ready before time to serve the soup, drain them out of the hot water, and put them, still in separate vessels, in cold water. Add them to the soup a long enough time before serving to heat them thoroughly.

This is a very pretty and delicious soup.

SPRING SOUP.

In June or July clear soup, with the addition of peas, asparagus tops, and young onions, is called a "spring soup."

MACARONI SOUP.

This is made by the addition of macaroni cut in two or three-inch lengths and boiled until tender in well salted water, to good beef stock.

VERMICELLI SOUP

is exactly the same except the vermicelli is not cut.

POTAGE À LA REIM, OR CHICKEN SOUP.

Boil an old fowl in four quarts of water until reduced to two quarts; add one carrot, an onion stuck with four cloves, a tablespoonful of salt, a little white pepper, and a scrape of nutmeg. Remove the chicken, and strain the soup. Take the breast of the fowl, chop it fine and rub it, with one cupful of rice boiled very soft, through a sieve. Add it to the soup, first skimming off every particle of grease. Let it come to a scald; stir in one-half pint of thick sweet cream, and serve at once. Do not let it boil after the cream has been added. It should just become hot enough to use. Add more salt if necessary.

AMBER SOUP.

(*Mrs. Henderson.*)

This soup is served at almost all company dinners. There can be no better choice, as a heavy soup is not then desirable.

Ingredients.—A soup bone of two or three pounds, a chicken, a small slice of ham, an onion, two sprigs of parsley, half a small carrot, half a small parsnip, half a stick of celery, three cloves, pepper, salt, a gallon of cold water, whites and shells of two eggs, and caramel for coloring.

Let the beef, chicken and ham boil slowly for five hours; add the vegetables and cloves to cook the last hour, having first fried the onion in a little hot fat and stuck the cloves in it. Strain the soup into an earthern bowl, and let it remain over night. Next day remove the cake of fat on the top; take out the jelly, avoiding the settlings, and mix into it the beaten whites of the eggs with the shells. Boil quickly for half a minute; then, placing the kettle on the hearth, skim off carefully all the scum and whites of the eggs from the top, not stirring the soup itself. Pass this through the jelly bag, when it should be quite clear.

The soup may then be put aside and reheated just before serving. Add then a large table-spoonful of caramel, as it gives it a richer color, and also a slight flavor.

BOUILLON.

This is simply a strong, clear extract of beef, or stock, which is often served in small cups at evening parties shortly after the guests have arrived. One quart of water to four pounds of meat and bone is the right proportion. It is just double that of ordinary stock jelly. As a rule no seasoning is added, except salt and pepper.

FRENCH GUMBO.
(*Louisiana Receipt.*)

Cut up one large fowl; season it with salt and pepper; dredge it well with flour. Put in the kettle a table-spoonful of butter, one of lard, and a chopped onion. Fry the fowl to a good brown; then add to this four quarts of boiling water; cover close and let it simmer two hours. Fifty oysters with their liquor is a good addition. Add a bunch of soup herbs and several pods of gumbo. Season high with cayenne; salt to taste.

BEEF SOUP.

Boil a soup bone the day before wanting it, according to directions for preparing stock. Skim the grease off next day, and melt the jelly; add spices to taste, a little Worcestershire sauce, a small tea-cup of butter rubbed in brown flour, a little vermicelli, and a grated carrot. Boil three eggs hard, mash smooth, put in turreen, and pour over them.

TURKEY SOUP.

Take the turkey bones and cook for one hour in water enough to cover them, then stir in a little of the dressing and a beaten egg. A little chopped celery improves it. Take from the fire, and when the water has ceased boiling add a little butter, with pepper and salt.

Of course the bones are removed and the soup strained before the dressing and egg are added.

ECONOMICAL WHITE SOUPS.

1. MILK SOUP.—To make this you will require two pounds of potatoes, two leeks or onions, two quarts of boiling water, one pint of milk, two ounces of butter, three dessert-spoonfuls of crushed tapioca, and pepper and salt to taste.

The potatoes and leeks must be pared and put into two quarts of boiling water, in which they must continue to boil until quite tender; pass both water and vegetables through a sieve, and put them back into the stew-pan; now add the milk, butter, and seasoning, place it on the fire and keep stirring, at the same time sprinkling in the crushed tapioca; another ten minutes' boiling will be necessary, after this is all added, to cook the tapioca; then serve. Care must be taken to keep stirring to the end, or the tapioca will stick together and be lumpy.

2. RICE-CREAM SOUP.—Take one pound of loin of veal, one-fourth of a pound of Carolina rice, a small quantity of onion, and two quarts of new milk.

Cut the veal into small pieces and put it on to stew with the other ingredients, adding a little white pepper and salt to taste; then pass it through a sieve, when it should be of the consistency of rich cream. The soup must be warmed again after straining, but great care must be taken that it does not boil, or it will curdle. If more flavor is liked, a very small, thin piece of lemon peel, a little cut celery, and a blade of mace, may be added when the seasoning is put in.

3. POTATO SOUP.—For this you will require a small breast of mutton, from which the fat should be trimmed; it should also be well jointed, as it makes an excellent dish when taken out of the soup.

Place the mutton in a stew pan with three quarts of water; as soon as it boils draw it to the side of the fire, skim it carefully, and season the broth with a very little pepper, and salt to taste. Peel and cut into quarters six large sound potatoes and three turnips, slice three onions and three heads of celery, and throw all these into the broth with a good sized handful of sweet herbs. Let all stew gently together for four and a half hours over a slow fire; take out the mutton, placing it in a covered dish near the fire, to keep hot till required; strain off the liquid, and force as much as possible of the vegetables through a coarse sieve with a wooden spoon, to be added to the soup; beat up the yolk of an egg with a quarter of a pint of milk; stir all together and warm it up for sending to the table, taking care that it does not now boil for fear it should curdle. Should you wish to make this soup richer, add another yolk and use cream instead of milk.

CREAM OF RICE.

To make cream of rice: Have three pints of rice, wash it well to take the dusty smell off; put it in a stew-pan with two ounces of butter, a little salt and grated nutmeg, and three quarts of boiled milk; set on the fire, heat slowly, stirring once in a while; when it boils cover it and let it simmer gently an hour or so; when done, pass it through a fine wire sieve by rubbing vigorously with a wooden spoon; put the residue in a stew-pan, add more boiled milk to give the soup the proper consistency; warm it, stirring continually; do not let it boil; finish with two ounces of table butter and half a pint of boiling cream; taste, season lightly, and serve with small, thin lozenge-shaped pieces of white bread fried in clarified butter and thrown into it.

VEGETABLE SOUP.

Take three pounds of shin of beef and stew it gently for an hour in two quarts of water, add two large onions cut in slices, one large tomato, two middle-sized vegetable marrows cut in small pieces, and half a peck of green peas; season with pepper and salt, and stew the whole for two hours longer. Neck of mutton may be used instead of shin of beef.

TOMATO SOUP.

Ingredients.—Three pounds of beef, one quart canned tomatoes, one gallon of water.

Let the meat and water boil for two hours, or until the liquid is reduced to a little more than two quarts. Then stir in the tomatoes and stew all slowly for three-quarters of an hour longer. Season to taste, strain, and serve.

CHICKEN SOUP.
(German Way.)

The chicken is singed, scalded, dredged with a handful of flour, and allowed to stand one hour in water. It is then put on the fire in this water with salt (the interior of the chicken must also be well rubbed with salt), skimmed, and then boiled four hours with vegetables.

Dumplings for this soup.—For three persons take two eggs, two spoonfuls of flour and a little salt. Then put a little butter into a small sauce-pan, add the mixture and stir it until it comes clean off the sauce-pan. When cold add the yolks of two eggs, and sugar, and knead it well; then cut out in little dumplings with a spoon, put them in the soup and let them boil five minutes. The soup must be strained before the dumplings are put in.

OYSTER SOUP.

Take one quart of water, one tea-cup of butter, one pint of milk, two tea-spoonfuls of salt, four crackers rolled fine, and a tea-spoonful of pepper. Bring to full boiling heat as soon as possible, then add two quarts of oysters. Let the whole come to a boiling heat quickly and remove from the fire.

The crackers serve the purpose of thickening, instead of flour.

OYSTER SOUP.

To one quart of oysters add a half pint of water. Put this on the fire, and as soon as it scalds, strain the liquor and set on the back of the stove to keep warm until needed. Put into another sauce-pan a heaping table-spoonful of butter, and when it bubbles add a table-spoonful of sifted flour; stir well and cook a few moments but do not let it brown; then add half a pint of rich milk, the oysters, salt, and cayenne pepper, and a sprinkle of mace. When this is just at the boiling point, add to the hot liquor strained from the oysters. Taste to see that it is sufficiently seasoned, and serve at once.

MOCK TURTLE SOUP.

(South Kensington School.)

Ingredients.—Half a calf's head, three ounces of butter, half a table-spoonful of salt, one-quarter of a pound of lean ham, one shallot, one clove of garlic, six mushrooms, one carrot, half a head of celery, one leek, one onion, half a turnip, a sprig of thyme, marjoram, parsley, and a bay leaf, one blade of mace, six cloves, three ounces of flour, two wine-glasses of sherry, the juice of half a lemon, one dozen force-meat balls.

Wash the calf's head well in water to remove all blood and impurities; cut all the flesh from the bones and tie it up in a clean cloth; put it over the fire, in a large stew-pan, with the bones, and four quarts of cold water, and half a table-spoonful of salt. As soon as it boils skim it well, and remove the stew-pan to the back of the stove to simmer gently for three hours, skimming occasionally. Now take out the calf's head, and strain the stock and set it aside to cool. When cold remove every particle of fat; then put one ounce of butter in a stew-pan and put it on the fire to melt; slice the ham, clean the vegetables and slice them, and fry all in the butter ten minutes, adding also the spices and herbs; then add three ounces of flour and stir well; now add the stock and stir until it boils, then reduce the heat and let it simmer about ten minutes. ˙ Remove every particle of scum and strain the soup into another sauce-pan. Take the meat from the calf's head out of the cloth and cut it up in small, neat pieces, and add these, two glasses of sherry, and the force-meat balls to the soup, and squeeze in through a strainer the juice of half a lemon.

FORCE-MEAT BALLS.

Ingredients.—Two ounces beef suet, one tea-spoonful of chopped parsley, one-fourth of a tea-spoonful of chopped thyme and marjoram, a little grated lemon-rind and nutmeg, salt and pepper, one egg, four ounces raw beef.

Chop the suet very fine; chop the beef also and put it in a bowl; rub three ounces of bread crumbs through a sieve and add it with one tea-spoonful of chopped parsley, a quarter of a tea-spoonful each of thyme and marjoram, to the beef. Grate half a tea-spoonful of lemon rind and nutmeg into the basin; season well with pepper and salt, add one egg, and mix all well together. Form into balls, egg and bread crumb and fry brown.

PEA SOUP.
(Appledore Cook Book.)

Pick the peas over that there may be no blemished ones among them. Wash and soak over night. In the morning turn off the water and put them in the soup pot. For one quart of peas allow eight quarts of cold water, one pound of lean salt pork, a small piece of celery, a little pepper, and half an onion; boil gently eight hours, being very careful that it does not brown. Have a large wooden spoon to stir it with. When done it should be thin enough to pour. In boiling it may become too thick; if so, add boiling water. When cooked, it is smooth and rather mealy. If not cooked enough, after standing a few minutes the thick part will settle and the top look watery. Have ready six slices of bread toasted brown, and cut into pieces an inch square; throw about a dozen of these pieces into a turreen, and the remainder send to the table dry. Strain the soup through a sieve and serve. If the pork does not salt it enough, use salt. This soup is even better warmed over than at first. Some persons use soup stock and butter, but it is rich enough in this way, and much healthier.

CORN SOUP.

Boil one quart of corn, cut from the cob, in one and one-half quarts of water, until perfectly tender. Rub two table-spoonfuls of butter with one table-spoonful of flour; let it bubble over the fire, then stir it into the corn and boil fifteen minutes longer. Just before serving beat up an egg and stir it in. Do not let it boil after the egg is put in. Season to taste with salt and pepper.

MULLIGATAWNEY SOUP.

Put a chicken, cut as for fricassee, into the stock pot, with a knuckle of veal and four quarts of water. Let this boil until the chicken is tender; take out the pieces of chicken, trim them neatly, and set them by to serve with the soup; let the veal simmer three hours. Fry an onion, a carrot, and a little celery in butter until a light brown, then add a table-spoonful of flour and brown that; now stir in a level table-spoonful of curry powder, and add slowly the stock. Return to the fire and simmer one hour. Twenty minutes before serving, strain the soup, skim off all the fat, and return to the fire with the pieces of chicken. Serve with boiled rice.

EGG BALLS FOR SOUP.
(Home Cook Book.)

Boil four eggs; put into cold water; mash yolks with the yolk of one raw egg, and one tea-spoonful of flour; add pepper, salt, and chopped parsley to taste; make into balls and boil two minutes.

CARAMEL FOR COLORING SOUPS.

Put one ounce of sugar in a sauce-pan over the fire; stir constantly until colored a rich, dark brown; add slowly one-half pint of boiling water; let it boil a few moments, then bottle for use.

MEATS.

GENERAL REMARKS.

The best roasts are the sirloin, the porterhouse, or thin end sirloin and the rib roasts. The most delicate roast is the fillet, or tenderloin. Never allow your butcher to *skewer* your meat. Have it *tied* carefully into shape, and then cut and remove the strings before dishing. Wooden skewers invariably give an unpleasant taste to the beef through which they pass, and any skewer makes a hole for the flow of the juices. Never wash meat in a pan of water. If it is dusty, wring a cloth out of cold water and wipe it off. Many a careless cook wastes a good proportion of the best part of the roast in a pan of water which is thrown away.

The best pieces for boiling, stewing, á la mode, etc., are from the round, the chuck rib, and the cross rib.

The choice cuts of steak are the porterhouse and the sirloin. The origin of both names is curious. The porterhouse steak is cut from the small end of the sirloin, and is so named from having been first used by the proprietor of a "Porter House" in New York city. The small size of the steak when trimmed makes it very convenient to be served to one or two persons at a time, and it soon became very popular. It is not to be recommended as an economical steak for family use, however, as there is more waste in the trimming for the table than in either the sirloin or round.

The word "sirloin" is said to have originated with Charles II, who, on returning from a hunt ravenously hungry, was so delighted with a choice roast of beef that was served him from the loin, that he jocularly knighted it, dubbing it "Sir Loin." This is indeed a delicious morsel, and can be cut either into fine roasting pieces or large, handsome steaks.

The round steak is also a favorite with many, and is perhaps the most economical piece for ordinary family use. There is a larger proportion of meat to bone, and less waste than in either of the other pieces.

All steak should be cut from one-half to three-quarters of an inch thick. It should never be pounded, since then the fibres are so torn and lacerated as to afford ready escape to all the juices.

I have used the word "roast" in the following receipts, although not strictly correct, because it is the word most generally used among housekeepers and will be perfectly understood. My receipts are all for baking meats, as so few have conveniences for roasting.

TO ROAST BEEF.

No. 1.—Make a bed of vegetables and sweet herbs for the bottom of the dripping-pan, by cutting in small pieces one-half a carrot, one-half a turnip, one small onion, and adding to these a sprig of parsley, a little thyme, and a bay leaf. The vegetables will do without the herbs if you cannot procure them. A piece of celery (the green top will do) is also a pleasant addition. Place these in a little mound, or bed, in the dripper (the dripper should be furnished with a rack), and, after tying the roast in good shape, place it on this bed. Do not put any water in the pan, and do not season the meat at first, as the salt extracts the juices. The temperature of the oven should be high at first. After the surface of the roast is well seared over, and the juices locked in, season the meat, reduce the heat, baste often, and cook slowly the requisite time.

TO ROAST BEEF.

No. 2.—Tie the roast in proper shape, rub it well with salt and pepper, then dredge it thoroughly with flour, and put it on the rack in the dripping pan. If the meat is very dry and lean, a little boiling water may be poured in the pan, but this must never be enough in quantity to touch the beef. The heat should be regulated according to instructions in *No. 1.* The basting should be frequent and regular after the first fifteen minutes.

Allow ten minutes to the pound if liked rare; fifteen or twenty if preferred well done.

The juice of the beef is the best sauce to serve it with, but if a made gravy is desired proceed as follows:

11

If the meat is baked after the first plan, take the vegetables out; if the roast is very fat, skim the most of this off; then put the pan on the top of the stove, stir in smoothly a table-spoonful of flour, and add, *very gradually*, stirring all the time, sufficient boiling water to make it of the proper consistency.

If baked after the second plan, proceed in the same way, except that there will be no vegetables to remove.

BEEF À LA MODE.

Remove the bone from a small round of beef (five or six pounds); cut lardoons of dry-salted pork, or sweet, fat bacon, one-half an inch square and two or three inches long; make gashes in the beef, and insert these at regular intervals; fill the opening from which the bone was taken with rich force meat, or good bread-crumb dressing, and sew it up; rub the beef well with a mixture composed of the following ingredients: one grated nutmeg, one table-spoonful of black pepper, one of ground cloves, one of allspice, and two of salt; add parsley, thyme, and sweet marjoram (it is a good plan to roll the lardoons in this, also, before inserting them). Put the trimmings of the pork in a saucepan, and when they are tried out, skim them from the grease, and put the beef, securely tied in shape, into the hot fat; brown it well on all sides, then dredge it with a heaping table-spoonful of flour, and turn it until that, too, is well browned; now pour in enough boiling water to about half cover the meat; pare and cut in pieces a carrot, a turnip, and an onion, and put these on top of the beef. If there is danger that the beef may burn or stick to the bottom of the kettle, slip a kitchen plate or saucer under it. Put the kettle on the back of the stove, to simmer gently and evenly four hours. Serve with the pieces of vegetables arranged on the platter around the beef with a portion of the sauce in which it is stewed; or baked onions may be served on the platter with it.

FILLET OF BEEF.

The fillet must be well trimmed and freed from fat and skin. Then lard it neatly; put the trimmings of pork or bacon with which you have larded it in the bottom of the dripping pan; pour into the pan a cupful of good beef stock, **or** hot water, though the stock is much the better, sprinkle salt and pepper over the fillet, put it in the pan, and bake from half to three-quarters of an hour, according to the size of the fillet, basting frequently, and adding, if necessary, a little stock occasionally. Serve with mushroom sauce.

Mushroom Sauce.—Put a table-spoonful of butter and a table-spoonful of flour in a saucepan over the fire. Stir until the flour is well browned. Add very slowly the juice from half a can of mushrooms, and sufficient hot beef stock to make the sauce the proper thickness; season with pepper, salt, and a tea-spoonful of lemon juice; add a half can of mushrooms, simmer a few moments, pour over the fillet and serve.

BOILED BEEF, NO. 1.

Plunge the beef into a small quantity of boiling water, about half enough to cover it, and boil rapidly in a tightly covered kettle for ten minutes. Then remove the kettle to the back part of the stove and simmer gently, allowing twenty minutes to the pound. Do not season until half an hour before it is done; then the water should have boiled away sufficiently to allow the meat to brown in the bottom of the pot. Now put in a table-spoonful of butter or sweet beef drippings, and a table-spoonful of flour rubbed together. Turn the beef until thoroughly browned. If necessary add more hot water after the meat is browned, or, better still, a ladleful of good beef stock.

BOILED BEEF, NO. 2.

Put some trimmings of pork, or a table-spoonful of other sweet fat into the stew-pan; have ready a saucerful of sliced carrot, turnip, and onion; brown these slightly in the fat, and then skim them out. Put now the piece of meat into the hot fat and brown it well; when a rich brown dredge it with a table-spoonful of flour, and gradually, stirring all the time, sufficient boiling water to make the gravy just thick enough. Season with salt and pepper and return the vegetables to the pot; remove to the back part of the stove and simmer gently until done. Serve with the vegetables neatly arranged around the meat, and a part of the gravy poured over them.

YORKSHIRE PUDDING.

To be baked under a roast of beef. It is put in the bottom of the pan, the roast lying on the rack. Bake half an hour.

Ingredients.—One pint of milk, two large table-spoonfuls of flour, two eggs, one salt-spoonful of salt.

Mix the flour and eggs well together; add the milk by degrees, and lastly the salt. Put it in the oven to set, then put it under the meat till one side is thoroughly browned, then turn and brown the other side.

BEEF STEW.

(Miss Parloa.)

Ingredients.—Two pounds of beef (the round, flank, or any cheap part (if there is bone in it, two and one-half pounds will be required), one onion, two slices of carrot, two of turnip, two potatoes, three table-spoonfuls of flour, salt, pepper, one generous quart of water.

Cut all the fat from the meat, and put in a stew-pan and fry gently for ten or fifteen minutes. While the fat is frying, cut the meat in small pieces, and season well with salt and pepper, and then sprinkle on two table-spoonfuls of flour. Cut the vegetables into very small pieces, and put them in the pot with the fat; fry them for five minutes, stirring all the time to prevent burning. Now put in the meat, and move it about in the pot until it begins to brown; then add the quart of boiling water. Cover over, let it boil up once, skim, and set back where it will just bubble for two and one-half hours; then add the potatoes cut in slices, and one table-spoonful of flour, which mix smooth with half a cup of cold water, pouring about one-third of the water on the flour at first, and when perfectly smooth adding the remainder. Taste now to see that the stew is seasoned enough, and if not add more salt and pepper. Let the stew come to a boil again, and cook ten minutes; then add the dumplings. Cover tight and boil rapidly ten minutes longer.

Mutton, lamb, or veal can be cooked in this same manner. When veal is used, fry out two slices of pork, as there will not be much fat on the meat. Lamb and mutton must have some of the fat put one side, as there is so much on these kinds of meat they are very gross.

DUMPLINGS.

Ingredients.—One pint of flour measured before sifting, one-half tea-spoonful of soda, one of cream tartar, one-half of salt, one of sugar.

Put all into a sieve, mix thoroughly, and run through the sieve; then wet with a small cup of milk; sprinkle a little flour on the board, turn the dough (which should have been stirred into a smooth ball with a spoon) on it, roll about half an inch thick, cut into small cakes, and cook ten minutes, as directed.

Things to be carefully noted: That the dumplings boil just ten minutes; that they do not sink too deep in the stew; that the stew is boiling rapidly when they are put in; that the cover fits tight on the pot, so that the steam shall not escape; and that the pot boils all the time, so that the steam shall be kept up. These few directions carefully followed will insure success every time.

BEEFSTEAK.

For broiling, the coals should be clear and bright. The broiler should be heated before the steak is put on it, and then exposed to the fiercest heat of the coals and turned frequently. As soon as the surface of the steak is seared over perfectly on all sides, it can be moved a little farther from the coals and cooked more slowly. It can be tested in the following manner: Press the flat part of the blade of a kitchen knife against the surface of the steak. If on removing it the fibre springs immediately back to its place, the steak is still very rare; if it resumes its natural appearance after a second or two, it is medium rare, but if it retains the impression of the knife, it is thoroughly well done. Never stick a fork into a steak. If you have not a double broiler turn the steak either by putting the fork under the slice and the flat blade of the knife above it, or you may put your fork into a portion of the fat, being sure not to pierce the muscular fibre. Do not season the steak until it is cooked. Then place it on a hot platter and put a lump of butter, and salt and pepper on its upper surface; then carefully turn and treat the other side in the same way. A little chopped parsley and a few drops of lemon juice or vinegar mixed with the butter, before seasoning the steak, makes what is known as *Maitre d' Hotel* butter, which is considered a very great improvement upon simple butter for steak.

If the conveniences for broiling are lacking, or if it is not easy to get good coals, there is a way of cooking it in a spider or skillet that is next to broiling, and as different as possible from the ordinary fried steak. Have the spider *very hot.* Do not put one particle of grease in it, but when hot put in the steak and turn continually, as in broiling, until the surface is seared; then reduce the heat as before and cook gradually until done. Of course, the precise point when it *is* done varies with individual taste. It can be tested in the same way as the broiled steak. Seasoned like broiled steak after it is done.

TO MAKE TOUGH STEAK TENDER.

Prepare a *Marinade*, or pickle, of one table-spoonful of vinegar, one of olive oil or melted butter, and a salt-spoonful of pepper. Soak the steak in this for an hour or more, turning it occasionally. The vinegar softens the fibre, the oil or butter keeps it soft, and the pepper seasons it somewhat. Never add any salt. It would be injurious in two ways: it would aid in extracting the juices, and would harden the fibre. The oil is better than the butter, as the latter hardens so soon. If butter is used, the dish containing the pickle must be kept in a warm place. The flavor of the steak will not be unpleasantly affected by this process, and the result is sure if thoroughly tried. If the steak is very tough, it is well to prepare the pickle in the evening before the meat is needed for breakfast, and allow it to remain in it all night. It is much better to treat tough steak in this way than to pound it. When ready to broil it, drain it out of the pickle, and proceed exactly according to the preceding directions.

BEEFSTEAK PUDDING.
(*English Receipt.*)

Line a basin with thin, plain pastry. For a small pudding, take three-fourths of a pound of rump steak, cut into thin slices without fat or gristle. Make a powder of pepper and salt; dip each slice into it, and lay round in layers in the basin until nearly full. Fill up the center with oysters or mushrooms, tie it tight in a cloth, and boil for three hours. Add water in the saucepan as required, but it must not reach the top of the pudding basin. Fill up the basin with good stock.

BEEFSTEAK ROLLS.

Cut a beefsteak quite thick, then split open lengthwise and cut in strips four or five inches wide; rub over the inside with an onion, and in each strip roll up a thin slice of bread buttered on both sides; stick two cloves in the bread, and sprinkle over it some salt, pepper, and celery seed (cut, or thin slices of celery stalk, if in season). Tie each roll with a thread; dredge it with flour, and fry it in hot butter. Then put these, when a delicate brown, into a stewpan, with only water enough to stew them. Make a nice thickened gravy from the liquor in which the steaks were stewed, and serve with the rolls, very hot. The rolls should stew slowly two hours. Veal or mutton is good prepared in this way.

FRIZZLED BEEF FOR BREAKFAST.

Brown a piece of butter the size of an egg in a saucepan, add a cup of cream or milk, one tea-spoonful of flour, mixed with a little cold milk. Have ready one-half pound of thinly shaved smoked beef, add it to the mixture, let it just come to a boil, serve.

HASH AND TOAST.

Toast slices of bread and put on a platter. Hash very fine cold beef or mutton; put in a saucepan, season with salt, pepper, and butter, add as much water or stock as the toast will absorb; boil ten minutes, pour over the toast, and serve immediately.

TO HASH BEEF.

(English Method.)

Cut slices of raw beef, put them in a stew-pan with a little water, some catsup, pepper, and salt; stew them till done, thicken the gravy with a lump of butter rubbed into brown flour.

POLISH HARE.

Take one pound of raw beef and one pound of sausage meat, two rolls or two good slices of bread softened in milk and squeezed out well, a little onion, salt, and ground allspice, cloves, and black pepper—all to taste, and three eggs and grated bread so as to make a nice dough; form it into a loaf and fry in butter. This is most excellent.

KLOPS OF BEEF.

Take the lean part of the raw meat, from the leg, cut in thin slices, and if you have a machine for chopping use it, if not, scrape the beef free from the gristle and sinews with a knife, and chop it fine with a chopping knife.

Take one-third the quantity of meat, of finely chopped suet, one-fourth of bread crumbs which have been boiled thick in a little butter, water, pepper and salt, with one or more eggs; form therefrom round balls the size of a small apple, press them rather flat, smooth them with the blade of a knife dipped in water and "criss-cross" them with the sharp end of a knife. Then put into a bread pan, parsley, a little onion, with tarragon, all chopped very fine, and let them stew slowly in butter; add the juice of a lemon with some white wine; lay in the klops, cover them over and then stew slowly for some minutes over a gentle fire; turn them over so the under side comes up and then stew slowly until done. Take them out and lay them in regular shape on a round dish, and mix with the sauce in which they have been stewed, some of Crosse and Blackwell's sardine or anchovy sauce; let it boil up and pour all over the klops and serve with little round potatoes fried brown in butter.

BEEF OMELET.

Ingredients.—Three pounds round steak put through the sausage mill, six butter crackers (rolled), three eggs (well beaten), one table-spoonful of salt, one tea-spoonful of sage, one tea-spoonful of pepper.

Mix with two table-spoonfuls of butter and water and bake one hour.

LANGUE DE BOEUF AU GRATIN, OR BAKED TONGUE.

Chop very fine a little parsley, lemon thyme, tarragon, capers and three anchovies. Soak a piece of crumb of bread in some good gravy; put it in a mortar with the herbs and a small piece of butter and thoroughly pound it together. Place a layer of this stuffing in the bottom of a fire proof baking dish. Then put slices of cooked tongue on the top of it, then another layer of stuffing. Pour over the surface a little butter melted in stock; place the dish in the oven until a nice color.

STEWED TONGUE.

(English Receipt.)

Cut up a slice of bacon into lardoons; sprinkle the pieces with salt, pepper, chopped parsley and a little allspice. Lard an ox tongue with these and lay it in a saucepan with two slices of bacon, four small bunches of parsley, two sprigs of thyme, two carrots cut into small pieces, two small onions, a few cloves, salt and pepper. Cover with stock to which has been added a glass of sherry. Simmer five hours, keeping the saucepan well covered. Strain the sauce on the tongue.

POTTED MEAT.

Remove all gristle, hard pieces, and fat from the meat; mince it very fine, and pound it in a mortar with a little butter, some gravy, well freed from fat, and a spoonful of Harvey or Worcester sauce; beat it to a smooth paste, seasoning during the process with pounded clove or allspice, mace, or grated nutmeg, salt, and a little cayenne; put it into pots, press it close down and cover with clarified butter or with marrow fat.

MEAT PIE WITH POTATO CRUST.

Cut beef or mutton (either raw or cooked), season with pepper, salt, and a finely shred onion. Line a buttered dish with mashed potato, put in the meat, with half a tea-cupful of boiling water; cover thickly with mashed potato, and bake an hour and a half.

TO MAKE TOUGH MEAT TENDER.

Soak it in vinegar and water; if a very large piece for about twelve hours. For ten pounds of beef use three quarts of water to three-quarters of a pint of vinegar; and soak it for six or seven hours.

TO ROAST A LEG OF VEAL.

Take out the bone, and fill the cavity with a dressing made as follows: three tea-cupfuls of grated bread crumbs, one cupful finely chopped suet, one-half cupful of chopped green parsley, one table-spoonful of sweet marjoram, and summer savory, one-half tea-spoonful of pepper, one tea-spoonful of salt, one egg, beaten. Put scraps of pork or bacon in the dripping-pan. Dredge the veal thoroughly with salt, pepper, and flour; lay slices of pork over it, and bake, allowing twenty minutes to the pound. *Baste often.*

VEAL CUTLETS.

Veal cutlets should be cut from the leg. They should be of an equal size, and must be pressed into shape with the blade of a knife, or a cutlet bat. Fry some thin slices of ham in their own fat; remove them from the saucepan; egg and bread the cutlets, and fry in the same fat. Make a gravy by adding flour to a part of the fat, then a little hot water, as in directions for beef gravy. Season with salt and pepper and a tea-spoonful of lemon juice. Serve in alternate slices of veal and ham, garnish with slices of lemon and the gravy.

FRICANDEAU OF VEAL.
(*Miss Corson.*)

Ingredients.—Two pounds of veal, one-fourth pound of larding pork, vegetables and seasonings, one-half peck of spinach.

Choose a thick, compact slice of veal from about the middle of the leg, and lard it as follows: Cut the pork in strips an eighth of an inch thick and two inches long; lay the veal on a folded towel on the left hand; put a strip of pork in the larding needle, and take a stitch with it in the upper surface of the veal; as you draw the needle out, the strip of pork, or lardoon, will remain in the meat. Insert the lardoons in even rows along the cutlet, making as many rows as its width will permit. Put into a pan some scraps of vegetables and the trimmings of pork; lay the cutlet on them and cook it in a moderate oven, taking care not to let it burn, and seasoning it when half done with white pepper and salt. Meantime wash and trim the spinach, put it into well salted boiling water, and boil it rapidly, with the cover off, until it is tender, which will be in from three to seven minutes, according to the age of the spinach; while it is boiling press it under the water with a wooden spoon. As soon as it is tender drain it in a colander, run plenty of cold water over it, chop it fine, and rub it through a sieve with a wooden spoon. When the veal is done, warm the spinach with a table-spoonful of butter and a salt-spoonful of salt; or take up the meat and keep it hot while you strain its gravy and warm the spinach in it. Arrange the *purée* of spinach neatly on a dish, lay the *fricandeau* on the spinach, and serve it hot.

FRICANDEAU OF VEAL.

Cut slices an inch thick and six inches long, lard them with slips of lean bacon, bake them a light brown, stew them well in seasoned stock made as thick as rich cream, serve them up hot, and lay around the dish sorrel stewed with butter, pepper and salt till quite dry.

VEAL CROQUETTES.

Dredge pieces of cold veal with flour; season with salt and pepper, and chop very fine; add enough warm water to bind together, form into cork-shaped rolls, dip into well beaten egg, roll in cracker or fine bread crumbs, and fry in hot lard.

BLANQUETTE OF VEAL.

(*Miss Corson.*)

Ingredients.—Three pounds breast of veal, two eggs, one ounce of butter, flour, vegetables, and seasonings.

Cut three pounds of breast of veal in pieces two inches square, put them in enough cold water to cover them, with one salt-spoonful of white pepper, one tea-spoonful of salt, a bouquet of sweet herbs, half a carrot scraped, 'a turnip peeled, and an onion stuck with three cloves; bring slowly to a boil, skim carefully until no more scum rises, and cook gently for thirty or forty minutes until the veal is tender; then drain it, returning the broth to the fire, and rinsing the meat in cold water to whiten it. Meantime make a white sauce by stirring together over the fire one ounce of butter and one ounce of flour until they are smooth, then adding a pint and a half of the broth gradually; season with a little more salt and pepper if they are required, and a quarter of a salt-spoonful of grated nutmeg. When the sauce has boiled up well, stir into it with an egg-whip the yolks of two raw eggs, put in the meat and cook for five minutes, stirring occasionally. A few mushrooms are a great improvement to the *blanquette;* or it may be served with two table-spoonfuls of chopped parsley sprinkled over it after it is put on a hot platter.

VEAL OLIVES.

Take the bone out of the fillet and cut thin slices the size of the leg, beat them flat, rub them with the yolk of an egg well beaten, lay on each piece a thin slice of boiled ham, sprinkle salt, pepper, grated nutmeg, chopped parsley and bread crumbs over all, roll them up tight, tie them, rub them with egg, and roll them in bread crumbs, lay them on a tin dripping-pan, and set them in the oven. When brown on one side turn them, and when sufficiently brown cover them with stock and simmer until tender.

TO STUFF AND ROAST A CALF'S LIVER.

Take a fresh calf's liver, and, having made a hole in it with a large knife run in lengthways, but not quite through, have ready force meat, or stuffing, made of part of the liver parboiled, fat of bacon minced very fine, and sweet herbs powdered; add to these some grated bread and ground spice, with pepper and salt. With this stuffing fill the hole in the liver, which must be larded with fat bacon, and then roast, flouring it well and basting with butter till it is cooked enough. This is to be served hot with gravy sauce.

VEAL LOAF.

Ingredients.—Three pounds of veal and two thick slices of pork, chopped fine, two eggs, two Boston crackers rolled, three tea-spoonfuls each of salt and pepper, one-fourth of a nutmeg.

Make into a loaf, dredge with flour. Bake from two and one-half to three hours. Baste often, and serve with meat gravy. Very nice hot or cold for tea.

SWEET-BREADS.

Sweet-breads, if properly cooked, make one of the most delicate dishes that can be put upon the table, but care must be taken in selecting them as there are two kinds, and it is only one kind that is very good. Ask for the " heart sweet-bread" and select the largest. There are many ways to cook them. This is a good way: Parboil the sweet-breads and put them into a stew-pan, and season with salt and cayenne to taste; place over a slow fire; mix one large table-spoonful of browned flour with a small piece of butter, add a leaf of mace; stir butter and gravy well together and let all stew for half an hour; then set the stew-pan in the oven and when the sweet-breads are nicely browned place them on a dish. Pour the gravy into half a pint of stewed tomatoes, thickened with a tea-spoonful of flour and a small piece of butter, and season. Strain it through a wire sieve into a stew-pan, let it come to a boil, and stir until done; then pour over the sweet-breads and serve very hot.

HOW TO DRESS SWEET-BREADS.

1. When well washed and cleared from skin, they may be larded with delicate strips of very fresh bacon or not, according to taste. Boil till nearly done, then put them into a thickly buttered deep dish which will stand the oven (metal or earthenware), strewing the bottom of the dish with thin slices of carrot and onion, add a ladleful of good broth, salt and pepper, and brown in the oven till of a dark golden color. Take out the sweet-breads, strain the juice, adding some good veal stock and a few drops of lemon juice, and serve.

2. Butter a stew-pan or good-sized saucepan thickly, line it with slices of carrot and onion, put in the sweet-breads prepared as above, i. e., washed and freed from skins, and larded, but not boiled. Let them brown well over in a brisk oven, shaking occasionally to prevent adherence, and turning if necessary, so that they may brown evenly on all sides. When of a deep golden hue all over moisten with three or four table-spoonfuls of thick cream, add enough veal stock to nearly cover the sweet-breads, cover tightly, and put live coals on the lid (this can be best done in a braizing kettle); place over a moderate fire, and let them stew gently for nearly an hour. To serve them, strain the sauce and add a little lemon juice. They are very good also when cooked in this way and served upon fresh young peas, spinach, or sorrel done in the French way. It is essential that the stock used should be veal stock, because one of the first rules of all good cookery is that all meats should be cooked in their own sauces, i. e., that the sauce should be of the same meat as the thing cooked.

TO FRY LIVER.

Fry first some thin slices of bacon; take them out and keep them warm until required.   Plunge the slices of liver for a moment into boiling water, drain and roll them in flour; fry in the fat left from the bacon.   Arrange the liver and bacon in alternate slices; garnish with lemon and parsley and serve smoking hot.   If the flavor of onion is liked a sliced onion may be fried with the liver.

ROAST LEG OF MUTTON.

Bone the leg, or take out the first joint, and fill the cavity with a bread crumb or force meat dressing.   Dredge with flour, salt, and pepper, and roast the same as beef.   Allow fifteen minutes to the pound.

BOILED LEG OF MUTTON.

Plunge into boiling water sufficient to cover it well; let it boil up and skim; add a little salt, remove to the back of the stove and simmer until tender.   A handful of rice thrown into the pot whitens the meat.   Serve with caper sauce. (See *Savory Sauces.*)

MUTTON CHOPS.

Broil like beefsteak, and serve with parsley.

AN EXCELLENT WAY TO COOK A BREAST OF MUTTON.

(Mrs. Buton.)

Ingredients.—Breast of mutton, two onions, salt and pepper to taste, flour, a bunch of savory herbs, green peas.

Cut the mutton into pieces about two inches square, and let it be tolerably lean; put it into a stew-pan with a little fat or butter, and fry it a nice brown; then dredge in a little flour, slice the onions, and put them with the herbs in the stew-pan; pour in sufficient water *just* to cover the meat, and simmer the whole gently until the mutton is tender.   Take out the meat, strain, and skim off all the fat from the gravy, and put both the meat and gravy back into the stew-pan; add about a quart of young green peas, and let them boil gently until done.   Two or three slices of bacon added and stewed with the mutton give additional flavor; and to ensure the peas being a beautiful green color, they may be boiled in water separately, and added to the stew at the moment of serving.

HARICOT MUTTON.

Cut pieces from the breast or scrag of mutton and fry them a good brown; dredge well with flour and add enough boiling water to cover them. Stick an onion with three cloves; prepare a bouquet of herbs; pare and cut in dice a turnip and two carrots; put these with a blade of mace, salt and pepper to taste in the stew, and simmer gently until the mutton is tender. Remove the herbs and the mace. Serve on a hot platter surrounded by the vegetables and a part of the gravy.

RICE CUTLETS.

One-quarter pound of boiled rice, one-quarter pound of bread crumbs, one-quarter pound of mutton, one-quarter pound of beef, one small onion chopped very fine, one gill of stock or cream, salt and pepper to taste. Shape into cutlets, egg and bread crumb, and fry in hot lard. Serve with fried parsley.

BOILED LEG OF LAMB.
(English Receipt.)

Time, one hour and a quarter after the water simmers. Select a fine fresh leg of lamb weighing about five pounds; soak it in warm water for rather more than two hours, then wrap it in a cloth and boil it slowly for an hour and a quarter. When done, dish it up and garnish with a border of carrots, turnips, or cauliflower around it. Wind a cut paper around the shank bone and serve it with plain parsley and butter sauce poured over it.

ROAST LEG OF LAMB.

Leg of lamb may be stuffed and roasted like leg of mutton. It is just as well not to stuff it, however. It should be done rather rare, just pink on the inside. Serve it with mint sauce. (See *Savory Sauces.*)

SHOULDER OF LAMB.

The shoulder blade should be removed, and the opening stuffed, then the shoulder is roasted according to the directions for roast leg of mutton.

LAMB CHOPS.

These are broiled for ten or fifteen minutes, turning often, season well with butter, salt, and pepper.

LAMB CROQUETTES.

These are made exactly like chicken croquettes, substituting cold lamb for the cold chicken.

ROAST PORK.

Roast the same as beef, except sage is added to the flour with which pork is dredged. Pork also requires to be very well done —from twenty to thirty minutes should be allowed to the pound, according to the thickness of the roast. Serve with baked apples.

BOILED HAM.

Scrub it well with a brush kept for the purpose. Mere washing will not suffice. Put over in cold water and boil from three to five hours, according to size. A ham weighing twelve pounds will take five hours. When done take out of the boiling water and plunge in cold water; remove the skin carefully and trim the underside of the ham. Then put it in a dripping-pan, and cover with grated bread crumbs and chopped lemon, and set it in the oven to brown. Trim the bone with cut tissue paper.

PORK SPARE RIBS.

Broil or fry them and serve with apple sauce. They are more delicate broiled. Make sure they are well done.

TENDERLOINS.

Broil or fry; serve without gravy and with baked apples.

TO FRY SALT PORK.

Cut the slices very thin; soak them in sweet milk an hour, or in boiling water a few moments; cut off the rinds; have the spider hot, and brown them quickly on both sides.

TO BROIL SALT PORK.

Prepare in the same way and broil in a double broiler over a good clear bed of coals; serve immediately on a hot platter *Very nice.*

TO FRY HAM.

If the ham is salty and hard, soak some time in sweet milk, cut the slices thin; have the spider hot and fry quickly. Serve at once with a fried or poached egg on each slice of ham.

BROILED HAM.

Prepare as to fry, and broil quickly and serve at once.

BACON.

This is broiled or fried like salt pork.

PORK AND BEANS.

(Miss Parloa.)

Examine and wash one quart of dry beans (the pea bean is the best), and then put them in a pan with six quarts of cold water; let them soak in this over night; in the morning wash them in another water, and place them on the fire with six quarts of cold water and a pound of salt pork. If they are the present year's beans, they will cook enough in half an hour; if older, one hour. Drain them and put half in the bean pot; then gash the pork, put it in, cover with the remainder of the beans, one table-spoonful of molasses, and one of salt, and cover with boiling water. Bake ten hours; watch them carefully, and do not let them cook dry.

DEVILED HAM.

One pint of boiled ham chopped fine with a good proportion of fat, one table-spoonful of flour, one-half cup of boiling water. Press in a mold, and cut in slices.

HAM OR TONGUE TOAST.

Cut a slice of bread, toast and butter it, take a small quantity of the remains of either ham or tongue, and chop *very fine;* have ready chopped, also very fine, two hard-boiled eggs; put both meat and eggs into a stew-pan with a little butter, salt, and a dash of cayenne pepper. When thoroughly hot, spread it on the toast, and serve immediately.

POULTRY AND GAME.

ROAST TURKEY.

Dressing.—To one cup of fine bread crumbs allow one-third of a cup of finely chopped suet, four sprigs of parsley, a tea-spoonful of sweet marjoram, summer savory and thyme, half a tea-spoonful of salt, a salt-spoonful of pepper, and half a beaten egg. Use no water, and be sure that the crumbs are very fine. Good dressing is never solid and leathery, but crumbs in the spoon when it is taken from the fowl. If the flavor of onion is liked, a tea-spoonful of chopped onion may be added to the above. Never put sage in stuffing for fowls. It is too strong, and should only be used with such rich and greasy meats as pork.

The turkey should be carefully picked, singed and drawn. In drawing, the first cut should be made lengthwise in the back of the neck. The windpipe and crop should be drawn from this opening; then cut inside the right thigh as you hold the turkey towards you, down carefully to the vent and clear around it, taking great pains not to cut into the entrails, and to loosen them, at the vent, perfectly from the body. Now put the forefinger in the opening at the neck and loosen the liver, heart, etc., from the carcase. Then introduce the hand into the opening below, loosen the ligaments that bind the entrails to the back, and then grasp firmly the mass from the top, and draw evenly and gently the whole contents of the body out. The next step is to separate the liver, etc., from the rest. This must be done with care, so as not to break the gall bladder, which lies directly under the liver. The heart must also be cut away and squeezed gently between the fingers, to force out any clot of blood that may have lodged there; and, lastly, the gizzard must be freed from the surrounding membrane and fat, and carefully cut open so as not to split the inside skin which holds the contents, as then the little sack can be removed whole. Unless the turkey is very rank it does not need other washing than is recommended for beef. If it is rank, wash it in strong soda water and wipe dry. The giblets should, in this latter case, be soaked in soda water ten or fifteen minutes. Now stuff the craw, pat it into shape, and draw the skin over the neck, lap it in the back where the opening was

made, and fasten it with a single stitch, tying the ends. Then
fill the body of the fowl and sew the opening up. Now press
the legs back towards the upper part of the body, and put your
trussing needle clear through the carcase, just at the second
joint, then draw the cord the needle is threaded with through,
and take the next stitch through the wings, putting the needle
first through the upper joint, and then bending the tip of the
wing back and pushing the needle through that, then through
the body just below or inside of the wishbone, then through the
tip of the other wing, and finally through the upper joint. Now
take the needle off, and tie the thread which you have brought
through the upper part of the body to that which you started
with on the same side of the body. Now turn the turkey over,
and after threading the needle again, take one stitch through
the back, just above the oil sack, which must always be cut out,
and, turning the fowl back, tie the ends of the legs down close
to the body. A long trussing needle is, of course, needed to prepare a fowl in this manner. It is something like a mattress
needle, and a very good home-made one can be manufactured
from one of the springs that give an umbrella shape. Take one
of these wires from an old umbrella, sharpen the end, and you
have a capital trussing needle.

The turkey is now ready for the oven. Put some scraps of
pork in the bottom of the dripping-pan, put a slice of pork under
each wing and a slice over the breast; then put the turkey in the
dripping-pan, in a pretty hot oven for the first fifteen minutes.
After that moderate the heat, and allow from fifteen to twenty
minutes to the pound, according to the age of the fowl, in a slow
oven. Baste frequently with the hot drippings from the pork.

A turkey should be cooked *slowly* and *basted frequently*. A
large turkey needs four hours at least. Rub the inside with salt
and pepper before stuffing. Half an hour before taking out
dredge well with flour and baste with melted butter.

Gravy.—When the turkey is in the oven, put the giblets, or
the heart, liver, gizzard, and neck, over the fire in cold water; let
them come gradually to a boil, and then simmer until tender.
Then chop the heart and gizzard fine, and mash the liver, and
put all into the bottom of a gravy boat. Now brown a table-
spoonful of flour and a table-spoonful of butter in a saucepan,

and then add very gradually the liquor in which the giblets were boiled. When the turkey is taken up, the threads removed, and it is ready for the table, pour the hot gravy into the gravy boat, over the giblets, and serve.

Serve with cranberries or with currant jelly.

Sausages are often used to garnish turkeys and chickens.

BOILED TURKEY WITH OYSTER SAUCE.

Select a plump turkey for boiling; clean and singe carefully; cut off the head and neck and the first joint of the legs. Stuff with a dressing made of bread, chopped celery, a little pork or' butter, salt and pepper, and a generous allowance of raw oysters. Truss carefully, so as to make it look round and plump. Sew it tightly in a strong cloth, cover with boiling water, and simmer gently two hours. Be careful to skim thoroughly; if boiled hard it will be tough. When done take out of the cloth and garnish with green celery tops.

For the oyster sauce or gravy, take two dozen large fresh oysters, put them in a stew-pan, drain the liquor on them; let them just come to a scald, but not boil. As soon as they are scalded take out the oysters; have ready a tea-spoonful of flour, mix smooth with a small cup of milk, and salt and pepper to taste, and a tea-spoonful of butter; add this to the liquor in which the oysters were scalded. Let all boil up once, put in the oysters, and serve.

TO BOIL A TURKEY WITH OYSTER SAUCE.

Grate a loaf of bread, chop a score or more of oysters fine, add nutmeg, pepper and salt to your taste, mix it up into a light force meat, with a quarter of a pound of butter, a spoonful or two of cream, and three eggs; stuff the craw with it, and make the rest up into balls and boil them; sew up the turkey, without stuffing the body, dredge it well with flour, put it in a kettle of cold water, cover it, and set it on the fire; skim it, let it boil very slowly an hour, then take off your kettle and keep closely covered; if it be of a middle size let it stand in the hot water half an hour, the steam being kept in will stew it enough, make it rise, keep the skin whole, tender, and very white; when you dish it pour on a little oyster sauce, lay the balls around, and serve it up with the rest of the sauce in a boat. The turkey should be set on in time so that it may stew as above; it is the best way to boil one to perfection. Put it over the fire to heat iust before you dish it up.

OYSTER SAUCE FOR TURKEY.

Put a pint of oysters in a bowl, wash them out of their own iquor and put them in another bowl; when the liquor has settled pour it off into a saucepan with a little white gravy and a tea-spoonful of lemon juice; thicken it with flour and a good lump of butter, boil it three or four minutes, put in a spoonful of good cream, add the oysters, keep shaking them over the fire till quite hot, but don't let them boil, for it will make them hard and shrivel them.

ROAST CHICKEN.

A chicken is drawn, stuffed, and baked exactly like a turkey.

BROWN FRICASSEE OF CHICKEN.

Try the grease from scraps of pork and put into a spider or saucepan. Cut up the chicken into as even sized pieces as possible, wipe dry, and then brown evenly and thoroughly in the hot fat. Add a heaping table-spoonful of flour, and turn the pieces of chicken several times until the flour is browned, being very careful not to scorch it. Now pour over the whole enough boiling water to cover it, and remove to the back part of the stove, add pepper and salt to taste, and let it simmer until tender. This is very nice served in a border of rice.

WHITE FRICASSEE OF CHICKEN.

Cut up the chicken as before, cover with boiling water, and let simmer until tender. Add a cupful of sweet cream, salt and pepper to taste, and a table-spoonful of flour wet in a little cold milk, and stirred until perfectly smooth. Let it boil up, and then pour over slices of biscuit arranged nicely on a platter.

FRIED CHICKEN.

Cut up the chicken as for fricassee. See that every piece is wiped dry. Put equal quantities of lard and butter into a spider and set it on the stove to heat. Have a plate with a cupful of sifted cracker crumbs which are well seasoned with pepper and salt. Roll the pieces of chicken in this, and then fry them in the hot grease, turning often, and browning evenly and well.

PRESSED CHICKEN.

Boil two chickens until dropping to pieces. Pick the meat off the bones, taking out all skin; season with salt and pepper, put in a deep tin or mold. Take one-fourth of a box of gelatine dissolved in a little warm water, add to the gravy left in the kettle, pour over the chicken in the mold, and set away to cool. When cold remove from the mold and cut in slices.

JELLIED CHICKEN.
(Canadian Receipt.)

Boil the chicken as above and until the water is reduced to a pint. Pick the meat from the bones in fair sized pieces, removing all gristle, skin, and bone. Skim the fat from the liquor, add an ounce of butter, a little pepper and salt, and half a packet of Nelson's gelatine. Put the cut up chicken into a mold, wet with cold water, and when the gelatine has dissolved pour the liquor hot over the chicken. Turn out when cold.

CHICKEN PATTIES.

Mince cold chicken and stir it into a white sauce made of milk thickened with corn starch and flavored with pepper, salt, and butter. Line small patty pans with puff paste, bake first, then fill with the mixture and set in a hot oven a few minutes to brown.

CHICKEN LOAF.
(Canadian Receipt.)

Boil a chicken in as little water as possible, until the meat can be easily picked from the bones. Cut it up finely, then put it back into the saucepan with two ounces of butter and a seasoning of pepper and salt. Grease a square mold, and cover the bottom with slices of hard boiled egg; pour in the chicken. Place a weight on it and set it aside to cool, when it will turn out.

MACARONI AND CHICKEN.

Line a tin quart mold with butter about one-half an inch thick. Cut macaroni, previously parboiled in salt and water, into inch lengths and stick them close together all over the mold. Chop cold chicken or turkey very fine, moisten it with milk or gravy and season well with curry or pepper. Fill the mold with this mixture, cover closely, and cook long enough to make the macaroni very tender. Serve with a white sauce made as follows:

White Sauce—Ingredients.—One tea-spoonful of butter, one table-spoonful of flour, one pint of milk, salt and pepper to taste, one table-spoonful of grated cheese.

Rub the butter and flour together in a saucepan over the fire, until the mixture bubbles, add the milk very slowly, stirring all the time until of the proper consistency. Add salt and pepper and a table-spoonful of grated cheese.

CHICKEN CROQUETTES.

Chop the meat off from one cold boiled chicken very fine; add one-half a tea-cupful of chopped suet, one tea-spoonful of chopped parsley, one-fourth of a nutmeg, grated, one tea-spoonful of chopped mushroom, one tea-spoonful of chopped onion, one tea-cupful of boiled rice (fresh boiled and hot), the juice and grated rind of half a lemon, salt, cayenne, and black pepper to taste; mix well together, and add just enough sweet cream to make it right for molding. Form into balls, or rolls, and fry in hot lard.

Cold beef, cold veal, and cold lamb can be made into croquettes in exactly the same way, substituting either for the chicken. The canned mushrooms can be used, or they can be omitted altogether.

CHICKEN CURRY.

Cut one large onion, or two small ones, in slices; put a heaping table-spoonful of butter in a stew-pan, and when it bubbles, add the onions and brown them; now skim out the onions, put in the pieces of chicken, cut as for a fricassee (one chicken), and brown them thoroughly on all sides; when they are brown, dredge them with a table-spoonful of flour, and turn until this too is brown. Pour boiling water slowly over this, stirring all the time, using enough to just cover the chicken; return the onions, add a bouquet of herbs if possible, and simmer slowly until the chicken is tender. Half an hour before serving mix a table-spoonful of curry powder to a smooth paste with some of the gravy, stir it into the stew, add the juice of half a lemon, and take out the herbs. Cover tightly until done. Serve in a border of rice. A sour apple fried with the onion is an improvement. Half a tea-cupful of grated, fresh cocoanut is also frequently added.

ROAST GOOSE.

Select a goose with a clean white skin, plump breast, and yellow feet; if the feet are red the bird is old. Pluck, singe, draw, and carefully wipe the goose; cut off the neck close to the back, leaving the skin long enough to turn over. Cut off the feet at the first joint, and separate the pinions at the first joint. Beat the breast pin flat with a rolling-pin, and after stuffing truss according to directions for turkey. Prepare the stuffing according to directions, adding sage and onion, a tea-spoonful of the former, a dessert-spoonful of the latter. Dredge the top of the goose with salt and pepper. Put a cupful of boiling water in the bottom of the dripping-pan. Baste often. A large goose will require two hours. If you have any suspicion that it is tough, pour over it a cupful of vinegar and rub it well in, before putting it in the pan.

DUCKS.

These are prepared, stuffed and baked in the same way. They are generally preferred under done, half an hour being allowed for an average sized duck. If they are old it is better to parboil them slightly before baking.

STEWED QUAIL.

Halve them, lay them in a deep kettle, cover with boiling water, and stew gently; skim thoroughly, season with salt and pepper, and when nearly done thicken with butter and flour rubbed together, made into a paste, and poured slowly in. Boil for five minutes after.

TO ROAST QUAIL DOWN IN A FLAT BOTTOMED POT.

Stuff the birds with a bread crumb dressing, seasoned according to directions and adding a little nutmeg; tie them up; rub them well with salt, pepper, butter, and flour, and put them in the pot, adding a little boiling water, and a heaping table-spoonful of butter; cook them very slowly, closely covered, turn often, and make them a light brown. Serve in the gravy from the pot.

BROILED QUAIL.

Split them open down the back; dip them in melted butter, and broil, turning frequently. Have ready slices of buttered toast; lay each quail on a slice, butter it well, add salt and pepper, and serve.

A still nicer way is to have a stew-pan over the fire containing hot cream salted to taste; when the quail is broiled, lay it for a moment in the cream, put it on the toast, and then cover with the hot cream.

PRAIRIE CHICKENS.

These can be cooked in exactly the same way as quails.

SADDLE OF VENISON.

No. 1.—Select a saddle of fresh juicy venison weighing about eight pounds. Season with pepper and salt; lard it with pork according to directions for larding; dredge with flour; sprinkle a little water over it, and put it into a hot, steady oven, with a cupful of hot water in the bottom of the dripping-pan. Bake it according to directions for roast beef, basting *very* often. Allow fifteen minutes to the pound. Always serve it steaming hot, and with currant or grape jelly.

A haunch of venison, the neck, and the leg are roasted in the same way.

SADDLE OF VENISON.

No. 2.—Rub it well with butter; make a paste of flour, salt, and water; roll it out and entirely cover the saddle; put it in a moderate oven and baste often; allow twenty minutes to the pound; fifteen minutes before serving, take off the paste, dredge the saddle well with flour, baste well, and then when nicely browned and frothed on top, serve with jelly.

VENISON STEAK.

Have the gridiron hot and well greased with butter or the fat of steak, turn often, and allow from five to ten minutes, according as the steak is liked rare or well done. When cooked to your taste take it off the gridiron, season with salt, pepper, and butter, and cover it up for five minutes in the oven.

CHAPTER XIII.

SAVORY SAUCES.

DRAWN BUTTER.

ALLOW three times as much butter as flour by weight. Put two-thirds of the butter in a saucepan and stir until it bubbles; then mix in the flour and stir constantly for about five minutes, being very careful the flour does not brown. When the flour is well cooked add slowly, stirring constantly, enough boiling water, or white stock, to make the sauce like thick cream. Let this boil up, then draw to one side of the stove and stir in the rest of the butter. Serve at once.

This is the foundation of many white sauces. Add hard boiled eggs chopped fine and you have *egg sauce;* add capers and *caper sauce* is the result; so a flavoring of anchovy gives *anchovy sauce,* etc., etc.

. CAPER SAUCE.

Put two ounces of butter in a saucepan with two table-spoonfuls of flour and stir well on the fire until the mixture assumes a brown color; add rather less than a pint of stock, free from fat, season with a little pepper, salt, and Worcester sauce. When the sauce boils throw in plenty of capers, let it boil once more, and it is ready.

MINT SAUCE FOR LAMB.

Two table-spoonfuls of chopped mint, one table-spoonful of sugar, one-fourth of a pint of vinegar; add water and heat.

CHILI SAUCE.

Eight good sized ripe tomatoes, one onion, one green pepper. Pare and slice the tomatoes and chop the onion and pepper.

Stew all together until the peppers are done, two-thirds of a cup of vinegar, one-half a cup of sugar. Spice to taste with cloves, allspice, cinnamon, and mace. After adding these cook till thick.

CHILI SAUCE.

Ingredients.—Forty-eight ripe tomatoes, ten peppers, two large onions, two quarts of vinegar, four table-spoonfuls of salt, two tea-spoonfuls each of cloves, cinnamon, allspice, and nutmeg, one of sugar.

Slice the tomatoes, chop the peppers and onions together; add the vinegar and spices, and boil until thick enough. Mustard and curry powder improves this.

SAUCE FOR COLD SALMON.

The yolks of two eggs, half a tea-cupful of cream, a little cayenne pepper and salt. Mix them together and simmer in a pan, stirring all the time till it thickens. When cold add two table-spoonfuls of vinegar.

TARTARE SAUCE.

Put the yolks of four eggs into a basin with salt and mustard to taste, and stir olive oil into them, one table-spoonful at a time. After each table-spoonful of olive oil put in one tea-spoonful of tarragon vinegar. Keep on doing this until the sauce is of the desired consistency; then add pepper, the least bit of cayenne, and a couple of shallots or a few pickled gherkins or onions chopped very fine.

SAUCE FOR FISH.

Ingredients.—Two ounces of butter, one-half cup of vinegar, one tea-spoonful of ground mustard, one tea-spoonful of salt, a little pepper.

Let this boil and add one cup of milk and yolks of two eggs. Let this just boil, stirring all the time.

EGG SAUCE FOR A SALT COD.

Boil four eggs hard; first, half chop the white, then put in the yolks and chop them both together, but not very small; put them into a pint of good drawn butter and let it boil up, then pour it on the fish.

FISH SAUCE.

Yolks of two raw eggs; add salad oil, drop by drop, until it is of the consistency of thick cream; add the juice of half a lemon.

MOCK OYSTER SAUCE.

Ingredients.—One tea-cupful of good gravy, one tea-cupful of milk, three dessert-spoonfuls of anchovy sauce, two dessert-spoonfuls of mushroom ketchup, two ounces of butter, one tea-spoonful of pounded mace, whole black pepper. All to be boiled until thoroughly mixed.

BREAD SAUCE.

Put into half a pint of cold milk one small onion, three or four cloves, a blade of mace, a few pepper corns, and a little salt. Set the whole to boil, then strain the milk over a tea-cupful of fine bread crumbs. Stir well on the fire for a few minutes, adding at the time of serving either a small pat of butter or a table-spoonful of cream.

WHITE SAUCE FOR GAME.

Boil an onion in a pint of milk until it is like a jelly; then strain and stir into the boiling milk sifted bread crumbs, enough to make it like thick cream when well beaten. Beat while boiling, and season with salt, black and cayenne pepper, and a little nutmeg.

SAUCE FOR TURKEY.

Cut the crumb of a loaf of bread into thin slices, put it in cold water with a few pepper corns, a little salt and onion; then boil till the bread is quite soft, beat it well, put in a quarter of a pound of butter and two spoonfuls of thick cream, and put it in the dish with the turkey.

CELERY SAUCE.

Wash and pare a large bunch of celery very clean, cut it into little bits, and boil it gently till it is tender; add half a pint of cream, some mace, nutmeg, and a small piece of butter rolled in flour; then boil it gently.

This is a good sauce for roasted or boiled fowls, turkeys, partridges, or any other game.

MUSHROOM CATSUP.

Put alternate layers of mushrooms and salt in an earthen jar, using at least a quarter of a pound of salt to two quarts of mushrooms. Let them stand for half a day, then cut the mushrooms in small pieces, and let them stand for three days, stirring them well once a day; then strain them, and to every quart of juice add half an ounce each of allspice and ginger, half a tea-spoonful of powdered mace, and one tea-spoonful of cayenne pepper. Put this all in a stone jar, set in a kettle of boiling water, and let it boil for five hours briskly; then let it simmer in a porcelain kettle for three-quarters of an hour; let it stand all night in a cool place; in the morning drain off the clear liquor and bottle it. Cork the bottles and seal tightly. The smaller bottles you use the better, as the catsup will not keep its distinctive flavor long if exposed to the air.

CURRANT CATSUP.

Six pounds of currants, three pounds of brown sugar, one pint of vinegar, one table-spoonful each of cloves and cinnamon, one-half table-spoonful each of allspice and black pepper, and a little cayenne pepper. Boil all together well from a half to three-quarters of an hour.

TOMATO CATSUP.

Take a bushel of tomatoes, and cut them in small pieces and boil until soft; then rub them through a wire sieve, add two quarts of the best cider vinegar, one pint of salt, one-quarter of a pound of whole pepper, one-quarter of a pound of allspice, one table-spoonful of black pepper, one good-sized pod of red pepper (whole), and five heads of garlic. Mix together and boil until reduced to one-half the quantity. When cold strain through a colander and bottle, sealing the corks. It will keep for two or three years as fresh as when made.

TOMATO CATSUP.

Ingredients.—One peck of tomatoes, one quarter of a pound each of pepper, allspice, and white mustard seed, two ounces of cloves, six table-spoonfuls of salt, half a gallon of vinegar.
Boil slowly six hours; cool and then bottle.

CHAPTER XIV.

FISH AND OYSTERS.

TO BAKE FISH.

O not remove head or tail; stuff, sew, or wind a string around the fish. Lay pieces of sliced pork across the top; sprinkle with water, salt, pepper, and bread crumbs; pour hot water into the pan; baste often while baking; serve with drawn butter sauce. If not frequently basted, the fish will be too dry.

BAKED FISH.

A fish weighing from four to six pounds is a good size to bake. It should be cooked whole to look well. Make a dressing of bread crumbs, butter, salt, and a little salt pork, chopped fine (parsley and onions if you please); mix this with one egg. Fill the body, sew it up and lay it in a large dripper; put across it some pieces of salt pork to flavor it; put a pint of water and a little salt in the pan. Bake it an hour and a half; baste frequently; after taking up the fish, thicken the gravy and pour over it.

CREAM GRAVY FOR BAKED FISH.

Have ready in saucepan one cup of cream diluted with a few spoonfuls of hot water. Stir in carefully two table-spoonfuls of butter and a little chopped parsley; heat this in a vessel filled with hot water. Pour in the gravy from the dripping-pan of fish. Boil thick.

TO BOIL FISH.

Except salmon. Place in a fish-kettle with salted *cold* water. Add a little vinegar or lemon juice. Boil gently, not to break.

13   193

Remove from the water as soon as thoroughly done, and drain before the fire. A little onion, parsley, carrots or cloves, with seasoning, adds to flavor and appearance.

Sauce.—Egg sauce, or *Sauce Hollandaise.* (See chapter on savory sauces.)

BOILED FISH.

Choose a good sized fish; lay it in the fish-kettle with plenty of well salted cold water; when the water boils draw the kettle aside, lift up the fish and let it drain, covered up, over the water until the time of serving. Serve with

White Sauce.—Melt an ounce of butter in a saucepan, add to it a dessert-spoonful of flour, mix thoroughly; add salt and white pepper to taste, and about a tumblerful of boiling water; stir on the fire until it thickens. Then take the saucepan off the fire and stir in the yolks of two eggs, beaten up with the juice of a lemon, and strained.

TO FRY FISH.

Cut this fish in even sized, regular pieces, egg and bread crumb and fry in hot lard.

SCALLOPED FISH.

Take any remains of cooked fish and pick them to pieces; put fine bread crumbs in the bottom of a deep dish, then a layer of the fish with a few table-spoonfuls of drawn butter, then the bread crumbs, and so on, alternately, until the dish is full. Let the top layer be bread crumbs, over which scatter little lumps of butter. Bake half an hour.

RUSSIAN FISH.

Take a pound of any cold fish, remove the bones and skin and flake it; place at the bottom of a pie dish about an inch thick, then put a layer of cold boiled rice (half a tea-cupful is sufficient for the quantity of fish), salt and pepper each layer; then, if no sauce be left, stew the bones in some milk, thicken with a little flour, pepper, salt, and a dessert-spoonful of anchovy sauce, pour over the rice layer; put a layer of cold hard boiled eggs cut in thin slices (two are enough), another layer of fish, rice, sauce and eggs, and when your dish is full, having eggs at the top, scatter a few finely chopped capers, a few small pieces of butter; warm thoroughly before the fire or in the oven and serve.

COD PIE.

Ingredients.—Any remains of cold cod, oysters, melted butter sufficient to moisten, mashed potatoes enough to fill up the dish.

Flake fish from the bone and take all the skin away. Lay in a pie dish, pour over it the melted butter and oysters with sauce; cover with mashed potatoes. Bake for half an hour, and send to table of a rich brown color.

Instead of melted butter use cream, if preferred.

HOW TO USE CANNED SALMON.

Cut round the top of the tin, which place in boiling water for a few minutes, until thoroughly heated through, taking care, however, that the water does not reach sufficiently high to be in danger of flooding the contents. Have ready some nicely mashed potatoes, which arrange in a border around a very hot dish; turn the salmon into the center of this, removing quickly any pieces of bone which may appear amongst the meat. Sprinkle a few capers over it, interspersed with morsels of fresh butter, and serve immediately before it has time to chill. This dish, if properly dressed, could not possibly be told from the remains of fresh salmon. Rice, boiled same as for curry, may be substituted for potato, and is preferred by many.

BROILED MACKEREL.

Soak over night in cold water, to which is added a little vinegar. Scrape all the black skin from the underside; broil over a quick fire, season with butter, and serve.

FRIED MACKEREL.

Soak as above, and scrape also; then put into a hot spider with a little butter; turn often till browned; when cooked pour over the fish, in the spider, one cupful of sweet cream. Dish up the fish and pour the gravy over it.

FISH BALLS.

Allow twice as much mashed potato as fish; mix well together, form into balls, and fry. Use any remains of cold fish.

CODFISH FOR BREAKFAST.

Take the fish and soak over night in cold water made slightly acid with vinegar. Wash in clean water; put into a saucepan with a lump of butter, and just heat through; then dredge with flour and stir well; then add slowly enough rich milk to make sufficient gravy. Have some hard-boiled eggs ready; save out the yolk of one, and garnish the platter, in the center of which the fish is served, with slices of egg, and pass the yolk through a sieve over the top of the fish.

CLAM CHOWDER.

Put in a pot a layer of sliced pork, chopped potatoes, chopped clams, salt, pepper and lumps of butter, and broken crackers soaked in milk; cover with the clam juice and water, stew slowly for three hours; thicken with a little flour. It may be seasoned with spices if preferred.

OYSTER STEW.

Put one quart of oysters in their own liquor on the fire. The moment they begin to boil skim oysters out and add to the liquor half a pint of hot cream, salt, pepper, and mace to taste. Skim well, remove, add to it the oysters and one and one-half ounces of butter. Serve hot with toast or crackers.

FRIED OYSTERS.

Select large, even-sized oysters; strip them and drain; beat two eggs slightly; dip the oysters first in the egg, then roll them in sifted bread or cracker crumbs; see that they are thoroughly coated with the egg and cracker, then fry in hot lard. Salt and pepper the crumbs.

SCALLOPED OYSTERS.

Be sure to have enough oysters. The trouble with scalloped oysters often is that crackers predominate so largely as to entirely smother the oysters. Strip the oysters, and strain the liquor. By stripping the oysters is meant taking each one in the fingers and quickly making sure there are no pieces of shell adhering to it. Cover the bottom of a deep dish with sifted cracker crumbs, pour over these a little of the liquor; next a

layer of oysters; season with salt, pepper and butter, and a very
little mace; then more crumbs and oysters, seasoning as before,
alternately, until the dish is filled. The top layer should be
crumbs, seasoned with lumps of butter. Now pour over the
whole half a tea-cupful of thick, sweet cream. Bake three-
quarters of an hour, keeping the dish covered half the time;
then remove the cover and brown.

OYSTER PATTIES.
(Home Messenger Receipt Book.)

Make a rich puff paste, cut in small squares, place a layer of
oysters, which have been dried on a napkin, on the paste, dust a
little salt, powdered mace, and cayenne pepper over them, covering with another piece of paste; wet the edges of the paste with
cold water, using a paste brush, and pinch tightly together; bake
in a rather quick oven to a delicate brown.

CHICKEN AND OYSTER CROQUETTES.

Take equal quantities of chicken, oysters, and bread crumbs.
Chop the chicken and oysters very fine; season with salt and
pepper and a little mace; moisten with one well-beaten egg and
enough thick, sweet cream to make just thick enough to handle.
A lump of butter should be added and stirred well in before the
egg and cream are used. Egg and bread crumb after forming
into balls or rolls, and fry in hot lard.

OYSTERS À LA CRÈME.

Use one pint of cream, rich and perfectly sweet, for one quart
of oysters. Strip the oysters, and drain them from the liquor;
strain the liquor. Put the cream over the fire and thicken it with
a dessert-spoonful of flour, made into a smooth paste with a little
cold milk; season with salt, pepper, and a little mace; when the
cream boils, add the liquor from the oysters, which has been
scalded and skimmed until clear; then put in the oysters, leaving
them just long enough to heat through. Have ready a platter
covered with thin slices of toast.

OYSTER SHORT-CAKE.

Prepare the oysters as above, and have ready a short-cake crust.
Split it open while hot, pour the hot oysters on the bottom
layer, cover, send piping hot to the table.

OYSTERS IN THE SHELL.

Open the shells and keep the deepest ones for use. Melt some butter, season with minced parsley and pepper; when slightly cool roll each oyster in it, using care that it drips but little, and lay in the shells. Add to each shell a little lemon juice, cover with grated bread crumbs, place in a baking-pan and bake in a quick oven; just before they are done add a little salt. Serve in the shells.

OYSTER FRITTERS.

Time, five or six minutes. Some good sized oysters, four whole eggs, a table-spoonful of milk, salt and pepper, crumbs.

Bread some good sized oysters, make a thick omelet batter with four eggs and a table-spoonful of milk, dip each oyster into the batter, and then into the grated bread, fry them a nice color and use them to garnish fried fish.

CHAPTER XV.

VEGETABLES.

THE POTATO.

HE potato is three-fourths water. The greater part of what remains is starch with a little fibrine, albumen and a small amount of mineral salts, fat, etc. It will be seen from its composition that it is not fit to be eaten as an exclusive article of diet. It is too poor in the muscle making elements. We also see that bread cannot be made from potato meal, since it is too deficient in gluten to be capable of vesciculation. As I have said before, a small quantity may be added with advantage to bread sponge, as the starch is eagerly appropriated by the yeast plant and the activity of the sponge is thereby increased. In the composition of the potato will also be found the reason for the addition of fat, milk, eggs, buttermilk, cabbage, etc., which are made by those who live chiefly on it. Being deficient in fat, in gluten, and other albuminous materials, instinct has led the Irishman, for instance, to increase its nutritive power by cooking with it cabbage, which is rich in gluten, and adding likewise a little pork or bacon for its fat. This combination of cabbage, fat, and potato, makes the famous Kol-kannon, which gives to the Irish laborer who lives on it, just what he requires, a cheap and nutritious food, which yields to him in proper proportion all that he needs to make him vigorous. Buttermilk, too, which is often combined with the potato in Ireland, containing as it does the casein and salts of the milk, adds to its value as food, and when it is enriched still more by the addition of some fat cheaper than butter, offers an article of diet which is cheap and at the same time sufficient for the needs of the body.

199

A laboring man can sustain life on potatoes and salt, but he will certainly lose vigor and capacity for long continued exertion.

The potato is one of the most valuable of vegetable foods and has many qualities to recommend it to the rich and the poor. It is one of the few articles found on the tables of both, esteemed as a luxury by the former, as a necessity by the latter. It is easily cultivated, yielding nearly always a rich return for comparatively little labor, and requires no great extent of land to supply the wants of an ordinary family. It can be kept from one season to the next without great expense and with a reasonable degree of care, and it never wearies the palate. It is like bread in the universality of its use, and a knowledge of the proper methods of cooking it is, therefore, of great importance.

Its history you are, doubtless, acquainted with. It is thought to be a native of Chili, and was brought to England by Sir Walter Raleigh in the sixteenth century. The story of his attempts to introduce it as food is interesting. It was planted in his garden in the county of Cork in Ireland, and the gardener, mistaking the seedballs that grew on the plant for that which was to be cooked, brought them to the cook to be prepared for her master's table. They were declared unpalatable and the gardener ordered to dig up the plant and throw it away, Sir Walter imagining he had brought home the wrong vegetable. Upon digging it up, the potatoes were discovered and a new trial made. This time they were so badly cooked, or rather so little cooked, being sent to the table nearly raw, that they stuck like wax to the teeth of those who tried to masticate them. They would have been again rejected had not some guest at the table, who had happened to have seen them elsewhere, explained the mistake and caused them to be returned to the fire. It was not, however, until more than a hundred years later that they came into anything like general use.

No vegetable is, perhaps, as a rule, more carelessly and wretchedly cooked than the potato. The most economical method is to cook them in their jackets. The waste caused by paring is at least 14 per cent, while cooked in the skins it is but 3 per cent. The salts moreover which add flavor to the potato lie next the skin and they are largely lost when this is cut off. We thus impair the taste as well as diminish the quantity when

we remove the skins before cooking. There is considerable dis-
cussion as to whether they should be thrown into hot or cold
water to be boiled. So high an authority as Dr. Edward Smith
says: "Potatoes and similar vegetables should be well cooked
with a considerable degree of heat. If it be intended to boil them
they should be placed at once in hot water, and if to be roasted
the oven should be moderately hot. When peeled and soaked
in cold water a larger proportion of the fecula will be extracted
than is desirable, and with a slow oven the peel will be hardened
and thickened."

TO BOIL POTATOES.

Throw them at once into boiling hard water, to which salt
in the proportion of a tea-spoonful to one quart has been added.
When tender the water should be well drained off and the kettle
placed on the back of the stove and covered with several thick-
nesses of cloth, a clean kitchen towel folded two or three times
answering this purpose. This cloth allows the steam to pass
through and at the same time keeps the potatoes warm and dry.
If left for a few moments to dry off in this way they will become dry and mealy. Boiled potatoes should never be served
in a covered dish. The cover will confine the steam, which will
condense and fall back on the potatoes rendering them sodden
and waxy. The best way to bing them to the table is in a dish
in which a warm napkin has been placed. The ends of the
napkin can then be folded over the potatoes. This will serve
every purpose of a cover and at the same time will not be impervious to steam.

Boiled potatoes should be eaten the moment the starch cells
are burst and the potato is tender. The skin acts upon the interior of the potato just as the cover of a vegetable dish acts upon
the potatoes it contains. It keeps all the moisture inside the
potato.

TO BAKE POTATOES.

Select as even sized and regular shaped potatoes as possible;
cut a thin rim of skin off as for boiled potatoes. Put them on
the grate in the middle of a very hot oven and bake rapidly for
half an hour for ordinary sized potatoes. They should be eaten
the moment the starch cells are burst and the potato is tender.

MASHED POTATO.

Boil according to preceding directions. When perfectly tendeı remove to an earthenware bowl or a very bright tin pan. Be sure to have this and everything that is to be added as seasoning hot. Heat the milk and butter together. Let salt and pepper be near at hand. Then mash thoroughly and when every lump is out, season with salt and pepper and stir in the heated milk and butter. Make the mixture quite soft, and now comes the most laborious and important part of the process. After the seasoning is all in, and most persons would consider the potato ready for the table, it should be beaten to a creamy snow-white froth, with a large fork. It needs a strong arm and plenty of energy. Do not feel entirely satisfied until the mixture looks light and foamy, like the beaten whites of egg. Potatoes mashed after this method will not be recognized as the same article as the heavy, stiff, lumpy food often offered as "mashed potato."

POTATO SNOW.

After the potato is prepared according to the above directions, press it through a colander into the vegetable dish in which it is to be served, and it will not only be extremely palatable, but will be "a thing of beauty" as well, adorning the table, and giving pleasure to the eye, while at the same time it appeals to the "inner man."

DUCHESSE POTATOES.

When the potatoes are boiled, press them at once through a colander. Season with salt, pepper, butter and a very little nutmeg. To two cupfuls of mashed potato, add the beaten yolks of two eggs. Now flour your pastry board. Take half of this mixture at once, flour your hands, and press it into a long roll. Cut round cakes from the end of this, brush the top of each with the white of eggs, and brown in the oven, or put the entire roll in a greased pan, brush it over with the white, and brown.

POTATO PUFF.

Press the hot potatoes through the colander as for Duchesse potato. Season with salt, pepper, butter and milk, as for Mashed potato. To two cupfuls of this, take two eggs; beat yolks and white separately. Mix in the yolks and lastly the stiffly beaten whites. Have ready a greased pan or pudding dish, and put this mixture in it by spoonfuls, heaping them up in a light and uneven way. Brown in the oven.

LYONNAISE POTATOES.

Cut cold boiled potatoes into even and rather thick slices. Cut, also, an onion in the same way. Put a spoonful of butter, or any sweet drippings, into a saucepan, over the stove. When it is hot, drop in the sliced onion and shake it about until it is a very delicate cream color, hardly a brown; then put in the sliced potato and shake until that, too, is delicately colored; add salt and pepper, and lastly a spoonful of chopped parsley. When this is thoroughly mixed with the potato and onion, place on a small platter, or in a shallow vegetable dish, and serve at once.

POTATO CROQUETTES.

Ingredients.—Three cups of cold mashed potato, one cup of sweet cream, a little salt, and two well-beaten eggs.

Mold into balls, egg and bread crumb and fry a delicate brown in hot lard.

POTATO MUFFLE.

Potatoes mashed fine, butter and salt as for table. Add one cup of sweet cream, six eggs beaten separately whites and yolks. Bake in a pudding dish until browm.

POTATO BUMPO.

Boil some mealy potatoes, mash them with butter and cream, season well, and put a layer of this in the bottom of a pudding dish; then put a layer of any kind of cold chopped meat or fish well-seasoned, then another layer of potato, and so on until the dish is full, making the last layer one of potato. Strew bread crumbs over the top with little pieces of melted butter. Bake until well browned.

SARATOGA POTATO.

Shave thin, soak in ice-water thirty minutes, dry, and fry in boiling lard to light brown; drain and salt. Serve hot in folded napkin.

PARISIENNE POTATOES.

Cut small balls with the potato-cutter described in the chapter on utensils; parboil in hot water well-salted, and then fry brown in hot lard.

SWEET POTATO.

Take those that are nearly of the same size, that they may be done equally; wash them clean, but do not peel them; boil them till tender, drain the water off and put them in the oven for a few minutes, to dry.

SWEET POTATOES BROILED.

Cut them across without peeling, in slices half an inch thick; broil them on a griddle and serve them with butter.

TO STEW CABBAGE.

Parboil in milk and water and drain it; then shred and put into a stew-pan with a tea-spoonful of butter, a tea-cup of cream, pepper and salt to taste, and stew until tender.

DRESSING FOR CABBAGE.

One half cup of vinegar, table-spoonful of butter, one egg. Beat the egg, heat all together, and pour on the chopped cabbage.

CABBAGE Á LA CRÉME.
(English Receipt.)

For this entrée, which is very delicate if carefully prepared, it is necessary to choose a cabbage as firm and white as possible. Throw the vegetable into some boiling water with some salt and boil till it is almost done, but not quite tender. Take it out and drain it thoroughly from all moisture. Then cut it up lengthwise into several pieces. Melt about an ounce of butter in a stew-pan. The quantity of butter must be regulated by the size of the cabbage; sufficient must be used to make a rich sauce. Add salt, white pepper to prevent any discoloration, and a spoonful of flour; then put in the cream, according to taste, in any case not less than a quarter of a pint. Lay in the pieces of cabbage, and finish cooking in the sauce until perfectly tender. Arrange symmetrically on the dish, and place some fried croûtons round.

CABBAGE FARCI, OR STUFFED.

(English Receipt.)

Cook the cabbage in salt and water sufficiently to open the leaves, and insert between them ordinary veal stuffing, slices of sausage meat, or some highly-spiced force meat; then tie it securely round with thread to prevent the force meat falling out. Replace in the stew-pan, and cook briskly at first, then simmer until completely tender. Serve with a little gravy poured over the whole. In winter roast chestnuts hidden in the center are sometimes added, when it is termed "chou en surprise."

CABBAGE.

Cabbage takes two hours in cooking. Cut it in quarters and examine it carefully to see that there are no insects or worms concealed between the leaves; then pour boiling water over it and let it stand half an hour; then put it in boiling, well-salted water, and boil till tender. It is well to set the dish containing it in the wood-shed while it is soaking the half hour, as then the odor does not fill the house, and soaking in this way and changing the water prevents, in a great measure, the strong smell which is such an annoyance in the usual method of boiling cabbage. When the cabbage is done, drain thoroughly in a colander, and then pour over it a little melted butter. Or cut the cabbage as for salad, and then pour the boiling water on it and let it stand as before, then put in fresh boiling water to cook until tender, then drain and boil up once in cream or milk.

COLD SLAW.

Sprinkle a quart of finely-chopped cabbage lightly with salt, and let it stand one hour; drain off the brine into a saucepan; add to it one cupful of strong vinegar, a tea-spoonful of butter, a tea-spoonful of mustard mixed smoothly with a little cold water and a salt-spoonful of pepper. When it boils stir in two well-beaten eggs and three table-spoonfuls of rich sweet cream; pour hot on the cabbage. Let it stand until cold, and serve. It is exceedingly nice.

ONIONS.

New onions can be boiled in one hour. Late in the fall and all winter the time must be increased to two hours. Throw them into boiling, well-salted water. After boiling half an hour change this water; renew the water, using boiling water each time, three times. Fifteen minutes before time to serve put a little sweet cream, a half a tea-cupful for eight or ten onions, over the fire in a stew-pan, and heat. Add a spoonful of butter, and stir it all the time until the butter is melted. Season with salt and pepper. Drain the onions out of the water, and boil them up once in this hot cream.

BAKED ONIONS.

Boil until tender in well-salted water, according to directions; then arrange them in a baking dish, put a lump of butter on the top of each onion, and sprinkle over them some sifted bread crumbs; pour half a cupful of sweet cream into the dish and bake slowly half an hour.

FRIED ONIONS.

Slice the raw onions into a saucepan; add a heaping table-spoonful of sweet drippings; fry thirty minutes, turning often.

TO STEW TOMATOES.

If the tomatoes are fresh throw them in boiling water and re-move the skins. Then cut away all the hard pith in the center and slice the tomato very fine. Put in a saucepan and stew gently half an hour. Long boiling makes the tomato very dark colored and very acid. Season with salt, pepper and butter, and if liked thickened, add a few very fine bread or cracker crumbs.

If the tomatoes to be stewed are canned instead of fresh, they need not stew more than fifteen minutes. After the can is opened examine its contents, and see that there are no hard, green pieces left in when you put the tomatoes on to stew. Cut them into fine pieces, and stir and mash them until they are re-duced to an even, fine pulp. Season as before, and serve hot.

BAKED TOMATOES.

Have a quantity of fine bread or cracker crumbs prepared as for scalloped oysters. Put a layer of these crumbs in the bottom of a greased baking dish or bright tin pan, and cover with a layer of tomatoes; sprinkle salt, pepper, and place little lumps of but-ter over this layer. Add also a few small pieces of raw onion—

just enough to flavor slightly; then another layer of bread crumbs and another of tomatoes, seasoned as before. Alternate in this manner until the dish is filled. The top layer should be crumbs. Put a little butter on this layer so as to brown the crumbs. Now put in a slow oven; allow an hour and a half for the baking if the tomatoes are fresh, one hour if canned. Keep the dish covered the first hour. Remove the cover half an hour before time to serve and allow the dish to brown nicely.

TO BROIL TOMATOES.

Broiled tomatoes make a delicious dish; select those that are not over ripe, and cut them in halves crosswise; dip the cut side into beaten egg, and then into wheat flour, and place them upon a gridiron, whose bars have been previously greased. As they become well browned turn them over and cook the skin side until thoroughly done. Put butter, salt, and pepper upon the egg side and serve upon a platter.

STUFFED TOMATOES.

Get them as large and firm as possible. Cut a round place in the top, scrape out all the soft parts; mix with stale bread crumbs, onions, parsley, butter, pepper, salt; chop very fine and fill the tomatoes carefully; bake in a moderately hot oven; put a little butter in the pan and see that they do not burn or become dry. Serve on slices of buttered toast.

GREEN TOMATOES FRIED.

Cut the tomatoes in slices about one-fourth of an inch thick and soak one hour in brine strong enough to season them. For every three tomatoes add one onion, of about the same size, sliced. Fry together in sweet drippings with a little butter added. Fry until tender or until they can be pierced with a broom straw.

TURNIPS.

Winter turnips need to be cooked two hours in well salted, boiling water. When they are perfectly tender, either mash and season well with salt, pepper, and butter, and then place smoothly and in good shape in a vegetable dish and finish by dotting with sprinkles of red pepper; or, cut in slices, arrange neatly in a vegetable dish, and pour over them a little melted butter; sprinkle with salt and add a small quantity of red pepper as before.

TURNIPS À LA CRÈME.

Boil them as directed; slice them evenly; have a saucepan with hot cream, slightly thickened with flour and seasoned with salt and pepper, over the fire; heat the sliced turnip in this and serve in a hot dish.

EGG PLANT.

The purple ones are best; get them young and fresh, pull out the stem and parboil them to take out the bitter taste; cut them in slices an inch thick, but do not peel them; dip them in the yolk of an egg and cover them with grated bread and a little pepper and salt—when this has dried, cover the other side in the same way—fry them a nice brown.

SUMMER SQUASH.

Gather young squashes, peel and cut them in two; take out the seeds and boil them till tender; drain off the water and rub them through a colander with a wooden spoon; then put them in a stew-pan with a cupful of cream, a small piece of butter, some pepper and salt; stew them, stirring frequently until dry. This is the most delicate way of preparing squashes.

WINTER SQUASH.

Cut in pieces, pare, and cut away the soft, stringy part. Cover with boiling water and cook till tender; then drain, return to the hot kettle, mash, season with butter, pepper and salt, and stir a few moments till thoroughly hot and dry. Squash is also good steamed.

BAKED SQUASH.

Cut in pieces; do not pare, but cut away the soft part as before directed. Bake until done; then scrape the squash away from the rind, season, heat, and serve.

SPINACH.

Pick and wash perfectly clean two or three pounds of spinach, put into a saucepan with a little water and let it boil till quite done. Turn it out on a hair sieve to drain, throw the water away and pass the spinach through the sieve. Put a good lump of butter into a saucepan with a pinch of flour, mix well, add the spinach, pepper and salt to taste, and a little milk; stir well and serve.

BOILED ASPARAGUS.

Place heads one way; tie in small bundles and cut off in equal lengths; put into salted boiling water and boil until tender; when well drained arrange upon thin slices of toast; pour over them drawn butter sauce; cook eighteen minutes.

BEETS.

Wash but do not scrape or cut at all, or you will injure the color. Old beets cannot be boiled too much; allow at least five hours. Young beets will cook in half that time. When tender, plunge into cold water, and the skin will come off easily.

STRING BEANS.

Cut into inch lengths after stringing them; put into boiling, well salted water; boil one hour; season with butter, salt and pepper.

PEAS.

Throw into well salted, boiling water; cook from twenty to thirty minutes; season with salt, pepper, butter, and add a little sweet cream.

BOILED PARSNIPS.

Scrape and boil one hour. If very large it is well to cut them in lengthwise slices. They can be served with drawn butter, or simply seasoned with butter, salt, and pepper.

FRIED PARSNIPS.

Boil as above, and then fry the slices in hot lard or pork fat.

BOILED CARROTS.

Scrape and boil until tender (from one to two hours). They should be cut in slices before boiling, and thrown into boiling, well salted water. Pour over them drawn butter.

14

CORN.

Remove the husks and silk and throw into boiling water. Young corn will boil tender in half an hour. Serve covered with a napkin.

TO BOIL CORN ON THE COB.
(Mrs. Henderson.)

At the Saratoga Lake House there is a third specialty of good things. The first is the fried potato, the second is the fresh trout, the third is boiled corn, which is served as a course by itself. The corn is boiled in the husk. The latter imparts sweetness and flavor to the corn, besides keeping it moist and tender. The unhusked corn is put into salted boiling water, and when done, and well-drained, some of the outside husks are removed, and the corn is served with the remaining husks about it; or, the cobs may be broken from the husks just before sending to the table, which would save this trouble afterward.

CORN CUT FROM THE COB.

Cut the corn from the cob, scrape the cob so as to be sure of getting all the juice or milk of the corn. Cover with boiling water and cook one hour; then pour in a tea-cupful of sweet cream, or rich milk, season with butter, salt and pepper and serve.

CORN PATTIES.

Twelve ears of corn, grated, one tea-spoonful of salt, one tea-spoonful of pepper, one egg beaten into two table-spoonfuls of flour. Fry in hot butter or lard.

MOCK OYSTERS.

One pint of grated green corn, three table-spoonfuls of milk, one tea-cup of flour, one half tea-cup of drawn butter, one tea-spoonful of pepper, one egg. Drop a table-spoonful into hot butter and fry from eight to ten minutes, or can be baked on a griddle. Can be made without eggs and butter.

CAULIFLOWER.

Trim off the outside leaves, and cut the stalk off flat at the bottom. Put the cauliflower, head down, in salt and water, and leave it to soak one hour to free it from vermin; then rinse off, put into salted boiling water and boil rapidly until tender. Serve plain, or pour drawn butter over them.

COOKED CUCUMBERS.

Peel and cut into quarters. Remove the seeds. Put into salted boiling water and boil until tender. When done, place on buttered toast and spread with butter.

SLICED CUCUMBERS.

Slice thin and soak in ice-water, well salted, at least an hour before serving. Drain them from the ice-water and send to table.

MACARONI.

Look over carefully one-half pound of macaroni, but do not wash it unless absolutely necessary. Break it as little as possible. Plunge it into well-salted boiling water and let it boil rapidly twenty minutes. While it is boiling, melt together in a saucepan, over the fire, one table-spoonful each of butter and flour. When they are thoroughly blended, add by degrees, one pint of sweet milk, stirring constantly so that the mixture will be perfectly smooth. Season with salt and white pepper. Drain the macaroni and put a layer of it in the bottom of an earthenware or tin baking dish; cover this with a few spoonfuls of the sauce, and a sprinkle of grated cheese, Parmesan being the best, then another layer of macaroni, sauce and cheese, until the dish is full, having a good layer of cheese on top of the dish. Now brown in the oven and serve hot. The macaroni can be prepared simply with the sauce, omitting the cheese.

MACARONI WITH TOMATO SAUCE.

Boil the macaroni as above, cover with tomato sauce and set in the oven ten or fifteen minutes, long enough for the macaroni to absorb the sauce. (For Tomato Sauce, see chapter on "Savory Sauces.")

MACARONI CROQUETTES.

Boil one half pound (or one half a paper) of macaroni in salted water the usual way. When done and drained, chop it *very fine*, then add pepper, salt, two eggs and a cupful of grated cheese. Put a tea-spoonful of butter in a saucepan and when it is bubbling hot add the macaroni mixture and let it cook about five minutes, stirring all the time. When the mixture is cool enough, form into shape, roll in egg and cracker crumbs and fry in boiling lard. Serve with tomato sauce.

CHAPTER XVI.

SALADS.

MAYONNAISE SAUCE.

UT the uncooked yolk of an egg into a cold bowl. Beat it well with a wooden spoon, then add two salt-spoonfuls of salt, and one salt-spoonful of mustard powder. Work them well a minute before adding the oil, then mix in a little good oil which must be poured in very slowly, a few drops at a time, at first alternated occasionally with a few drops of vinegar. In proportion as the oil is used the sauce should gain in consistency. When it begins to have the appearance of jelly, alternate a few drops of lemon juice with the oil. When the egg has absorbed a gill of oil finish the sauce by adding a very little pinch of cayenne pepper and one-half a tea-spoonful of good vinegar. Taste it to see if there are enough salt, pepper, mustard, and cayenne; if not, add more very carefully.

FRENCH SALAD DRESSING.

Ingredients.—Three table-spoonfuls of salad oil, one table-spoonful of vinegar, one salt-spoonful of salt, one-half salt-spoonful of pepper.

Mix the oil, pepper, and salt together; add the oil stirring well.

SALAD DRESSING.

To six eggs well beaten add one small tea-spoonful each of salt and pepper, one table-spoonful each of mustard and sugar, one cup of sweet cream, piece of butter the size of an egg. Of this make a custard and when cold add one coffee-cup of cider vinegar.

213

SALAD DRESSING.

Beat up two hard boiled yolks of eggs, mix with them one salt-spoon of table salt, one mustard-spoon of raw mustard, one tea-spoonful of soft sugar, one cayenne-spoon of cayenne pepper. When all is well pounded add, very gently, mixing all the time, four table-spoonfuls of cream or milk, and about two table-spoonfuls of vinegar; the last must be put in slowly, as it depends on the strength of the vinegar how much to use. Stop pouring in when the dressing becomes thick. The basin may be rubbed over with garlic or onion if the flavor is liked.

TOMATO MAYONNAISE.

Pare smooth even-sized, ripe tomatoes without scalding them. Slice rather thickly, keeping each tomato by itself so it can be put back in shape. *Marinate* the tomatoes by soaking them for a moment in the French dressing; arrange the slices so that the tomatoes seem to be whole, and put a spoonful of the Mayonnaise dressing on the top of each one. This makes both a beautiful and a delicious salad.

TOMATO SALAD.

Slice alternate layers of onion and tomato, and salt the onion sufficient to season the whole. Let it stand one-half hour and then pour over it the following:

FRENCH SALAD MIXTURE.

Ingredients.—Three table-spoonfuls of salad oil, one table-spoonful of vinegar, one salt-spoonful of salt, one-half a salt-spoonful of pepper.

Mix thoroughly the oil, salt and pepper, and add the vinegar, stirring well.

CELERY SALAD.

Ingredients.—The yolk of one egg, two table-spoonfuls of cream, one table-spoonful of white sugar, three table-spoonfuls of vinegar, one tea-spoonful of olive oil, one tea-spoonful of made mustard, a pinch of salt, celery.

Beat the yolk of the egg, add the other ingredients and pour it over the celery, cut into inch lengths.

CHICKEN SALAD.

Ingredients.—One boiled chicken cut in small pieces, four leaves of celery cut fine, two cucumber pickles cut fine, a small quantity of hashed cabbage, so that the proportion shall be one-third meat to two-thirds cabbage, etc.

Rub the yolks of four hard-boiled eggs to a paste, add two table-spoonfuls of melted butter, one table-spoonful of mustard, one table-spoonful of salt, one-half table-spoonful of black pepper and one-fourth as much cayenne, one tea-spoonful of vinegar, yolk of one egg, uncooked. Pour this dressing over the salad just before placing on the table.

RUSSIAN SALAD.

Cut into pieces about an inch long carrots, French beans, potatoes, cucumbers, onions, beet root, lettuce, endive, green peas, and a little tarragon—in fact any cold vegetables you may happen to have (but of course the tarragon, cucumbers, lettuce and endive are not to be boiled); mix all together with a very rich salad dressing. When all is mixed add the lettuce, endive, etc., and mix in with the cold vegetables small pieces of cold boiled salmon or lobster, or both if you have them. Turn the whole well over together, and put into the dish; garnish well with hard-boiled eggs cut in four, beet root according to your own fancy, and little sprays of parsley. The consistency of the salad dressing should be that of good cream.

RUSSIAN SALAD.

To make this in the greatest perfection, small pieces of the flesh of partridges, poultry, or cold salmon are required, a few anchovies filleted, turnips, carrots, asparagus heads, green peas, French beans, beet root, prauns, and capers—all finely chopped; eschallot, pepper, mustard, vinegar, and caviare. The cold vegetables should be cut in small dice, and the amalgamation must be so cleverly managed as not to allow any one flavor to predominate. Of course this receipt can be greatly modified and still be very appetizing.

CABBAGE SALAD.

Ingredients.—One small head of cabbage, one-half a bunch of celery, one-fourth of a cup of vinegar, one-fourth table-spoonful each of mustard, sugar, pepper, and salt, one egg well beaten.

Take a little of the vinegar to wet the mustard, put the rest over the fire; when boiling stir in the other ingredients and cook until it becomes thick; pour it over the cabbage while hot and mix it well. When cold it is ready for the table. The same sauce, when cold, will do for lettuce.

HERRING SALAD.

Ingredients.—Two dozen potatoes which have been pared and boiled, six salted cucumbers, two gherkins, two dozen apples pared, cold veal, the same quantity as of herring, and four salted herrings which have been soaked in cold water for some hours, then taken out, skinned, and boned.

Chop the veal, herrings, potatoes, apples, cucumbers and gherkins, and some capers, fine. Make the dressing of three table-spoonfuls of olive oil, one table-spoonful of vinegar, a salt-spoon of salt, a pinch of cayenne, one-half tea-spoonful of sugar, three-fourths of a tea-spoonful of dry mustard—mix all together; if too dry a little stock may be added.

This salad must be nicely formed on a dish, rather high in the center, and then can be garnished to taste with beets cut in different shapes; also small pickles, olives, capers, etc. This is excellent.

SAUERKRAUT SALAD.

Chop fine as much onion as is needed to flavor the salad, and salt it well. Mix it with the cold sauerkraut, and allow all to stand until the kraut has the flavor of the onion. Make a dressing of sour cream and a little vinegar, pour it over the mixture and serve.

SALMON MAYONNAISE.

Drain thoroughly half a can of salmon, and flake it into rather small pieces. Cover the bottom of a salad bowl with leaves of lettuce, drop in a layer of salmon, season with the French dressing, add small pieces of pickle, capers, or beets, also slices of hard-boiled eggs; put a few more leaves of lettuce, then another layer of salmon, seasoned as before, and so on until the bowl is full. Mask the top with the mayonnaise sauce, and garnish with lettuce, celery tops, beets, capers, eggs, or anything suitable.

Chicken, cold veal, cold beef, cold mutton, can be made into a mayonnaise in the same way, and all are exceedingly good.

CHICKEN SALAD.

Boil the chicken until tender, pick all the meat from the bones, and free it perfectly from skin, fat and gristle. Use half as much celery as chicken; do not cut either very fine; mix them thoroughly and marinate with the French dressing. Shape in a salad bowl, or on a platter, and mask with mayonnaise sauce. Garnish with the celery tops, capers, olives, beets, etc.

Cabbage (the hard part) can be used in the place of celery. In that case, season with celery salt.

CHAPTER XVII.

PICKLES.

FRENCH PICKLE.

NE peck of green tomatoes chopped fine, six chopped onions, one cup of salt stirred in. Let it stand over night. Drain off the water, then take two quarts of water and one quart of vinegar, boil all together twenty minutes and strain through a colander. Then take two quarts of vinegar, two pounds of sugar, one pound of white mustard seed, two table-spoonfuls each of ground pepper, cinnamon, cloves, ginger, ground mustard. Put all in a kettle and boil fifteen minutes.

MUSTARD PICKLES.

Ingredients.—One hundred small cucumbers, two quarts of silver skinned onions, two quarts of French beans, two cauliflowers, one pint nasturtiums, one dozen small red peppers, one-half pound ground mustard, two quarts vinegar.

Salt each of these vegetables twenty-four hours, then scald them well with vinegar separately and throw the vinegar away; then take one-half pound of ground mustard, beat it smooth with a little vinegar and pour over it two quarts of boiling vinegar.

Mix the pickles thoroughly and pack them as close as possible in bottles, fill with the vinegar and mustard, and seal. This makes an elegant pickle.

RIPE CUCUMBER PICKLES.

Ingredients.—One quart of vinegar, one pound of sugar, spices.

Peel the ripe cucumbers and take out the seeds, cut in lengthwise slices. Mix together the sugar, vinegar, and spices to taste, put in the fruit and let the whole stand over night. In the morning boil all together until the cucumber is tender.

CHOPPED PICKLE.

Ingredients.—Cut four cabbages as for slaw, one dozen green peppers, one peck of green tomatoes, one dozen cucumbers.

Chop all together; sprinkle with salt and let stand over night; drain off all the water. To every quart of the mixture add one pint of onions, chopped and scalded; stir them in with the other ingredients, put in a jar, and cover with vinegar, and let it stand twenty-four hours; then drain and put a layer of the mixture, a layer of ground mace, with black and white mustard seed alternately. Take vinegar enough to cover it, add spices, and to every quart of vinegar add one-half pound of brown sugar. Boil and pour over while hot. This makes a splendid pickle.

PICKLED PLUMS.

Ingredients.—One peck of plums, one pint of vinegar, one ounce of cloves, one ounce of cinnamon, four pounds of sugar.

Boil the vinegar, sugar and spices together; pour boiling hot over the fruit, leave two days. Drain the fruit, boil the liquor, and pour again boiling hot over the fruit.

SPICED CURRANTS.

Ingredients.—Seven pounds of currants, three and one-half pounds of sugar, one pint of vinegar, one table-spoonful of cloves, one table-spoonful of cinnamon, one tea-spoonful of mace.

Can while hot.

SPICED PEACHES.

To seven pounds of fruit add three pounds of sugar, one pint of vinegar, cloves, cinnamon, and a little mace. Pour this syrup boiling hot over the peaches for nine mornings.

GREEN TOMATO SWEET PICKLES.

Three pounds of white sugar to one quart of vinegar, and spice to suit the taste; put in a porcelain lined kettle and let it come to a boil; have ready six pounds of green tomatoes unpared, sliced or whole as you prefer; drop them in and cook until tender.

PICKLED CABBAGE.

Take the red cabbage, remove the outer leaves, and shred; sprinkle thoroughly with fine salt; let it remain with salt two days, removing the water; make a pickle with vinegar, four ounces each of ground pepper and ground ginger, and one ounce of cloves and boil it; put the cabbage in jars, packing closely; when the vinegar with spices is on the boil fill up the jars. Will be good to eat in a week.

GREEN TOMATO PICKLES.

Ingredients.—One peck green tomatoes, ten white onions, six green peppers, one small box of mustard, two quarts of vinegar, one and one-half pints of salt, one-half pound of white mustard seed, one-fourth of a pound of whole cloves, one table-spoonful of black pepper.

Cut the onions and tomatoes in thin slices and chop the peppers fine; make layers of them in a large stone pot and sprinkle each layer with salt; let them stand twenty-four hours and then drain off the brine. Put tomatoes, onions, and peppers in a preserving kettle, sprinkle on each layer the mustard seed, spice, and pepper, and so fill the kettle. The mustard should be thoroughly mixed with the vinegar and thrown into the kettle after everything else is in. Stew slowly over a moderate fire for three-quarters of an hour.

MIXED PICKLES.

Ingredients.—Half a peck of green tomatoes, one cabbage, one dozen onions, and other vegetables you may like; slice them and sprinkle with salt; let them stand one night; then wash them with cold water and wring dry in a cloth. Put them on to boil, covering well with vinegar, in which are mixed two tablespoonfuls of mustard, two ounces of white mustard seed, one ounce each of cloves, allspice, celery seed, and turmeric powder, and one-half a pound of brown sugar. Boil until tender.

CHAPTER XVIII.

EGGS, OMELETTES, AND CHEESE FONDUS.

FRIED EGGS.

F one has an *egg fry-pan*, it is an easy matter to fry eggs. Fill the little cups partly full of lard, or the grease from fried ham or salt pork; drop in the eggs, being careful not to break the yolks; turn them if liked that way, and slip carefully out.

If one has only a common spider, it is still no difficult matter to fry an egg properly. Have enough grease in the spider to nearly cover the eggs; dip it over the surface and fry carefully. Take out without breaking. Do not put more eggs in the spider than you can keep separated. It is a good plan to put muffin rings in the spider, or saucepan, and drop the eggs in these. This keeps them in good shape. If they are ragged when done, trim the edges.

POACHED EGGS.

Let the water boil *before*, but not *after* the eggs are dropped in. Salt the water and add a very little vinegar. Drop the eggs into muffin rings as above described, and when they are done take up on a skimmer, or on a pancake turner.

It is, of course, easier to poach them in a regular "egg poacher."

BEATEN OMELETTE.

Never use more than three eggs; beat the whites and yolks separately, the whites very stiff; the yolks but little; add a salt-spoonful of salt and half the amount of pepper to the yolks before beating; when both are beaten, whisk them delicately together; then put a spoonful of butter into a sauce-pan; let both butter and saucepan be hot; pour in the egg, heap it to one side,

223

and keep it free from the botttom by lifting it occasionally with a silver fork, and by shaking the pan; when brown on the under side, turn, then slip off on to a hot platter. One egg treated in this way will make an omelet large enough for one person.

FOLDED, OR ROLLED OMELETTE.

Break three eggs into a bowl, add a half salt-spoonful of pepper, and a salt-spoonful of salt. Give the egg seven or eight beats with the spoon; have ready on the stove a hot saucepan with a good lump of butter melted in it; pour in the egg; as it sets on the bottom prick with a fork, but do not stir; keep it free from the bottom of the saucepan, and when creamy in the center, either roll, or fold, serving at once on a hot platter.

These omelettes may be varied *ad infinitum.* Chopped parsley, mushroom, and onion sprinkled over the folded omelette, just before folding, gives an *"Omelette aux Fines Herbes."*

Chopped ham added in the same way, makes a *ham omelette.* And one may use jelly, or sweetmeats in the place of the herbs or ham, and so the omelette may be varied to suit the taste.

SCALLOPED EGGS

Ingredients.—Six eggs, five table-spoonfuls of minced ham, a little chopped parsley, a very little minced onion, three spoonfuls of cream and one spoonful of melted butter, salt and pepper to taste, one-half a cup of bread crumbs moistened in milk, and a spoonful of melted butter.

Line the bottom of a small dish, well buttered, with the soaked bread crumbs; put upon these a layer of chopped ham, seasoned with the onion and parsley. Set in the oven, closely covered, until smoking hot. Beat up the eggs to a stiff froth, season with pepper and salt; stir in the cream and a spoonful of melted butter; pour evenly upon the layer of ham. Put the dish, uncovered, back into the oven and bake until the eggs are "set."

SHIRRED EGGS.

Ingredients.—Six eggs, three table-spoons of gravy—from poultry is best—enough fried toast to cover the bottom of a flat dish, a very little grated cheese, one tea-spoonful of butter.

Melt the butter in a frying pan; when hot break into this the eggs; stir in the gravy, pepper and salt to taste, and continue to stir very quickly and well up from the bottom, until the whole is a soft yellow mass.   Have ready in a flat dish the fried toast, spread thinly with anchovy paste; sprinkle the grated cheese over this; heap the shirred egg in the center and serve before it has time to harden.

EGG ROLLS.
(German Receipt.)

Allow one egg for each person, three-quarters of a pint of milk and four tea-spoonfuls of flour for every three eggs. Beat whites and yolks separately; mix the flour smoothly with the milk, then add the eggs and whisk well. Try a little at a time in a buttered omelet pan. Roll as an omelet; serve very hot; to be eaten with sugar or molasses.

SWISS EGGS.

Butter well a dish that will stand the heat of the oven, line the sides of the dish with shavings of good cheese. Drop on to the already buttered dish five or six raw eggs; pour over them about three table-spoonfuls of good cream. Season with salt, cayenne and a small grate of nutmeg.

Sprinkle a little grated cheese over all and two table-spoonfuls more cream. Place in the oven for about seven minutes or until the eggs are set.

CURRIED EGGS.

Cut a couple of onions into slices and fry them to a light golden color in plenty of butter; add one table-spoonful of curry powder and a sprinkling of flour, moisten with a cupfull of stock and simmer gently for ten minutes. Then add six hard boiled eggs cut into slices; simmer for a few minutes longer and serve.

EGGS À LA CRÈME.

Boil twelve eggs just hard enough to allow you to cut them in slices—cut some crusts of bread very thin, put them in the bottom and around the sides of a moderately deep dish, place the eggs in, strewing each layer with stale bread grated and some pepper and salt.

Sauce à la crème, for the eggs.—Put a quarter of a pound of butter, with a large table-spoonful of flour rubbed well into it

15

in a sauce pan; add some chopped parsley, a little onion, salt, pepper, nutmeg, and a gill of cream; stir it over the fire until it begins to boil, then pour it over the eggs, cover the top with grated bread, set in the oven and when a light brown send it to the table.

TO KEEP EGGS FRESH.

(Our Continent.)

At a recent farmers' convention in Iowa it was decided that well-dried oats not less than a year old were the best medium for packing; and cold storage, at a temperature ranging from 40° to 42° was also an essential, though they must be used almost immediately when taken out of cold storage, as they soon spoil. If kept in paper cases they will become musty, as the eggs sweat in changes of temperature, the paper becomes damp, and in time taints the eggs. In all cases they should be stood upon the small end, as in this position they keep fully a month longer. Dry salt has been found good for storing small quantities for family use. Dipping the eggs in melted tallow, covering them with a brine made of one pint of slacked lime, one pint of salt, two ounces of cream tartar, and four gallons of water has proved very effectual; the rule for brine covering two hundred.

TOMATO OMELET.

Ingredients.—One-half can of tomatoes, drained and chopped fine, five eggs beaten together, one small cup of bread crumbs; season to taste.

Stir in spider until it thickens. Cook with plenty of butter.

BREAD OMELET.

Put into a tea-cup of bread crumbs, a tea-cup of sweet cream, a spoonful of butter and salt and pepper to taste. When the bread has softened break in four eggs, beat all together and fry like a plain omelet.

ANCHOVY OMELETTE.

Ingredients.—Two eggs, salt, pepper, half tea-spoonful of anchovy essence, four anchovies.

Season the yolks of the eggs with the salt, pepper and essence. Cut the four anchovies into small pieces. Beat the whites of eggs to a stiff froth, blend gently with the yolks and put in a well-buttered saucepan over the fire. Drop in the pieces of anchovy, and keep the egg well to one side of the saucepan. When it is browned on the bottom put in the oven to set.

CHEESE OMELETTE.

Two whites and three yolks beaten together. Add salt and pepper, and one ounce of Parmesan cheese, grated. Beat it thoroughly; add one table-spoonful of sweet cream; put into a well-buttered saucepan, stir from the bottom until it begins to thicken well, then heap it to one side of the saucepan and keep it in good shape until it is brown on the bottom and sufficiently firm. Put more butter in the saucepan if necessary. When done turn out on a warm plate.

CARROT OMELETTE.

Use rather more of potatoes than carrots. Boil well and run them through a sieve; stir well in a good table-spoonful of butter, one egg, and seasoning. Butter and crumb a pie dish; pour the mixture in, thickly crumb the top and spread with bits of butter. Bake and turn out.

CHEESE FONDU—MELTED CHEESE.

Ingredients.—One cup of bread crumbs, very dry and fine, two scant cups of milk, rich and fresh, one-half pound dry old cheese, grated, three eggs whipped very light, one small table-spoonful of melted butter, season to suit, a pinch of soda, dissolved in hot water and stirred into the milk.

Soak the crumbs in the milk, beat into these the eggs, the butter, seasoning, lastly the cheese. Pour the *fondu* into a buttered dish, strew dry bread crumbs over the top, and bake in a rather quick oven until delicately browned. Serve immediately in the baking dish, as it soon falls.

CHEESE SCALLOP.
(German Receipt.)

Soak a small tea-cupful of stale bread crumbs in fresh milk. Beat into this one large egg, a tea-spoonful of melted butter, and three ounces of grated cheese, pepper and salt to taste. Strew sifted crumbs on the top, and bake till it is a delicate brown.

COTTAGE CHEESE.

To be in perfection, cottage cheese must be made from fresh clabbered milk. Skim the sour milk, and set a gallon or two of it on the back part of the stove in a milk pan, and let it gradually heat until it is lukewarm all through. Stir it occasionally to prevent its hardening at the bottom. When it is a little warmer than new milk, and the whey begins to show clear around the curd, pour it all in a thin, coarse bag, tie it close, and let it hang up to strain two or three hours in a cool place; then take from the bag and keep the contents in a covered dish. When preparing for a meal, mix with the curd rich, sweet cream, sugar and nutmeg. It is even better to add a little fresh butter and salt, then those preferring sugar can use it in addition, and those who like it without the sugar can also be suited.

CHAPTER XIX.

FRUITS AND JELLIES.

PREPARING FRUITS FOR CANNING.

OIL cherries moderately, five minutes; raspberries moderately, six minutes; blackberries moderately, six minutes; plums moderately, ten minutes; strawberries moderately, eight minutes; whortleberries five minutes; pie plant, *sliced*, ten minutes; small sour pears, *whole*, thirty minutes; Bartlett pears, in halves, twenty minutes; peaches, in halves, eight minutes; peaches, whole, fifteen minutes; pine-apple, sliced, half an inch thick, fifteen minutes; Siberian or crab-apple, whole, twenty-five minutes; sour apples quartered, ten minutes; ripe currants, six minutes; wild grapes, ten minutes; tomatoes, twenty minutes.

The amount of sugar to a quart should be: for cherries, six ounces; raspberries, four ounces; Lawton blackberries, six ounces; field blackberries, eight ounces; whortleberries, four ounces; quince, ten ounces; small sour pears, whole, eight ounces; wild grapes, eight ounces; peaches, four ounces; Bartlett pears, six ounces; pine-apples, six ounces; Siberian or crab-apples, eight ounces; plums, eight ounces; pie plant, ten ounces; sour apples, quartered, six ounces; ripe currants, eight ounces.

CURRANT JELLY.

(Home Messenger Cook Book.)

This receipt is the only one which we will *warrant* to make good jelly against odds. We have made jelly by it on the fifth of July, and on the fifteenth, and each time it was a perfect success. While we recommend all persons to make their jelly from fresh fruit early in the season, we can still assure those who are

229

behindhand that they need not despair of jelly that will set firm
and hard later in the season.

Run the currants through your hand, picking out the leaves
and any stray thing that may adhere to them, but leaving the
currants on their stems. Weigh the fruit, being accurate in
remembering the number of pounds. Put a pint of water into
the preserving kettle, and add a bowl or two of currants, mashing and pressing them until you have sufficient juice to cover
the bottom of the kettle; then add the remainder of the currants;
let them come to a boil, and boil at least twenty minutes, of
course stirring and pressing them from time to time, that they
may not burn. Have a three-cornered bag of thin, but strong,
unbleached cotton, that has been well scalded and wrung till almost dry; hang it up and pour the boiled currants into it. Let
it drip into a stone crock all night, but by no means squeeze it;
the currants will drain perfectly dry. In the morning, pour
the strained juice into a preserving kettle without measuring;
let it come to a boil and boil throughly for three or four minutes, then pour in half as many pounds of sugar as you had
pounds of currants. For instance, a peck of currants will probably weigh twelve pounds, therefore, use six pounds of sugar.
The moment the sugar is entirely dissolved the jelly is done. To
make sure that the sugar is entirely dissolved, see that it begins
to jelly on the ladle. It will look thick, and drop thick and a
little stringy, but if let heat beyond this point it will lose its
thickness, and not jelly nearly so well, and always disappoints
you if you lose faith in your instructions and insist upon "letting it come to a boil," All the boiling is done *before* the sugar
is added.

RHUBARB JELLY

Peel and cut up quite small some fresh rhubarb, put it into a
preserving pan with a very little water, and the thin rind of
half a lemon to every pound of fruit. Boil until reduced to a
pulp. Strain the juice, weigh it, and allow one pound of pounded
sugar to every pound of juice. Boil up the juice, add the sugar,
boil, skim, and when it jellies on the skimmer pour into pots,
and tie down when cold.

CLARET JELLY.

One bottle of claret. Put the rind of one lemon, one tea-cupful of red currant jelly, half tea-cupful of brandy, seven ounces of lump sugar, one ounce (or two and one-fourth ounces if liked rather stiff), of isinglass; boil five minutes and strain. Serve with whipped cream.

LEMON JELLY.

Wet quite one-half package of Cox's gelatine. Soak in cold water half an hour. Add the juice of one lemon, one cup of sugar, one pint of boiling water. When the gelatine is all dissolved, strain through a cloth into molds or cups and set in a cold place.

APPLE JELLY.

Boil sour apples until tender in as little water as possible without burning. Strain through a flannel bag. To every pint of juice use one pound of granulated sugar. Boil the juice seven minutes, then add the sugar and boil three minutes longer. Put in tumblers and seal up when cold.

ICELAND MOSS JELLY.

Soak for an hour four table-spoonfuls of the moss in cold water enough to cover it; then stir into it a quart of boiling water and simmer gently until it dissolves; strain, sweeten to taste, flavor with the juice of two lemons and a glass of wine; strain into molds and cool.

CALF'S FOOT JELLY, WITH WINE.

(Francatelli.)

Split two calf's feet, break up the bones, and put the whole into a gallon sized stew-pan, or stock-pot, then add two quarts of cold water and set it on the fire to boil; remove the scum as it rises to the surface, and when the stock has been thoroughly skimmed set it on the back part of the stove, to continue gently boiling for about five hours. The stock must then be strained off through a sieve into a basin or pan and set aside in a cool place until it has become firm. The grease should be scraped off the surface with a spoon, and a little boiling water thrown over it in order to wash away any that may remain. It should then be wiped with a clean cloth and put in a stew-pan to melt over the fire. Next add one pound of loaf sugar, half a pint of sherry, one glass of brandy, six cloves, a half a stick of cinnamon, the rind of two lemons peeled very thin and without any of the pith as this is bitter; then pour in the whites of three eggs and one whole egg whipped up with a little cold water and the bruised shells; whip this well together over the fire, and when it is nearly boiling throw in the juice of four lemons, stir the jelly with the whisk for a minute or so, and then set the stew-pan down by the side of the fire, put on the lid with some live embers upon it and allow the jelly to stand by the side of the stove fire for a quarter of an hour longer, to set the eggs; next throw the jelly into a jelly-bag, fixed on a stand, ready with a basin placed under to receive the jelly as it passes through the bag; continue pouring the jelly back again through the bag until it runs quite bright and clear; then cover over the stand with a cloth and leave the jelly to run until the whole is passed.

This kind of jelly may either be served in glasses or set in molds imbedded in ice; when it has become quite firm, dip the mold in hot water, wipe it and turn the jelly out carefully on its dish.

CLARIFICATION OF CALF'S FOOT JELLY, FOR GENERAL PURPOSES.

Put the prepared stock of two calf's feet into a stew-pan with a pound of sugar, the rind of two lemons and the juice of four; whip three whites and one whole egg together, with a quarter of a pint of spring water, throw this in with the stock, and whisk the whole together over the fire until it is on the point of boiling, then add the juice of half a lemon and a little spring water; withdraw the jelly from the stove and set it down by the side, to continue gently simmering for about ten minutes longer, covered with the stew-pan lid containing some live embers of charcoal. The jelly may then be passed through the bag in the usual way, and when it has run through perfectly bright, let it be kept in a cool place to be used as occasion may require.

This kind of foundation or stock jelly, prepared without any decided flavor, may be used for making all kinds of jellies, it will then be only necessary to add, to the quantity required to fill a mold, a gill and a half of any kind of *liqueur*, and if the jelly be too stiff, a little thin syrup may also be added. It may be used likewise to make fruit jellies, with the addition of a pint of the filtered juice of currants, raspberries, cherries, or strawberries, or half a pint of the clarified infusion syrup of peaches, apricots, or pine-apples.

PRESERVED CUCUMBERS.
(German way.)

Pick and cut in long slices fifteen cucumbers, sprinkle them with a handful of salt and let stand over night, then take them out and dry them on a napkin.

Put two quarts of vinegar on the fire and boil the cucumbers in it till tender. Let them stand over night in this vinegar, then take out and dry, and put in a jar with alternate layers of herbs and button onions, the upper layer being herbs; the herbs used are terragon and mint. Then boil one quart of wine vinegar with half a pound of loaf sugar, skim it and when cold pour over the cucumber and tie up the jar well.

PRESERVED PLUMS.
(German way.)

The plums are washed and dried, then put into a jar, and for one peck boil three-fourths of a quart of wine vinegar with one pound of sugar, skim it well and pour over the plums when cold. After one or two days strain off the vinegar and boil it up again and pour over the plums when cold. Repeat this operation three times, at intervals of one or two days. The last time boil some cloves and cinnamon with the vinegar; prick the plums with a fork in several places before the vinegar is poured over them to keep them from shriveling.

PRESERVED CRANBERRIES.
(German way.)

The cranberries are picked over, washed and dried on a colander; then they are boiled in their own juice. To one peck, one and one-fourth pounds of sugar are added, boil down and skim well. Then put them in a jar, mixing with them ground allspice, cloves and cinnamon.

PRESERVED MELONS.

(German way.)

The melons are pared, sliced, and put on a dish in layers with sugar, the upper layer being of sugar. Then, for a large muskmelon, boil one gill of vinegar with three pounds of sugar, skim it well. In this the slices of melon are put and boiled till tender, carefully skimming. Repeat this operation at intervals of one or two days, until the juice becomes thick.

SPICED CURRANTS.

Ingredients.—Five pounds of currants, four pounds of sugar, one pint of vinegar, four tea-spoonfuls each of cinnamon and cloves.

Boil three hours; no pepper or salt; delightful with venison or mutton.

MACEDOINE OF FRUITS.

Stew carefully some pears, apples, plums, cherries and apricots, or any variety of fruit that may be convenient, and cut up into pieces. Prepare a gelatine jelly, flavored with half a tumbler full of champaigne (or any wine which is convenient, good currant or sherry). Fill a mold with alternate layers of jelly and fruit and serve after freezing. If the fruit is very ripe it is better not to cook it. Indeed, no soft fruit, strawberries, etc., requires cooking for macedoine. The jelly may if preferred be flavored with lemon instead of wine.

APPLE MARMALADE.

Wipe the apples well, but do not peel them, core and quarter them and cut in thin slices. If the apples are very small ones, there will be an excess of skin in the marmalade; to counteract this and provide more pulp, a few large apples must be peeled and added to the rest. Have ready some syrup, made in the proportion of three pounds of sugar to a pint of water, and boil quickly for five minutes; moist sugar will do if a brown marmalade is not objected to, but loaf sugar makes it transparent and finer flavored. Into this boiling syrup throw the sliced apple, and boil rather rapidly for one hour, reckoning from the time of its first boiling up, stirring frequently. It should then be clear, jellified and rather stiff. The rapid boiling drives off the watery particles in steam, and on this depends much of the success in keeping the marmalade from fomentation. Allow three pounds of sugar to four pounds of apples. Some people like cloves, cinnamon or lemon peel added as flavoring; but in this marmalade the natural flavor of the apples is so nicely preserved that it is almost a pity to spoil it.

PEACH MARMALADE.

To make peach marmalade, pare, stone and weigh the fruit, heat slowly to draw out the juice, stirring up often with a wooden spoon. After it is hot, boil quickly, still stirring, three-fourths of an hour; add then the sugar, allowing three-fourths of a pound to each pound of fruit. Boil up well for five minutes, taking off every particle of skum; add the juice of one lemon to every three pounds of fruit, and the water in which one-fourth of the peach kernels have been boiled and steeped. Stew all together for ten minutes more, stirring to a smooth paste. Put it up hot in air tight cans, or if you prefer to, put it in glass jars, put it in them when nearly cold and put white paper on the top of each jar.

APPLE GINGER.

Seven pounds of apples, pared and cored; seven pounds of pounded loaf sugar, two ounces of ground ginger, the juice of three lemons, one pint of water. Boil slowly rather more than half an hour. Put in molds and cover.

STEWED APPLES FOR CHILDREN.

Peel and core as many apples as are required, take the peel and cores and put them in a baking dish, with as much water as is required to stew the apples in afterward, add two cloves and a table-spoonful of raw sugar; let them stew until tender, then pour the juice through a sieve upon the apples that are peeled and quartered, and put them in the oven and stew until tender. Do the same with the peels and cores when making pies or puddings with apples.

TO BAKE APPLES FOR CHILDREN.

Core, but do not peel them; into the hole that is made with the corer put plenty of sugar. Take a baking tin and strew it well with sugar, then pour a little water on it; then put the apples on the tin and bake them till thoroughly done. A delicious jelly will be thrown out, and if the sight of the tin is disliked, it must all be scraped up and served on the dish with the apples.

ICED APPLES.

Pare and core one dozen large apples, fill with sugar, very little butter and nutmeg or cinnamon; bake till *just done.* Let them cool and remove without breaking to another dish; have some icing prepared, lay on top and sides and return to the oven to brown slightly. Serve with cream.

CHAPTER XX.

BEVERAGES.

TEA MAKING.

IE the quantity of tea you think sufficient very loosely in a thin muslin bag, or inclose it in one of the little wire balls that are made for this purpose. Put it into an urn or silver kettle with a spirit lamp beneath; pour boiling water over it, and when it has stood a few moments take out the tea and light the lamp. Tea is none the worse for boiling or being kept hot, if the tea leaves have been removed.

The principle in good tea-making is to keep the infusion as free from tannin as possible, therefore it should not be allowed to draw for longer than three minutes at the most. A perfect cup of tea should be a delicate brown, with a golden tinge changing to a light yellow when the cream is added.

This is the English method. My way is to allow one tea-spoonful of tea to every person; enclose the tea in the tea ball, pour over it water *that has just come to the boil* and let it steep five minutes. Steep it always in an earthenware steeper. Let both steeper and tea be hot when the water is poured on. After the tea has steeped sufficiently, remove the tea ball, and serve, if possible, in the same pot in which it was steeped.

COFFEE.

Buy coffee by the quantity and always brown and grind it yourself. Use one-third Mocha and two-thirds Old Government Java. Brown evenly and thoroughly and only a little at a time, and keep it in a tightly covered can or bottle. Allow one table-spoonful of coffee for a person, if liked only medium strong. Beat an egg, shell and all, with the ground coffee, add enough

237

cold water to cover it, and let it stand an hour or so; it may be prepared in this way, for breakfast, the night before, if only it is kept closely covered. Half an hour before it is needed, pour boiling water over it, all that will be needed, stir it thoroughly, cover it tight, and cover the spout also, and put on the stove where it will keep boiling hot, but not actually boil. *Serve in the same coffee-pot in which it is made.* See that the spout is free from setlings.

Coffee is sometimes made in this way, and called,

GOLDEN COFFEE.

For two persons take two table-spoonfuls of ground coffee, tie up in a piece of Swiss muslin, leaving room for expansion, pour on one pint of boiling water, cover close and set on the back of the stove for twenty minutes. Beat one egg with a Dover egg-beater thoroughly, divide it into two coffee-cups, and add the usual quantity of sugar for each. Hold the coffee-pot high up, pour the boiling coffee on the egg, and add warm milk, and with the golden foam standing above the rim of the cup you will have a pretty picture to look at, and a delicious drink to partake of.

CHERRY SYRUP.

Pick the stems off some cherries, not too ripe, crush and leave them twenty-four hours; pass through a hair sieve first, thoroughly pressing the crushed fruit, then through a filter. To eighteen ounces of the liquid add two pounds of loaf sugar, in a copper preserving pan; just allow it to boil, clearing away any scum as it rises; when cool, pour into bottles, pint size being best.

RHUBARB WINE.

Cut in small pieces as you would for pies one peck of rhubarb; pour three quarts of boiling water on it and let it stand one week, stirring and mashing it every day; squeeze through a coarse cloth and add three pounds of good brown sugar to one gallon of juice; let stand in a jug loosely corked until October, then rack off and bottle tight.

Blackberry, currant, cherry, and other berries may be made into wine the same way, except that the proportion of water is, one gallon of boiling water to one gallon of fruit.

RASPBERRY VINEGAR.

To one gallon of red raspberry juice, add one quart of good cider vinegar, four pounds of white sugar; mix well and let it stand twelve hours, strain, put on the stove and let it boil up, then bottle and seal while hot. It will keep for years and it makes a delicious cooling drink for sick or well in hot weather.

RASPBERRY ACID.

Dissolve five ounces of tartaric acid in one quart of cold water, pour it on twelve pounds of fruit in a large jar, let it stand twenty-four hours, strain it from the fruit without pressing, and to every pint of juice put one and one-fourth pounds of pounded loaf sugar; stir with a wooden spoon until the sugar is all dissolved. Let it stand a day or two, then take off the scum and bottle.

GOOSEBERRY SYRUP.

Four pounds of gooseberries, not too ripe, one pound of ripe cherries, and one-half pound of red raspberries; crush all together and then leave them to ferment in an earthen jar for twenty-four hours. After this, if the juice looks fairly clear, put the fruit in a large clean hair sieve and press the juice through with the hands. Weigh the liquid thus passed, and to one and one-fourth pounds of liquid add two pounds of white sugar; melt over a clear fire, and after boiling up four separate and distinct times, take it off the stove, skim, and pour gently in a large earthen vessel. When quite cold, pour it off into pint bottles, well cork them, and keep in a cool place.

BARLEY WATER.

Add two ounces of pearl barley to half a pint of boiling water; let it simmer five minutes, drain, and add two quarts of boiling water; add two ounces of sliced figs and two ounces of stoned raisins; boil until reduced to a quart; strain for drink. This is very nutritious for an invalid.

JELLICE.

One-half a tea-spoonful of currant, lemon, or cranberry jelly put into a goblet; beat well with two table-spoonfuls of water;

fill up with ice water, and you have a refreshing drink for a fever patient.

ROOT BEER.

Take one pound of yellow dock roots, one pound of burdock, one pound of sarsaparilla, one pound of hops, a quarter of a pound of spruce twigs, all boiled together in three gallons of water. Strain off the liquor, add six gallons more of water, one gallon of molasses, and one pint of good yeast; fill the cask full that it is put in and leave out the bung for the skum to overflow. When the fermentation ceases, stop it up tight and you will have a healthy, blood cleansing and refreshing beverage that will strengthen and invigorate the system. Add ice in the summer.

GINGER BEER.

Take one table-spoonful of ginger, one of cream tartar, one pint of yeast, one pint of molasses, and six quarts of water. Stir well together and set in a warm place. When it begins to ferment bottle it up and in eight hours it will be good to use and will keep good several days.

RASPBERRY WINE.

To every quart of ripe fruit put one quart of soft water. Mash them and let them stand two days, then strain, and to every gallon put three pounds of sugar. In two months bottle it and to each bottle add a wine-glass of brandy.

ORANGE AND LEMON SYRUP.

Put one pint of cold sugar syrup in an earthen jar with the rind of six oranges and three lemons, or *vice versa;* cover the jar, and let the contents infuse for twenty-four hours. Press the juice from the oranges and lemons into a quart of water, pass the whole through a tammy, a silk one, if possible. Put three pounds of cut loaf sugar and the juice as above into a preserving pan on a clear bright fire; let the whole melt and heat until it arrives at a heat corresponding to thirty-two degrees of a saccharometer. Pour into an earthen jar and let it cool. Then bottle for use.

SWISS BLACKBERRY WINE.

(Said to be excellent and medicinal.)

To one bushel of berries put two gallons of water and express the juice. To each gallon of the liquid add one pound of refined white sugar; put in a cask a peck of freshly burned charcoal broken up in small pieces; then pour the liquid upon it. Let it ferment; when done, close the cask tight. Let it remain till January, then draw off and bottle.

BLACKBERRY WINE.

To every gallon of crushed berries add one quart of boiling water; let it stand twenty-four hours, then squeeze through a jelly bag. To every gallon of juice add two pounds of good brown sugar, the whites of two eggs well beaten and stirred in the juice. Pound some cloves, cinnamon and nutmeg together. tie them in a muslin bag and drop them into the juice. Put the mixture in a jug or cask till done working, then cork close and in four months bottle. It will improve with age.

16

CHAPTER XXI.

MISCELLANEOUS.

BEEF TEA.

(By Dr. Chambers.)

AKE the cook understand that the virtue of beef tea is to contain all the contents and flavors of lean beef in a liquid form; and that its vices are to be sticky and strong, and to set in a hard jelly when cold. When she understands this, let her take half a pound of fresh killed beef for every pint of beef tea required, and remove all fat, sinew, veins and bone. Let it be cut up into pieces under half an inch square, and soak for twelve hours in half a pint of cold water. Let it then be taken out and simmered for two hours in one pint of water, the quantity lost by evaporation being replaced from time to time. The boiling liquor is then to be placed on the cold liquor, in which the meat was soaked. The solid meat is to be dried, pounded in a mortar, freed from all stringy parts, and mixed with the rest.

When the beef tea is made daily, it is convenient to use one day's boiled meat for the next day's tea, as thus it has time to dry and is easier pounded.

A wholesome flavoring for beef tea is fresh tomato. A piece of green celery stalk, or a small onion, and a few cloves, may also be boiled in it.

Beef tea and broth should not be kept hot, but heated up as required.

BEEF TEA.

Cut a pound of the round steak into small pieces; pour over it a cup of cold water and let it stand one hour; pour them into a glass fruit jar, screw on the cover, put over the stove in cold water and bring *nearly* to a boil. Strain the liquor off, after it has remained at nearly the boiling point for an hour or so, season with salt, and it is ready to use.

TOMATO BUTTER.

Ingredients.—Nine pounds of tomatoes, three pounds of brown sugar, one pint of good vinegar, three table-spoonfuls of cinnamon, one table-spoonful of cloves.

Cook well. Boil three hours.

CANNING SWEET CORN.

Cut the corn raw from the cobs; to every six quarts of corn allow one ounce tartaric acid dissolved in water; put the corn, with sufficient water to keep it from burning, over the stove; when it boils add the tartaric acid; when the corn is parboiled can as you can tomatoes, using, however, glass jars instead of tin. When the corn is opened for use, turn it into a colander and pour cold water over it until the sour taste is removed. Add a small lump of soda when cooking.

PASTE FOR CLEANING BRASS.

Quarter of a pound of soft soap, one ounce of spirits of wine, four ounces of well ground rotten stone, one tea-spoonful of sweet oil. Mix and keep in a jar. This has been in use fifty years.

TO CLARIFY DRIPPING.

Take the dripping hot from the fire and pour it into a basin with half a pint of boiling water, stir well, and let it stand until cold. The impurities will settle in the water and at the bottom of the cake of fat; this can be scraped off with a knife, when the dripping will be quite pure.

TO PRESERVE MEAT OR FISH FRESH.

Cover with a solution of borax and water—one-fourth of a pound of borax to one gallon of water. Add a little salt if you choose. Dissolve the borax in a little hot water, and then add the rest of the water cold. Cool the whole, and it is ready to use.

RECEIPT FOR BRONCHITIS.

Ingredients.—One pound of baking pears, half a pound of raw sugar, one pint of vinegar. Simmer all together four or five hours and bottle.

TO DETECT ADULTERATION IN MUSTARD.

Drop a few drops of ammonia on it. If red pepper is present it will turn red; if not it will remain a greenish yellow.

POMADE.

Ingredients.—Two ounces of white wax, six ounces of castor oil, two ounces of lard, one ounce of oil of sweet almonds, one-half ounce of citronella.

Melt and mix together, and beat to a light froth.

JAPANESE CREAM.

(Very good for cleaning men's clothing and dark dresses.)

Ingredients.—Four ounces each of white castile soap and ammonia, two ounces each of alcohol and ether, and one ounce of glycerine.

Cut the soap thin; dissolve it in one quart of soft water over the fire; when dissolved add four quarts more of cold soft water, then add the spirits.

TABLE OF DOMESTIC MEASURES OF FLUIDS.

(For medicinal or other purposes.)

Sixty drops, one tea-spoonful or drachm; two tea-spoonfuls, one dessert-spoonful; two dessert-spoonfuls, one table-spoonful, or half an ounce; four table-spoonfuls, one wine-glassful; two wine-glassfuls, one tea-cupful, or one gill.

CANDY.

Ingredients.—One pound of white sugar, two table-spoonfuls of vinegar, one tea-spoonful of cream tartar, one tea-spoonful of butter, one tea-cup of cold water, flavor to suit the taste.

Do not stir until it is done. Fresh lemon may be used in the place of cream tartar.

CARAMELS.

Ingredients.—Two cups of sugar, one cup of molasses, one-half pound of French chocolate, one cup of rich cream, butter the size of a hickory-nut, vanilla.

SUPERIOR CANDY.

Ingredients.—One pound of white sugar, two-thirds of a common tumbler of water, one table-spoonful of good sharp vinegar or lemon juice, a piece of butter the size of a walnut.

Let it dissolve and slowly boil, but do not stir it any. Try it by dipping a little out occasionally from one side until it stiffens in water, then pour out and cut in small pieces.

LEMON TOAST.

Beat the yolks of three eggs and mix them with half a pint of milk. Dip slices of bread into the mixture, then fry them to a delicate brown in butter. Take the whites of two eggs, beat them to a froth, add to them three ounces white sugar and the juice of a small lemon. Stir in a small tea-cup of boiling water and serve as a sauce on the toast.

APRICOT TOAST.

Take some ripe, but not over-ripe, apricots, halve and stone them. Make a syrup with plenty of white sugar and some water; when boiled for a couple of hours strain; lay the pieces of apricot in the syrup and add a glass of white wine; simmer for a few minutes. Cut out of the crumb of a milk loaf some rounds a little larger than the apricots. Fry them a pale yellow in fresh butter, drain and arrange them in a circle on a dish with a piece of apricot on each round, concave side uppermost; put a kernel in the center of each, pour the syrup well over, and serve with some whipped cream in the center of the dish.

CHAPTER XXII.

FOOD.

BY DR. D. S. FAIRCHILD,

Professor of Pathology, Histology, etc., Iowa State College of Agriculture and Mechanic Arts, Ames, Iowa.

FOOD.

ONE of the weightiest influences which determine the life of the individual is the nature of the food he eats. The value of this influence can be plainly traced all along the line of man's advancement from a condition of barbarism up to the highest point of his present civilization; the strength of his muscles, the course of his thoughts and his whole mental tone are determined by the nature of his food. The sum of the factors which influence the welfare of the individual must in like manner influence the welfare of the nation. Accepting the fact that an abundance of nutritious food is necessary to the development of the physical and mental energies of the individual, and that the present welfare and future progress of the nation is dependent upon the physical and mental qualities of its individual members, it is clearly apparent that the first importance should be attached to the quantity and quality, as well as the preparation of the foods which make up our diet.

The economy of nature as illustrated in the development of our digestive organs is directed as far as possible to the reduction of the quantity of the material ingested to the narrowest limits consistant with the character of our diet which is, or should be, selected from every kingdom of nature. Appreciating this fact civilized communities adopt various methods of improving the

quality of grains and vegetables, selecting such varieties as contain the largest amount of nutritive matter and the least amount
of fibrinous or innutritious material, and they also select such
breeds of animals for food purposes as contain the largest amount
of nutritive juices and fat, in the finest and most delicate fibrous
framework. Civilized communities, furthermore, find it greatly
to their advantage to employ the best methods of preparing their
food, consulting both the stomach and the palate in such a
manner that the food shall become palatable and at the same
time digestible. The increasing difficulty of obtaining good
food imperatively demands that the best methods be employed
in utilizing all the nutritive principles therein contained in the
most economical manner. These considerations have already
been recognized in the establishment of schools of cookery in
various countries.

It is a fact well known to physiologists that a normal or
healthy diet cannot be made up of any one kind or class of foods,
but must, on the contrary, contain substances derived from all
classes. Therefore the notion which some people have of con-
fining their diet to some particular kind of food is a false one,
and usually, sooner or later, leads to imperfect nutrition, attended
by a train of difficulties resulting from a loss of balance between
waste and repair in the different tissues, and a consequent im-
pairment of the physical and mental strength and endurance.

The foods which science and experience have taught us to be
necessary for the perfect nourishment of the human body, are
divided into two groups, one of which contains nitrogen and the
other does not. The first, or nitrogenous group, as albumen,
casein, gluten and gelatin, is used in the system in building up
muscular and other tissue, and for the repair of waste or injury
sustained by them. The second, or non-nitrogenous group, as
starch and sugar, oils and fats, are employed largely in the pro-
duction of animal heat. To these must be added the inorganic
substances, as chloride of sodium (common salt), phosphate of
calcium, etc. Now as these substances have their specific offices
to perform in the physical economy, and as one cannot perform
the office of another with any degree of success, it becomes apparent that they must be mixed in varying proportions to form
a normal diet, for while albumen and gluten can supply the tis-

sues with nutritive material, they cannot generate animal heat, and the animal would sooner or later die. On the other hand, while oils and fats, starch and sugar, can produce animal heat and cause fat to be stored up in the system, they cannot supply the needs of the muscles and other tissues. The truth of these observations is established by experiments made in feeding, and furthermore by the fact that foods which form the exclusive diet at certain periods of life contain all of these elements in admixture, as milk and eggs.

The value of certain foods may depend quite as much on their digestibility as on the relative qualities of the necessary elements which they contain. Moreover, the quantity and kind of food to be taken with the greatest economy and advantage cannot be settled for each individual, except by a consideration of the exact quantities of certain elements that are required. Much will depend upon the habits and digestive powers of· the individual. Food, which to one person is appropriate, may be quite unfit for another, and the changes of diet so instinctively practiced by all to whom they are possible, further indicate that the varying necessities of the body are determined by the conditions of waste · and repair.

The adult human being does not find in any one kind of food all of the material the body requires, otherwise, one might suffice for all his wants. It is by a combination of foods that the requirements are met, each substance contributing to one or more of the wants of the system. Some foods are more valuable than others in that they supply a greater number of the substances which the body requires. Animal food, as flesh or muscular tissue contains the elements which our system needs as flesh-formers, and also as heat-generators, and life may be maintained for very long periods if it be eaten in large quantities. Since the source of flesh in animals used as food is found in vegetables, it follows that vegetables should have the same elements as flesh, and it is a fact of great interest that in vegetables we have foods closely analagous to the flesh of animals, hence our appetites and the demands of our system cause us to extend our choice to both the animal and vegetable kingdoms.

SAVORY GRAVY.

Mince one onion fine; fry it in butter to a dark brown, and stir in a table-spoonful of flour. After one minute add half a pint of broth, or stock, pepper, salt, and a very small quantity of Worcester sauce.

PLAIN DUTCH SAUCE, OR SAUCE HOLLANDAISE.

Pour half a pint of drawn butter into a small saucepan, add four raw yolks of eggs, a little grated nutmeg, a little pepper, two ounces of fresh butter, and a little salt; stir the sauce briskly on the fire in order to set the yolks; pass it through a fine sieve, add the juice of half a lemon, and serve at once.

SAUCE HOLLANDAISE.

(Dubois' Receipt as given by Mrs. Henderson.)

Pour four table-spoonfuls of good vinegar into a small stew-pan and add a few pepper corns and some salt; let the liquid boil until it is reduced to half; let it cool, then add to it the well beaten yolks of four or five eggs, four ounces of good butter, more salt if necessary, and a very little nutmeg. Set the stew-pan on a very slow fire, and stir the liquid until it is about as thick as cream; immediately remove it. Now put this stew-pan or cup into another pan containing a little warm water kept at the side of the fire. Work the sauce briskly with a spoon, or with a little whisk, so as to get it frothy, but adding little bits of butter, in all about three ounces. When the sauce has become light and smooth it is ready for use.

TOMATO SAUCE.

Stew six tomatoes, or half a can of tomatoes, with a spray of parsley (if it can be had), two cloves, a tea-spoonful of chopped onion, half a tea-spoonful of salt, and a salt-spoon of pepper, half an hour. Strain through a sieve and add a cupful of good beef stock, if you have it. It is, however, very good without. Now put a table-spoonful of butter and a table-spoonful of flour in a saucepan over the fire, and mix well and cook thoroughly. Add the tomato pulp by degrees, stirring constantly. Cook a few moments.

ANIMAL FOODS.

These may be divided into flesh, fish, and fowl, and their products, milk and eggs. Flesh may be divided into lean and fat, the former contains nitrogen and the latter does not. While all kinds of flesh contains nutritive qualities in common, the proportion in which these qualities exists varies. The lean meats are made up mainly of networks of fibres containing a greater or less amount of fat. The fibrous tissue gives rise to the toughness which varies with the age and breeding of the animal; in old animals the fibres are dense and firmer, in young animals more juicy and tender. The aim of modern breeding is to produce the greatest amount of muscle and fat at the earliest period of life, but while delicacy of flavor may thus be obtained, fullness and richness can be produced by age only. Good meat should contain a certain amount of fat mixed with the lean, the relative proportions of which vary both with the animal and the condition in which it is killed. The nutritive value of the fat and lean respectively is much the same in all animals used as food, so that the same weight of lean meat from one animal should nourish the body as well as the same weight from another. As, however, the influence of appetite and relish plays an important part in the phenomena of nutrition, reference should be had to the taste in selecting the particular kind of meat, as this fact will exercise an important influence in digestion and assimilation. All things being considered, beef is the most nutritious and the most easily digested.

The effect of cooking flesh is chiefly physical, rendering the meat more easy of mastication and digestion, but the object may be frustrated if the substance of the flesh be hardened in any appreciable degree. Cooking is also employed to make the food hot when it is eaten, with a view to improve its flavor and to stimulate the sense of taste. The effect of roasting or boiling meat is to decrease its bulk. This loss in bulk and weight is due to the extraction of the juices of so much of the mass of flesh as may be acted on by the heat. These are chiefly water containing salts and the peculiar flavor of meat, with a proportion of fat in a fluid state, gelatine, and perhaps some albumen. If these matters are collected there will be no real loss of nutriment. The difference between roasting and boiling lies chiefly in the fact that in roasting the outside is exposed to the hot air and becomes overcooked before the inside is sufficiently cooked. This occurs to a far greater extent in roasting than in boiling. Stewed meat occupies a position between that of boiled and roast. The degree in which extraction of juices takes place in cooking meat depends upon the method of applying heat and becomes a fundamental question in cookery.

Various methods have been employed for the purpose of preserving meat, the chief of which is salting. Salted meat is much less valuable for food than fresh. The salt extracts a considerable quantity of the juices and so much lessens the nutritive value and natural flavor of the meat. The flesh is also harder, this depending of course considerably on the strength of the saline solution. The introduction of so much salt into the system is prejudicial to health, by inducing a craving for fluids, and by causing indigestion or skin diseases. The capability to nourish the system is lessened by the various effects mentioned.

VEAL.

Veal, while it is sometimes a delicacy when properly killed, is not so valuable as a food as beef, and it is more difficult of digestion, being about equal to pork.

MUTTON.

Mutton is much more valuable than veal as a food, and is more easily digested, but not equal to beef. It is better suited to those who follow sedentary habits than to those who are engaged in much physical labor. Mutton broth has less nutritive value than beef broth, but having a more delicate flavor is preferred by many persons.

PORK.

Pork, having so very large a proportion of fat cannot be regarded as equal to beef or mutton in nourishing the system of those who make much muscular exertion. It is also digested with greater difficulty.

The frequent presence of parasites in pork is an objection to its use as a food, but the danger from these may be obviated by thoroughly cooking the meat.

LEBIG'S EXTRACT OF MEAT AND BEEF TEA.

In preparing these extracts the insoluble and most nutritious parts are left behind. They yield an agreeable flavor and are a valuable addition to other foods. They give a degree of exhilaration which may be useful to the feeble, but a great mistake is made if they are relied upon as a principal diet for the sick. While these substances are not nutritious in themselves, they modify assimilation and nutrition in a useful manner.

EGGS.

Eggs, from the large amount of nutritious matter contained in them, furnish an important article of food. The length of time required to digest them is about the same as for mutton. The manner of cooking eggs exercises an important influence upon their digestibility. When boiled to the extent of slightly hardening the albumen they are, undoubtedly, more easily digested than in any other form. The impression that a raw egg is more readily digested than a cooked one is a mistake. If taken raw they should be beaten thoroughly so as to expose the particles of albumen to the air, otherwise the unboiled white forms a viscid clotted mass of low diffusibility into which the gastric juice permeates with the greatest difficulty. For sick people a compromise may be made by adding a stimulent, both to render the compound more agreeable to the palate and more easily digestible, as for example, wine and egg, or brandy and egg. Poaching is an admirable way of cooking eggs.

POULTRY AND GAME.

The flesh of birds contains relatively less fat and juices than mammals and is, therefore, less nutritious and also less fitted for strong men than for invalids, who require a lighter diet. The flesh of wild birds is closer and firmer than domesticated birds, but the flavor is fuller and stronger. It contains more nitrogen but less fat and is probably less valuable as a food, although wild birds living on insects and grain are both rich and delicate food when properly cooked.

FISH.

Fish, for food purposes, are divided into two classes, white blooded and red blooded. The first may be represented by the cod, and the second by the salmon. The nutritive value of fish varies very considerably. The white fish contain but little oil and are, therefore, less nutitious, while in the salmon the oil is distributed throughout the muscular tissue, which consequently gives them a greater food value. Eels are a luscious and rich food, and possess a high nutritive value. The methods of preparing fish for the table are numerous and may exercise all the skill of the cook.

OYSTERS.

The oyster is not a food of high nutritive value, but its delicacy of flavor makes it useful to the sick. The mode of eating it may depend upon the taste of the individual. The raw oyster is much more easily digested than the cooked, hence in feeble conditions of the stomach, if it can be tolerated, it is to be preferred.

LOBSTER AND CRAB.

These are neither very nutritious nor easy to digest. Their tissues are coarse and tough, and while they are popular as a change of food and as a luxury, they are a frequent cause of indigestion.

CHEESE.

The value of cheese as an article of diet depends upon the variety. Rich cheese of proper age is highly nutritive, and while somewhat difficult to digest in itself, it promotes the digestion of other foods.

MILK.

This is one of the most valuable foods we have. It contains all the elements of nutrition within itself, and in the most digestible form. Whatever the source of milk, it contains essentially the same elements and has always the same qualities. The milk of one animal differs from another only in the relative proportions of these elements. The test of quality is usually the proportion of cream. Cow's milk is the most agreeable to the taste, and differs from human milk chiefly in having a larger proportion of fat and casein, and a less proportion of sugar. If a mixture be made of two-thirds of cow's milk and one-third of warm water, to which half an ounce of sugar of milk, or half that quantity of refined cane sugar, be added to the pint, we shall obtain a composition very similar to that of the mother's milk. Skimmed milk is more nutritive than is generally supposed. It differs from new milk in the removal of nearly all the cream. It is said that if one-fourth or one-half ounce of fat, as suet, to a pint, be added to skimmed milk, it is equal in nutritive value to new milk. The milk of all animals is more easily digested when eaten warm.

BUTTER AND FATS.

The value of these substances in the animal economy is very great, both chemically and physically. Fat supplies the heat forming elements of food, and is more readily transformed than starch. It supplies an essential element in growth, and in the daily use of the body it is necessary that there should be a full supply of fat in some of its forms. It supplies an agreeable flavor, without which bread and farinaceous food could not be readily eaten, and it lubricates the passages, through which the masticated food is more readily conveyed.

VEGETABLE FOODS.

The same nutritive elements exist in vegetables that exist in animal foods, and within certain limits the two classes are interchangeable. They are also divided into flesh formers and into heat givers. The former consists of seeds and vegetable tissues, whilst the latter consists of starch and sugar. That is, seeds when digested will produce flesh, and starch when transformed may produce fat, although the latter is denied by some chemists. The mineral and organic salts which are required for nutrition are also found in the vegetable kingdom. It will be seen that both kingdoms contain the same nutritive elements, and while we may subsist on substances obtained exclusively from one or the other, experience shows that the processes of nutrition can be performed better on a diet derived from both kingdoms in varying proportions. The cooking of flesh is desirable, although it is not necessary to its digestion, but the cooking of seeds is still more so in order to enable the stomach to dissolve and perfectly transform them. It is commonly supposed that the digestion of vegetables is easier than that of animal food, and that the process is more quickly performed, but the experiments of Dr. Beaumont have shown that mutton will be digested more quickly than bread, and an egg earlier than a potato. Another fact of importance is that a greater bulk of vegetable than of animal food is required to provide the necessary amount of nutriment, and hence those who live chiefly on the former must eat larger quantities; otherwise the difference would not be great. Vegetables also require a greater power of digestion, and the vital actions move more slowly.

PEAS AND BEANS.

The most highly nutritious seeds are peas and beans, as they contain a large percentage of nitrogen. It is well known that they must be thoroughly cooked. The time required to digest beans when boiled is from two and one-half to three hours.

INDIAN CORN.

While corn is less nutritious than the leguminous seeds it is more agreeable to the taste, and it is more readily eaten, and at the same time more readily cooked and digested. It contains a larger proportion of nitrogen than wheat and, hence, is a more stimulating food. The time required for the digestion of corn-cake or bread is from three to three and one-half hours.

WHEAT.

This is the most important of the vegetable products as a food. It is preferable to any others on which men chiefly live, since it is a far more agreeable food than corn, and more nutritious than rice. It contains nearly all the essential elements of nutrition. The quality varies with the seed, the cultivation, the season, and the climate. In hot climates and in hot seasons the product is harder and more nitrogenous than that of a wet or cold season. The outside layers of a wheat grain contains a considerable quantity of nitrogen, and are therefore nutritive. The inner part consists largely of starch, hence flour made exclusively of the interior of the grain is relatively poor in nutritive qualities.

The most improved methods of grinding, however, effect a compromise by which a large percentage of the nitrogen-containing-parts are retained in the finest and whitest flour.

Newly made bread is less digestible than that which has been kept for a certain time. This is due to a degree of toughness which renders the bread less capable of mastication, whilst after bread has been kept for a short time it has lost some of its water, and is more friable. It is also probable that new and hot bread is eaten rapidly with less mastication, and is consequently swallowed in larger lumps than old bread. Bread made from good flour is easier to masticate and digest than that made from poor.

RICE.

Rice consists almost exclusively of starch and is relatively deficient in nitrogenous elements, and is therefore inferior to wheat in nutritive value. New rice is said to be inferior in quality to old, as it is much less digestible, and is likely to produce indigestion, diarrhœa, and rheumatism. The time required for the digestion of boiled rice is from one to two hours.

OATMEAL.

Oatmeal is a strong and highly nutritious food, but requires much cooking to break its starch cells, in order to make it easily digested.

VEGETABLES.

The potato is the most important representative of this class, both for nutritive value and for its agreeable flavor. It forms an important article of food for many people. The chemical composition does not differ materially in the several varieties, although there is some difference in flavor which serves as the basis of choice in the different kinds. The relative value of potatoes is determined by their weight, for the heavier they are in relation to size, the more starch they contain. They are deficient in mineral matter and are therefore unfit to be a sole food.

New and waxy potatoes are less digestible than old and mealy ones. The time required for their digestion is from two and a half to three and a half hours.

Cabbage, mustard, radishes, turnips, onions, tomatoes, cucumbers, and pumkin, constitute the least nutritious class of vegetable foods, and are perhaps less valuable for their direct nutritive elements than for their indirect and medicinal and saline juices.

FRUITS.

These are less nutrient foods than luxurious, yet they are additions to a dietary. Their agreeable flavor moistens the mouth and stimulates the sense of taste. They differ in digestibility according to the proportion of fibrous tissue they contain. In such fruits as the strawberry, pine-apple, grape, and banana the cell-wall is very thin and easily broken up, hence digestion is easily performed. All fruits contain much fluid in relation to the solid matter, and supply sugar, acids, salts, and various volatile essences, upon which their flavor depends, and are extremely useful in preserving health and promoting the appetite. A great blessing has been gained by the development of the various methods of preserving fruits in such a manner as to retain their juices, salts, and flavor.

CONDIMENTS.

While condiments are not foods, they are extremely valuable adjuncts to food and useful medicines. They render the food more palatable, stimulate the appetite, and assist in preserving food.

17

CHAPTER XXIII.

FOOD ADULTERATIONS.

BY THOMAS E. POPE.

Professor of Chemistry, Iowa State College of Agriculture and Mechanic Arts, Ames, Iowa.

BAKING POWDERS.

AKING powders are a mixture of bicarbonate of soda with either tartaric acid, cream of tartar, or acid phosphate of lime. The adulterations are generally flour, starch, and alum. The flour and starch being used to increase the weight and bulk, and alum to make the bread white and stiffen the gluten of the flour, so that an inferior flour can be used to make good bread.

To detect flour, and starch, dissolve the powder in water. If nothing but cream of tartar, tartaric acid, and bicarbonate of soda have been used, the powder will dissolve completely. If tartaric acid has been used some flour has to be added to keep the powder from spoiling, and a small amount therefore must not be looked upon as an impurity. Tartaric acid is the most economical to use of the two, one half of the acid properties being neutralized in cream of tartar.

To detect alum see article on flour.

As the value of baking powders depends entirely on the amount of gas they will generate, an estimation of the amount will determine their comparative merits. This can be done roughly as follows:

Wrap some of the baking powder up in porous paper, then fill a pan with warm water, hold a tumbler inclined under the water, when filled with water raise the closed end out, and lift the tumbler as high as possible without letting the mouth come out from the water. Then insert the paper containing the powder quickly under the mouth of the tumbler. As soon as the water sinks through the paper gas will be formed, and the amount in the tumbler will show the value of the powder.

COFFEE.

Raw coffee when shaken up with cold water, allowed to stand for fifteen minutes and filtered, gives a filtrate nearly colorless. The coffee bean is not changed by soaking in warm water, but the imitated bean either crumbles, renders the water turbid, or else changes its color.

Roasted unground coffee when shaken with water floats, but the imitated bean sinks. The water remains colorless if the coffee has not been sprinkled with sugar to glaze before roasting. To test ground roasted coffee, shake three parts of the coffee up with twenty parts of cold water, set aside for half an hour, shake again and filter. The filtrate ought not to be bitter and should be colorless or slightly yellow. Adulterations give a yellow or brown tint and some a bitter taste to the filtrate.

To detect adulterations with wheat, rye, or any substance containing starch, shake up the coffee with a dilute solution of caustic potash, filter, dilute with considerable water, acidify with hydrochloric or sulphuric acid, and add a few drops of iodine solution. The solution will turn blue if starchy adulterations are present.—*From Fresenius' "Zeitscheifs."*

FLOUR.

To detect adulteration with alum, make a solution of logwood by soaking for twenty minutes about two parts of logwood in the form of sawdust, or raspings, with one thousand parts of rain water. This solution must be made up fresh when wanted, and the logwood from which the sawdust is made must be taken from the center of a large piece where it is not exposed to the air. Logwood chips will not do as well, and the extract is of no value at all. Make a solution of carbonate of ammonia by dissolving one part of the salt in three parts of water and one of ammonia. Take about half an ounce of the flour and mix with rain water to a thin paste, add about a table-spoonful of the logwood solution previously mixed with an equal bulk of the carbonate of ammonia; if alum is present the mixture will turn bluish black; if not it remains pink.—*Robbins' test.*

SUGAR.

Pure sugar is soluble in water, and some adulterations, such as starch, terra alba, gypsum, etc., can be detected by their insolubility. To detect glucose, add to the solution of sugar a few drops of a solution of copper sulphate, then enough of a solution of caustic potash to dissolve the precipitate first formed, and boil. A red precipitate proves the presence of glucose, the amount of precipitate depending on the quantity of glucose present.

A simpler method, though not as delicate, is to boil the solution of sugar with a solution of caustic potash; if glucose is present the solution will turn brown, the depth of color depending on the amount of glucose present.

Brown sugars, molasses, and syrups all contain some glucose, and powdered sugar some starch.

TEAS.

To detect coloring or facing material, agitate half an ounce or so of tea in a little warm water for a few minutes, and strain through muslin; the coloring matter will pass through, and, on standing, settle out. Green teas are more apt to be covered with injurious matters than black. Foreign leaves can best be detected after soaking in water, when they unroll and show their form; if the tea is powdered the microscope must be used.

VINEGAR.

To detect the presence of mustard, ginger, or any astringent principle used to give a fictitious strength, add carbonate of soda (washing soda) until there is no more effervescence; any acid or astringent taste will be the test for impurities.

To prove the presence of mineral acids, sulphuric, hydrochloric, etc., boil three or four ounces of vinegar twenty minutes with six or seven grains of powdered starch, then add one or two drops of diluted tincture of iodine; a blue color, the reaction of starch on iodine, will prove the absence of mineral acids. This test is based on the fact that boiling starch with mineral acids changes it to dextrine and glucose; if no mineral acids are present the starch is left unchanged, and gives its characteristic color with iodine.

The strength of vinegars can be roughly ascertained by weighing out one ounce of clear and transparent crystals of washing soda, and slowly pouring on it the vinegar to be tested until active effervescence ceases; this will take place as soon as enough acid has been added to neutralize the soda. One ounce of washing soda will neutralize one-half ounce of acetic acid, the acid of vinegar, and dividing this number by the number of ounces of vinegar used, will give its strength. Good vinegar ought to contain about four and one-half per cent of acid.

WATER.

Water when pure is odorless, colorless, tasteless, and not turned brown by Nessler's solution. The odor is best detected by heating the water nearly to boiling in a clean flask or bottle, shaking and smelling; heating makes the odor stronger. The color can best be observed by holding the bottle, which must be of clear white glass, up to the light, and no particles should be seen floating round in the water.

Nessler's solution had better be prepared at a drug store or by some chemist. The formula is: Dissolve four parts of iodide of potash in ten parts of distilled water, and add while warming powdered red iodide of mercury, until a little remains undissolved, then dilute with forty parts of water; filter and add seventy-five parts of dilute caustic soda solution (one part of soda to twenty of water); let it stand for two days, and decant from any residue that may settle.

Add about a tea-spoonful of the Nessler's solution to a couple of ounces of water in a wine-glass. A brown or red coloration is due to free ammonia, and though harmless in itself, indicates that the water has been contaminated with organic matter which has since been destroyed. Water showing much of a coloration is not fit to drink. A white precipitate is due to lime or magnesia, which makes a water hard but is not unhealthy.

Another simple test for organic impurities is to add a table-spoonful of granulated sugar to a pint of water, pour into a clean glass bottle and set in the sunlight; the bottle must be kept corked loosely. If the water remains clear, it is free from organic mater; if it clouds, it is impure. Water when freezing throws out lime and other inorganic impurities, but retains much of the organic matter, and ice made from impure water is unfit to drink.

CHAPTER XXIV.

ANTIDOTES TO POISONS.

BY PROF. T. E. POPE.

ANTIDOTES TO POISONS.

HERE are three general methods to be pursued: *First—* To remove the poison from the body by emetics and purgatives. Warm water and mustard is a safe and quick emetic. Salt and water may also be employed. Vomiting may be aided by tickling the throat with a feather. *Second*—To administer something that shall retard the absorption of the poison. White of eggs, flour, milk and lard, all act in this manner, and sometimes form harmless compounds with the poison. Lard or fats must not be given in cases of poisoning by phosphorus. *Third*—To administer some substance that shall act chemically on the poison and form a harmless compound or else combat its physiological action.

ACIDS.

Hydrochloric, called also muriatic; sulphuric, called also oil vitriol; nitric, called also aqua fortis; acetic acid and vinegar. *Antidotes.*—Some alkali, as carbonate of soda, or soapsuds. Very dilute nitric acid in sawdust is useful for cleaning brass.

ALKALIES.

Ammonia, potash, soda, and their carbonates. *Antidote.*—Vinegar or vegetable acids, lemons, milk. Ammonia is used to soften water and remove grease stains; potash and soda to make soap.

263

ANTIMONY.

Antidote.—Vomiting should be induced by large draughts of warm water. Chemical antidote—strong infusion of green tea, oak bark, or nut-galls have been recommended. Antimony is met with generally as tarter emetic.

ARSENIC.

Antidote.—Give an emetic and white of egg in milk. The chemical antidote is hydrated resquioxide of iron, prepared by adding ammonia to tincture of iron, and straining off the precipitate on muslin. A table-spoonful or more of this may be given at a dose. Arsenic in a poisonous form is found in arsenious acid, frequently called arsenic, fly powder or cobalt, Fowler's solution, Paris green, Emerald green, and a number of other substances.

COPPER.

Antidote.—Emetics and white of egg or milk. Vinegar must not be given. Copper in the form of copper sulphate, verdigris, and Paris green are all poisonous. Cases of poisoning are known from cooking acid food in copper or brass vessels.

LEAD.

Antidote.—Emetics; sulphate of magnesia or epsom salts; very dilute sulphuric acid; milk with white of egg. Lead in the form of white lead, sugar of lead, red lead and litharge are all poisonous, and rain water kept in contact with lead pipes in cisterns is unsafe to drink.

HYDROCHLORIC ACID—See Acids.

IODINE AND IODIDE OF POTASH.

Antidote.—Emetics; wheat flour; starch. Iodine forms an insoluble compound with starch. There is no chemical antidote to iodide of potash.

DOVER'S POWDER—See Opium.

LAUDANUM—See Opium.

MORPHINE—See Opium.

NITRIC ACID—See Acids.

OPIUM.

Paragoric, laudanum, Dover's powders and morphine are all made from opium.

Antidote.—Emetics. Keep the person awake; striking with wet cloths and dashing cold water over the head and chest are useful. As a stimulant strong coffee is recommended.

OXALIC ACID.

Antidote.—Powdered chalk, magnesia, white wash, large draughts of warm water; these should be given as soon as possible. Carbonate of soda is of no use.

Oxalic acid is used to remove ink stains and iron rust from white clothing, polishing marble, and looks very much like epsom salts; it differs in its acid taste.

PARAGORIC—See Opium.

PHOSPHOROUS.

Antidote.—An emetic as soon as possible. Fats must not be given. Purgatives may be given if the poison has passed into the intestines. Phosphorous is found on matches, and in rat poison.

POTASH—See Ammonia.

SILVER AS NITRATE.

Antidote.—Common salt administered as soon as possible. Nitrate of silver is used in indelible inks and also as a caustic.

SODA—See Ammonia.

SULPHURIC ACID—See Acids.

STRYCHNINE.

Antidote.—Emetic and use of chloroform as a chemical antidote; strong solution of green tea has been recommended. Used only as a poison.

ZINC.

Antidote.—Milk and white of egg; large amount of warm water, repeatedly given. Carbonate of soda has been recommended as an antidote.

CHAPTER XXV.

DANGEROUS ILLUMINATING OILS.

BY J. K. MACOMBER, B. SC.,

Professor of Physics in the Iowa College of Agriculture and Mechanic Arts, Ames, Iowa.

DANGEROUS OILS.

OIL lamps continue to explode. Life and property are destroyed almost every day because of accidents, with what are supposed to be kerosene oil lamps. The general public attributes the explosion to the upsetting of the lamp or some other carelessness. People are not aware of the fact that good kerosene oil will not explode. They seem slow to believe that an explosion or a sudden burst of flame from a broken lamp is certain evidence of a bad oil. It is the purpose of these pages to point out the nature of these substances, and the practical methods by which the dangerous can be detected and distinguished from the safe oils.

All these oils are the product of petroleum. Petroleum or "rock oil," occurs as a natural product in enormous quantities in Pennsylvania, Ohio, and other adjacent states. It is found in wells from which, in some cases, hundreds of barrels flow in a day. The native petroleum is a dark colored fluid, and from it by distillation are obtained a large number of substances which are used for illuminating purposes. All of these substances may be classed as "Hydro-carbons," being composed of hydrogen and carbon in various proportions. All are inflammable and all are sometimes used for burning in lamps. When petroleum is heated the first liquid driven off, that we need consider, is

GASOLENE.

This is a very clear transparent liquid with a specific gravity of about 66, calling water 100. It has a penetrating odor and is

267

so volatile that unless it is kept in a perfectly air-tight vessel it soon escapes. Its vapor is highly inflammable far below the freezing point of water, and if a quantity is once fired it blazes up with such violence that it can hardly be extinguished. Mixed with a certain proportion of air it forms a compound which explodes like gunpowder. This is the substance used in automatic gas machines for making gas. Air is pumped over the gasoline and mixed with the vapor. If the proportion of air to vapor is kept about right it burns much like ordinary gas, and by storing the liquid under ground far from a building, no special danger need be feared.

Stoves are now made in which gasolene vapor is burned. A reservoir holding about a gallon is placed several feet above the point where it is to be burned, and then by heating a tube containing the liquid, the vapor issues forth mixed with air and produces a very hot flame. In careless hands these stoves are certainly dangerous. And the greatest danger arises from the fact that those who use them must generally store some of the gasolene about the premises. If there exists the slightest defect in the vessel, the vapor steals out and a lighted lantern or lamp brought near will almost certainly result in a violent explosion. Lamps were formerly made which burned gasolene, and the same objection applies to them that does to stoves. No good insurance company will take risks on buildings where this substance is used.

The following article, clipped from a Chicago paper, illustrates the nature of gasolene:

"GASOLENE EXPLOSION.—A mixed case of bad judgment, heroism and suffering occurred at an early hour yesterday morning at the house of Mr. J. M—, Barber street. The husband and father of the family had gone away, and Mrs. M. subsequently went to light a gasolene stove, on which she had been accustomed to prepare her meals. As she bent over it with a lighted match an explosion occurred which was heard in several houses in the vicinity. Before Mrs. M. could realize her dangerous situation, the flames from the combustible material had enveloped her dress and were scorching her body. The flames had taken hold of some timber and spread rapidly to a bed near by, in which her twelve year old boy was sleeping. Before he awoke he was badly scorched. His mother in her despair ran to the back yard, her clothing ablaze, and crying for help in her frenzy. Her daughter pursued her with a blanket and threw it about her mother and smothered the flames, but not before her own face and hands were blistered. In the meantime the boy had been battling for himself and had succeeded in extinguishing the flames on his own clothing, but at the expense of intense suffering. The greater portion of his body was literally roasted and he was unable to speak. The mother was delerious. The fire department turned out and extinguished the fire. The boy and girl will recover, but there is little hope for the mother."—*Times.*

NAPTHA AND BENZINE.

The next product of petroleum is naptha. This substance is also highly inflammable, with a very pungent odor and clear transparent appearance. There are three grades of naptha in the market, A, B and C. These vary in specific gravity from 70 to 75. A light naptha is called "benzine." Both are used for removing grease from clothing. Naptha is used for making gas by forcing the liquid into a red-hot retort in the absence of air. It is then driven into a gas holder and mixed with about forty per cent of air. This process is used very successfully at the Agricultural College. In some countries naptha is mixed with earth and then used for fuel. All grades of naptha are dangerous, when used for illuminating purposes. Like gasolene, its vapor ignites far below the freezing point of water, and at the ordinary temperature of the air it burns with great fury. Its vapor mixed with air in certain proportions produces a compound as explosive and dangerous as gunpowder. If the spout of a can containing it is left open, fire is liable to run down into the vessel, following the vapor, and explode the can. If a lighted lamp containing this substance breaks, the entire room will be filled with flame in an instant, all light objects will be ignited and the results are always disastrous to life and property. The per cent of naptha in our American petroleums is very large; and since its uses are comparatively few, its cheapness offers a constant temptation for dishonest manufacturers and dealers, to mix it with the next and most valuable product of petroleum.

KEROSENE.

Good kerosene is almost as transparent as water when properly prepared. Some of it is of a yellowish color, and has a peculiar bluish tint when viewed by transmitted light. Its specific gravity is about 80, sometimes a little more or a little less. It evaporates very slowly, and does not give off any inflammable vapors until heated to 150 degrees Fahrenheit. Good, standard kerosene oil is perfectly safe. A lighted match can be thrust into it at any temperature below 150 degrees and it will not fire it. If spilled on a table and a match applied, it will be difficult to light it, and when ignited it burns very slowly at first. It is the mixing of naptha with kerosene which renders it so dangerous. Good kerosene sells at twenty-five to thirty cents per gallon, retail. Naptha can be purchased at 11 to 12 cents per gallon by the dealer. By selling naptha for kerosene enormous profits are made and the consumer is cheated in two ways. He is in constant danger of fire, and the naptha does not give near as much light as good oil. Formerly it was thought to be safe to use oil having a burning point of 110 degrees Fahrenheit. If lamps were always kept in good condition this would answer; but it frequently happens that the top portion of a lamp gets very hot. This raises the fluid up to the burning point and serious consequences may follow. The fire test should be 150 degrees Fahrenheit. Oil of this quality may be regarded as perfectly safe.

HOW TO TEST OILS.

With a little care any one can test a specimen of oil and determine whether it is fit for use. A common thermometer, a tea-cup, saucer, and a little warm water includes the apparatus needed. First remove all objects from the table which are inflammable. Put some boiling water in the tea-cup and gradually pour in cold water, until its temperature is about 145 degrees. Pour a little oil on the warm water and stir well until the oil has the same temperature as the water. Light a match and move it quickly two or three times over the surface of the oil.

Do not hold it still a moment. The test is for the purpose of determining the presence of inflammable vapors over the fluid. Finally plunge the match quickly into the oil. If it does not ignite the oil is all right. If it lights, reject it as below the standard and dangerous. To extinguish the oil when lighted place the saucer over the tea-cup. If the oil is suspected to be very bad, pour a little on water at about 60 or 70 degrees. If it contains naptha or gasolene it will ignite the moment a match comes over it and burn furiously. Again, pour a little good kerosene oil on a smooth board and apply a lighted match. It will ignite with great difficulty and probably go out. Now pour a little oil which contains naptha, or a little pure naptha, on a board and apply a lighted match. It will burst into a great flame instantly, and unless very little is used the flame will rise up several feet. All these tests should be made in a room where there is no light or fire near, as any specimen may be a dangerous one.

Below is presented a table, giving the specific gravities of a number of these substances, and also their burning points:

NAME.	SPECIFIC GRAVITY.	BURNING POINT.	CHARACTER.
Gasolene................	66.5	Below freezing point	Very dangerous
C Naptha............ ...	70	Below freezing point	Very dangerous
B Naptha.............	72	Below freezing point	Very dangerous
A Naptha....	74	Below freezing point	Very dangerous
Kerosene.....	80	150°	Perfectly safe
Paraffine....	84	Solid	....
"Safety Fluid".	69	Below freezing point	Very dangerous
"Kerosene" B........	77.5	40°	Dangerous

The specific gravities represent the relative weight compared with water, which is called 100. Paraffine is a white, wax-like substance sometimes used for making candles, and is the residuum from the distillation of some petroleums. The so-called " safety fluid " is a specimen sent me for examination after a lamp filled with it had exploded and burned two children to death.

The specimen marked " kerosene " B is another which was sent me for examination, and the person using it had been warned against it by having two slight explosions, or " puffs," which blew out the light. He had also noticed that the light

from it was very poor. It is vile, dangerous stuff, and the men
who sell such should be prosecuted to the extent of the law.
But the so-called "Safety Fluid" is one of the most dangerous
substances ever put into a lamp; a man could read by a lighted
candle stuck into a keg of gunpowder with more "safety" than
by a lamp fed with such fluid. Better have a powder magazine
under your bed than to store such safety fluids about your house.
There are certain dishonest dealers who put some substance into
low grade oils and claim that it renders them safe. Then some
such name as "safety fluid" is given it, and it goes forth on its
errand of death; for it can be depended upon, that no chemi-
cals put into a bad oil can make it safe. Accidents are most
likely to occur when using a lamp only partially full of the dangerous oil. When the lamp cools, air enters and mixes with the
vapor, and the next time it is lighted perhaps the flame will run
down beside the wick and an explosion results. In testing an
oil a bluish flame will sometimes be seen to run over the surface
of the fluid, and then go out at a temperature below where the
oil burns. This first temperature is called the "flashing point."
In some states the "flashing point" is used as the basis for testing oils. This is a lower temperature by five or ten degrees than
the "burning point."

The dangerous qualities of naptha and gasolene are inherent
in the nature of the liquids themselves, and no human device
can alter them, and yet there are men who go about pretending
to sell "non-explosive napthas," and "non-explosive" lamps and
stoves. "Safety lamps" and "safety fluids" are only safe when
the fluid used is good kerosene, and this is always safe. The
victims of these disasters are generally innocent women and
children. By purchasing oils in quantities of five gallons at a
time, and applying the tests as described in this paper, all danger
can be avoided.

INDEX.

18

274   INDEX.

www.ingramcontent.com/pod-product-compliance
Lightning Source LLC
Chambersburg PA
CBHW030345270326
41926CB00009B/968